"As an educator for 42 years, it is so refreshing to finally have a Principal's Desk Reference that provides the 'How To' in implementing these well-defined educational leadership standards. This book is very useful in providing support and enabling principals and educational leaders to continually grow and develop throughout their career."

Naomi Matsuzaki, *Hawaii's National Distinguished Principal, sponsored by NAESP*

"As a practitioner, I cannot think of a more timely, relevant, and useful resource for our nation's educational leaders. The authors of this book have over 60 years of experience upon which readers can draw reflection. Even the most seasoned leader will find this book to be useful in describing what effective leaders should know and be able to do to achieve success with each professional standard. The authors have done a tremendous job in paying close attention to what matters most in our work."

Kristi Wilson, *President of the American Association of School Administrators (2020–2021)*

"This book honestly and thoughtfully delivers specific solutions to many of the challenges and struggles educational leaders face today. The authors successfully recognize the value of gaining real-life support from proven effective school leaders who have experienced many of the same challenges and are eager to share their best practices and lessons learned. Most important is how the authors provide tangible ways to understand and implement the Professional Standards for Educational Leaders in ways that will support a successful career long term."

Lisa Strohman, *JD, PhD, author of* Digital Distress, Growing Up Online

"As you read Chapter 5 imagine a New Mexico feast. The beans, rice and enchiladas are superbly prepared—they represent curriculum, instruction and assessment so well researched and described. The spices are the success stories immersed in the chapter. Adjacent to your platter are your sopapillas and honey. They are eaten with the meal. The sopapillas and honey represent the constant care for adults and children immersed in Chapter 5."

Lee Jenkins, *author of* How to Create a Perfect School

The Principal's Desk Reference to Professional Standards

With the ever-changing, complex role of the principalship, school leaders are thirsty for a useful desk reference that aligns with professional standards. This actionable book brings the PSEL standards to life, providing leaders with support, mentorship, and practical advice. This book provides solutions to challenges and answers the hard questions associated with educational leadership alongside a host of tools, strategies, organizers, templates, and rubrics. Including voices from experienced leaders across rural, urban, suburban, tribal, and international settings, this book helps principals at all levels navigate challenges and make decisions that positively impact their students' futures. You will be inspired to strive for a better future for your school community as you continually develop skills leading to a long, successful career in educational leadership.

Robyn Conrad Hansen is Assistant Professor of Practice and Chair of the K-12 subunit for the Educational Leadership Department at Northern Arizona University.

Frank D. Davidson is Assistant Professor and co-chair of the Doctoral Steering Committee at Northern Arizona University.

Other Eye On Education Books Available from Routledge
(www.routledge.com/eyeoneducation)

Empowering Teacher Leadership: Strategies and Systems to Realize Your School's Potential
Jeremy D. Visone

Trailblazers for Whole School Sustainability: Case Studies of Educators in Action
Edited by Jennifer Seydel, Cynthia L. Merse, Lisa A. W. Kensler, and David Sobel

The Confident School Leader
Kara Knight

Get Organized Digitally! The Educator's Guide to Time Management
Frank Buck

Creating, Grading, and Using Virtual Assessments: Strategies for Success in the K-12 Classroom
Kate Wolfe Maxlow, Karen L. Sanzo, and James Maxlow

Leadership for Deeper Learning: Facilitating School Innovation and Transformation
Jayson Richardson, Justin Bathon, and Scott McLeod

A Practical Guide to Leading Green Schools: Partnering with Nature to Create Vibrant, Flourishing, Sustainable Schools
Cynthia L. Uline and Lisa A. W. Kensler

Building Learning Capacity in an Age of Uncertainty: Leading an Agile and Adaptive School
James A. Bailey

Rural America's Pathways to College and Career: Steps for Student Success and School Improvement
Rick Dalton

Bringing Innovative Practices to Your School: Lessons from International Schools
Jayson W. Richardson

A Guide to Impactful Teacher Evaluations: Let's Finally Get It Right!
Joseph O. Rodgers

A Guide to Early College and Dual Enrollment Programs: Designing and Implementing Programs for Student Achievement
Russ Olwell

A Leadership Guide to Navigating the Unknown in Education: New Narratives Amid COVID-19
Sally J. Zepeda and Phillip D. Lanoue

The Principal's Desk Reference to Professional Standards

Actionable Strategies for Your Practice

Robyn Conrad Hansen and
Frank D. Davidson

NEW YORK AND LONDON

Cover image: © Getty Images

First published 2022
by Routledge
605 Third Avenue, New York, NY 10158

and by Routledge
4 Park Square, Milton Park, Abingdon, Oxon, OX14 4RN

Routledge is an imprint of the Taylor & Francis Group, an informa business

© 2022 Robyn Conrad Hansen and Frank D. Davidson

The right of Robyn Conrad Hansen and Frank D. Davidson to be identified as authors of this work has been asserted in accordance with sections 77 and 78 of the Copyright, Designs and Patents Act 1988.

All rights reserved. No part of this book may be reprinted or reproduced or utilised in any form or by any electronic, mechanical, or other means, now known or hereafter invented, including photocopying and recording, or in any information storage or retrieval system, without permission in writing from the publishers.

Trademark notice: Product or corporate names may be trademarks or registered trademarks, and are used only for identification and explanation without intent to infringe.

Library of Congress Cataloging-in-Publication Data
A catalog record for this title has been requested

ISBN: 978-0-367-70269-4 (hbk)
ISBN: 978-0-367-70268-7 (pbk)
ISBN: 978-1-003-14533-2 (ebk)

DOI: 10.4324/9781003145332

Typeset in Optima
by Newgen Publishing UK

Access the Support Material: www.routledge.com/9780367702687

Contents

List of Illustrations ix
Acknowledgments x
Meet the Authors xii

1. **Introduction to the Professional Standards for Educational Leaders** 1
   Robyn Conrad Hansen and Frank D. Davidson

2. **Standard 1: Mission, Vision, and Core Values** 11
   Robyn Conrad Hansen

3. **Standard 2: Ethics and Professional Norms** 28
   Frank D. Davidson

4. **Standard 3: Equity and Cultural Responsiveness** 41
   Frank D. Davidson

5. **Standard 4: Curriculum, Instruction, and Assessment** 51
   Robyn Conrad Hansen

6. **Standard 5: Community of Care and Support for Students** 84
   Frank D. Davidson

7. **Standard 6: Professional Capacity of School Personnel** 94
   Robyn Conrad Hansen

Contents

8. **Standard 7: Professional Community for Teachers and Staff**   **116**
Robyn Conrad Hansen

9. **Standard 8: Meaningful Engagement of Families and Community**   **130**
Robyn Conrad Hansen

10. **Standard 9: Operations and Management**   **145**
Frank D. Davidson

11. **Standard 10: School Improvement**   **154**
Frank D. Davidson

12. **Mentoring as an Integral Part of a Comprehensive Evaluation System**   **166**
Robyn Conrad Hansen

13. **Grow Your Own: A Program for Aspiring Leaders**   **186**
Frank D. Davidson

14. **The Future of PK-12 School Administration**   **199**
Frank D. Davidson

Appendix A: Professional Standards for Educational Leaders (PSEL)   205
Appendix B: PSEL Knowledge and Skill Self-Assessment   208
Glossary   219
Contributor Biographies   220

Illustrations

Figures

1.1	Theory of Action—Standards-Focused Leadership	6
2.1	Vision and Mission Progress Check List	22
5.1	Force Field Analysis and the Three Stages of Change	56
5.2	The Interdependency of the Curriculum, Instruction, and Assessment Triad	60
5.3	Sample Walk-Through Results by Quadrant	68
7.1	Comparison of Distributive and Transformational Leadership Models	98
7.2	Example of a Distributive Leadership Cabinet	99
7.3	Concerns for a Balanced Health and Wellness	106

Table

12.1	Example of Mapping PSEL Expectations into Leadership Domains	175

Acknowledgments

We would like to acknowledge and thank the following people and State and National Associations for their contributions to this book.

Book Cover Inspiration:
Mr. Matthew P. Werleman, Advanced Marketing USA, www.advancedmarketingusa.com

Editing and Formatting:
Mr. Jimmy Hansen
Dr. Edie Hartin

Review, Feedback, Support, and Encouragement:
Mr. Rich Barbacane
Dr. Gracie Branch
Dr. Kristi Brinkerhoff
Dr. Amy Burgess
Dr. Brandie Burton
Ms. Suzie Carey
Dr. Catarina Song Chen
Dr. Karen Coleman
Dr. Walter Delecki
Dr. Andi Fourlis
Dr. Earl Franks
Dr. Danielle Fuchs
Ms. Blaine Hawley

Dr. Lee Jenkins
Ms. Kimberly Koda
Dr. Donna Lewis
Ms. Kimbrelle Barbosa Lewis
Ms. Naomi Matsuzaki
Ms. Marta Maynard
Ms. Dorsey Middaugh
Dr. Cort Monroe
Ms. Kas Nelson
Dr. Barbara Newman
Dr. Missie Patschke
Dr. Shannon Bruce Ramaka
Ms. Judy Andrews
Dr. Larry Rother
Mr. Darrell Rud
Dr. Michael Schwanenberger
Mr. Tom Shearer
Dr. Mary Kay Sommers
Dr. Lisa Strohman
Ms. Diana Wallace
Ms. Judy Wallace
Ms. Debbie Ybarra
Ms. Elena Zee

Resources, Support, and Encouragement:
American Association of School Administrators (AASA)
Arizona School Administrators (ASA)
International Council of Professors of Educational Leadership (ICPEL)
National Association of Elementary School Principals (NAESP)
National Association of Secondary School Principals (NASSP)
National Policy Board for Educational Administration (NPBEA)
Northern Arizona University (NAU) Colleagues and Graduate Students, past, present, and future
Frank's loving family and friends
Robyn's loving family and friends

# Meet the Authors

Robyn Conrad Hansen and Frank Davidson are colleagues at Northern Arizona University (NAU) working in the College of Education, Department of Educational Leadership. They both hold leadership positions within the department, teach courses at the master's and doctoral levels, supervise principal and superintendent interns, and chair doctoral dissertations. Robyn and Frank have a sincere desire to work with school leaders, cultivating an educational environment that is rigorous, relevant, and rich in real-life experiences taught by world-class educators preparing them for a career that excites them for a lifetime, better enabling them to be the successful leaders of tomorrow.

Robyn Conrad Hansen
Robyn Conrad Hansen was honored to serve on the workgroup for completing the PSEL with other members from the National Policy Board for Educational Administration. Robyn currently is a Professor of Practice and is the Chair of the K-12 subunit for the Educational Leadership Department for Northern Arizona University. She was the proud principal of Playa del Rey Elementary School from 2001 to 2016. Playa is a four-time Arizona A+ School of Excellence, a Title I Rewards School, and has earned an "A" Label from the Arizona Department of Education for academic growth and achievement. In the spring of 2015, Playa del Rey was honored by the US Department of Education as a Teach-To-Lead Lab School focusing on Distributed Leadership. Prior to leading Playa del Rey, she was the assistant principal at both the high school and middle levels earning the Arizona Assistant Principal of the Year Award in 2000 sponsored by the National

Association of Secondary School Principals (NASSP). Robyn was recognized as Arizona's National Distinguished Principal of the Year in 2010 sponsored by the National Association of Elementary School Principals (NAESP).

In 2016, Robyn was honored to serve as the President of the National Association of Elementary School Principals (NAESP) representing 65,000 principals in the United States and around the world. She served two years on the NAESP Board as the Zone 9 Director representing the eight Western United States, as well as Guam and Island of Samoa, prior to being elected President. Then she served three years on the NAESP Executive Board as an officer.

She completed her undergraduate degree in education from the University of Wisconsin (Eau Claire) and her graduate degrees at Northern Arizona University in educational leadership. Her doctoral research was in school improvement planning focusing on leadership and strategic planning.

Robyn has presented at over 30 state and national conferences, as well as international conferences in Dubrovnik, Croatia (2015), Bogota, Columbia (2015), Cape Town, South Africa (2016), and Prishtina, Kosovo (2017, 2018, 2019).

Connect with Robyn at: Robyn.Hansen@JRHIE.com, Robyn.Conrad@nau.edu, or on Twitter @RobynHansenAZ

Frank D. Davidson

Frank D. Davidson is a professor at Northern Arizona University. He earned his doctorate in educational leadership from the University of Arizona in 2005. His doctoral research involved a statewide study of superintendents' instructional leadership practices and the relationship of such practices to growth in student achievement.

Prior to joining Northern Arizona University in August of 2017, he served for 38 years as a public school teacher, principal, assistant superintendent for curriculum and instruction, and superintendent. He values the opportunity to work with practicing and aspiring leaders to assist them in developing their knowledge and skills.

Frank's research interests include the superintendency, the principalship, and instructional leadership. He is the editor of the *eJournal of Education Policy*, an international refereed journal providing perspectives on current policy issues facing both K-12 and higher education (available at in.nau.edu/eJournal/).

Meet the Authors

Frank received the Superintendent of the Year Award for Large School Districts from the Arizona School Administrators in 2000, the Business Leader of the Year Award from the Greater Casa Grande Chamber of Commerce in 2003, and the Arizona nomination for National Superintendent of the Year from the American Association of School Administrators in 2006. In 2014, he was named to the Southwestern College of Kansas Hall of Fame. In 2016, he received the Raymond Sterling Kellis Leadership Award from the Arizona School Administrators.

Connect with Frank at: Frank.Davidson@nau.edu

Introduction to the Professional Standards for Educational Leaders

Robyn Conrad Hansen and Frank D. Davidson

Introduction

This book focuses on helping principals effectively implement the standards and expectations of the Professional Standards for Educational Leaders (PSEL, 2015). In each chapter, we describe what an effective leader should know and be able to do to achieve success with each standard and its associated expectations. This book provides practical application of the standards that can then be used as the basis for a principal performance evaluation system, mentoring, and a grow your own leadership development program. The ten standards directly from the PSEL 2015 document developed by the National Policy Board for Educational Administration are provided in Appendix A or online (www.npbea.org/psel). We created an associated PSEL Knowledge and Skills Self-Assessment based on the PSEL expectations aligned to each of the standards for you to use throughout your leadership journey. It is provided in Appendix B.

The role of the principal has evolved over time from being a school manager to one of heightened complexity as an instructional leader with increased demands and expectations. With the ever-changing role of the principalship, school leaders are thirsty for a useful "Principal's Desk Reference" supporting the PSEL 2015 with actionable strategies for practice. Having this book at your fingertips provides support and mentorship from

DOI: 10.4324/9781003145332-1

experienced and successful principals and superintendents who truly understand the complexities of the leadership role. We use vignettes from these experts in the field of educational administration to bring the PSEL to life. These proven leaders have shared their contact information with you in the Contributor Biographies section of this book.

The most successful principals recognize the value of gaining real-life support from effective school leaders—those who have experienced many of the same challenges and are eager to share their best practices and lessons learned. The role of an educational leader can be very isolating and stressful. This book provides solutions to challenges and helps answer the hard questions. You will find stories shared by proven leaders from a variety of school settings, i.e., rural, urban, suburban, and international that you can relate to as an elementary, middle, high school or district administrator. Our goal is for you to be inspired to strive for a better future for your school community as you continually develop skills leading to a long, successful, healthy career in educational leadership knowing you are not on this journey alone.

Who Should Read *The Principal's Desk Reference?*

This resource is intended for both beginning and aspiring principals who would like a realistic view of the expectations that lie ahead of them. Our goal is to help practicing educational leaders who want ideas on how to implement the PSEL in their current role as a principal, assistant principal, dean, or other levels of educational administration. We focus on helping principals in effectively implementing the standards and the associated expectations contained within PSEL. Each of the ten standards provides a list of expectations that further outline what an *effective leader* should be able to accomplish. Moving from novice, to proficient, to expert over time. We dissect each expectation to provide you with practical ideas on how to implement them at your school. This information is also useful when you are using the PSEL as the basis for principal performance evaluations, mentoring, and your own leadership development programs. This book is a companion to the PSEL document and provides guidance to assist principals in regularly reflecting on their professional practice to consider

Introduction

one's own values, motivations, beliefs, and actions, and how these are viewed in light of professional standards.

History of Educational Leadership Standards

Educational leadership standards have been continually improving over the years. The original ISLLC standards (Council of Chief State School Officers, 1996) represented the first effort to develop national standards for school leaders. These standards and their subsequent update (Council of Chief State School Officers, 2008) initiated significant discussion among scholars in the years following their adoption, as they helped to shape leadership development programs, administrative evaluation instruments, and state licensure processes.

The next generation of standards are the Professional Standards for Educational Leaders (PSEL) adopted in 2015 by the National Policy Board for Educational Administration. They replace the ISLLC standards and have the potential to produce a more substantial impact on the profession.

Related to PSEL are the National Educational Leadership Preparation (NELP) standards (National Policy Board for Educational Administration, 2018). The NELP standards, adopted in 2018, while aligned to the PSEL standards, serve a somewhat different purpose than the PSEL standards. The NELP standards are focused on higher education programs and stipulate "what novice leaders and preparation program graduates should know and be able to do after completing a high-quality educational leadership preparation program" (National Policy Board for Educational Administration, 2018, p. 3). They are also intended to serve as the basis for the review of leadership preparation programs through the Council for the Accreditation of Educator Preparation (CAEP).

Professional Standards for Educational Leaders

"Bringing these standards to life" is our focus with this book. The chapters that follow capture the voices and stories of proven leaders and practitioners, and answer questions about the meaning that leaders ascribe to each of the standards in their daily lives. By studying the voices of school leaders that were part of the development of these standards, we are able to provide aspiring and practicing school leaders with examples of the methods by which leaders can bring practical meaning and relevance to the standards. Our goal is for these standards to become not just words on a page, but rather a concrete explanation of the ways in which leaders carry out their work on behalf of all students in the nation's schools.

Professional standards for educational leaders, of course, are intended to ultimately serve the object of leaders' efforts—students. Young and Perrone effectively articulate the purpose of standards as follows:

> Professional standards define the nature and the quality of work of persons who practice in a given profession. They are created for and by the profession to codify norms of conduct and ethics as well as provide guidance for how practitioners should be prepared, hired, developed, supervised, and evaluated. In most fields, they are used to inform government policies and regulations that oversee the profession. By articulating the scope and quality of work as well as the values and norms of the profession, standards suggest how practitioners can achieve the outcomes demanded by the profession and the public at large.
>
> (2016, p. 4)

There is ample evidence that two of the most significant factors that impact student achievement are the quality of teachers and principals (Day et al., 2006, 2016; Hallinger, 2018; Leithwood & Louis, 2012; Ylimaki & Jacobson, 2013). Given the fact that leadership matters, it is important to stipulate and define expectations for leaders, which is the first step in improving the quality of leadership in schools.

What Are the Major Changes from ISLLC 2008 to PSEL?

Smylie and Murphy (2018) identify areas of development that distinguish PSEL from ISLLC. First, practitioners played a more significant role in contributing to the PSEL standards than was the case with their predecessor standards. According to Smylie and Murphy, "this led to a more comprehensive, useful, and potentially influential knowledge base" (2018, p. 24). A second development has been the move toward a more positive, forward-focused, and aspirational view of leadership. This development reflects the larger trend in the field away from managerial views of leadership toward transformational and authentic models of leadership that are grounded in ethics and equity. Third, the standards focus more explicitly on principles and values. Murphy and colleagues note that:

> Not only do the new standards emphasize the personal "virtues" associated with effective leaders (such as integrity and trustworthiness), they are careful also to highlight the social nature of the work, noting ways in which personal relationships and interactions make it possible to lead schools successfully.
>
> (Murphy et al., 2017, p. 22)

Finally, the standards continue to emphasize the importance of success for every student but move to a definition of success that includes both academic success and student well-being.

We hope, through this book, to shed greater light on approaches toward leadership development as part of the professional standards. We wholly support steps being taken to align leadership preparation programs, state licensure requirements, and administrator evaluation processes, and we urge all states to formally adopt the PSEL standards. As an extension of these efforts, we view the self-directed learning efforts of practicing principals as an additional tool for improving school quality through aligning leader practices with the standards. In our view, leadership preparation programs, state licensure requirements, administrator evaluation processes, reflective practice, mentoring, and professional development are six levers that can serve to advance the alignment of school leadership with the standards. By sharing the perspectives of practicing leaders in this book, we aim to illustrate the ways in which principals' self-guided development can affect the course of their careers and the impact on schools and student learning. Figure 1.1 provides a graphical view of these six practical implementations for aspiring and practicing leaders.

Experience is a powerful teacher. As principals gain experience, they typically gain confidence in their abilities, and, provided they are reflective about their practice, they can become better able to appreciate their strengths and deficiencies. In other fields, work-based learning has

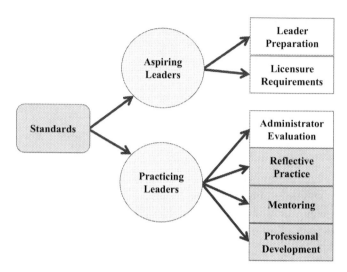

Figure 1.1 Theory of Action—Standards-Focused Leadership
Source: Created by Dr. Frank Davidson

been demonstrated to be a more powerful source of learning than formally organized training (Eraut, 2011). As we gain experience, we have the benefit of reflections on what was learned from past efforts to perform a task.

Over the last two decades, there has been an increasing interest in authenticity in leadership (Avolio & Gardner, 2005; Begley, 2003; Gardner et al., 2011), which is defined by Begley as follows:

> Authentic leadership implies a genuine kind of leadership—a hopeful, open-ended, visionary and creative response to social circumstances, as opposed to the more traditional dualistic portrayal of management and leadership practices characteristic of now obsolete and superseded research literature on effective principal practices.
>
> (2003, p. 1)

Authentic leadership is based on the maxim, "To thine own self be true" (Avolio & Gardner, 2005). The theory of authentic leadership argues that the leader's values closely guide their actions, that "self-knowledge of personal values is seen as a prerequisite for authentic leadership," (Branson, 2007, p. 226), and that self-knowledge can be cultivated through deep reflection on one's beliefs and values and the manner in which these influence one's actions.

Introduction

Laws, policies, and professional standards are not all the variables that determine whether desired outcomes are achieved. The internal motivation of individuals, their training, their ethics and values, organizational culture, the influence of professional organizations, and collegial support and accountability also play a role in determining the success of individuals, the profession, and organizations. Factors such as these will be examined in the coming chapters in the context of the standards, principals' workplace experiences, and the interpretation of these experiences.

Professional standards are the expression of aspirational ideals. They create an image of what we should expect in the highest possible performance of leadership responsibilities in each of the areas under consideration. While we can aspire every day to present the very best version of ourselves, experienced school leaders realize that one of the realities of the job is that, on some days, one must be satisfied with "good enough" solutions to many of the thorny problems of schooling that defy simple solutions. Being an effective leader does not require perfection as measured against a set of ideals; falling short of the ideal simply reflects the complexity of the job of school principal. Aspiring to the ideal, however, and reflecting on how to get there, can and should be the accepted norm for practicing leaders.

In developing the PSEL, there was a marked effort to engage practitioners more fully than was the case with earlier versions. Smylie and Murphy assert that this "has led to a more comprehensive, useful, and potentially influential knowledge base" (2018, p. 24). We concur, and we believe that practitioners' voices need to continue to be heard as our profession now strives to give practical meaning to the standards. Through this book, our vision is to illustrate the ways in which leaders integrate the standards as they engage both the trials and successes of school leadership. It is our hope that the stories we provide affirm our confidence in the capabilities of effective leaders and help all of us to grow through their examples.

How to Use *The Principal's Desk Reference*

In Chapters 2–11, you will find an overview of the ten standards accompanied by expectations of what an *effective leader* should know and be able to do to achieve success with each standard. The PSEL has

7

several expectations per standard that provide additional insight into what is "expected" of a successful educational leader. Within each chapter, we dissect these expectations and provide real-life examples of how they can be implemented in your leadership journey.

Chapter 12 discusses the use of the PSEL in the principal performance evaluation process and a need for mentorship, at least in the principal's first year. Chapter 13 provides guidance on the development of a "Grow Your Own" leadership development program. In Chapter 14, we share our views concerning the future of PK-12 administration.

This book was written by two authors with very distinct backgrounds and writing styles. Each chose to write about five of the ten standards within PSEL. Robyn spent the majority of her career as a practicing PK-12 administrator in elementary, middle level, and high school and applied this real-life experience in her chapters. Frank spent over half of his career in PK-12 as a superintendent and applied this unique perspective to his chapters. While our education and experiences are similar, and we each have a passionate interest in the ways that the standards can be applied to leadership, we each approach and communicate implementation of the standards from our own distinctive perspectives. We hope that our individual voices will help readers grow in their understanding and appreciation of the standards, just as we have grown through collaborating on this project.

Valuable contributions to this *Principal's Desk Reference* are the vignettes shared by award-winning, proven leaders who are effective principals and superintendents helping you better understand the "how" of implementing each of the standards. So often we get the theory, but not how to use in practice. These exceptional leaders have learned many lessons over the years and share their thoughts and personal stories with you. To help you get to know them better, a short introductory biography about the principal and their experience is included at the end of the book under Contributor Biographies.

This book is intended as a desk reference, to keep close at hand. You may wish to start at the beginning and read through the entire book or let the table of contents guide your reading and choose topics of most importance to your current situation. If you are looking for a source for a professional learning community book study, this would be an inclusive book to discuss focusing on solutions to the complexities of school leadership. We believe this book is very useful as a reference when carrying out a self-evaluation or when designing and reflecting on professional goals and action steps.

References

Avolio, B. J., & Gardner, W. L. (2005). Authentic leadership development: Getting to the root of positive forms of leadership. *Leadership Quarterly, 16*(3), 315–338. https://doi.org/10.1016/j.leaqua.2005.03.001

Begley, P. T. (2003). In pursuit of authentic school leadership practices. In P. T. Begley & O. Johansson (Eds.), *The ethical dimensions of school leadership* (pp. 1–12). Kluwer Academic Publishers.

Branson, C. (2007). Effects of structured self-reflection on the development of authentic leadership practices among Queensland primary school principals. *Educational Management Administration & Leadership, 35*(2), 225–246. https://doi.org/10.1177/1741143207075390

Council of Chief State School Officers. (1996). *Interstate School Leaders Licensure Consortium standards for school leaders.*

Council of Chief State School Officers. (2008). *Educational leadership policy standards: ISLLC 2008.*

Day, C., Gu, Q., & Sammons, P. (2016). The impact of leadership on student outcomes: How successful school leaders use transformational and instructional strategies to make a difference. *Educational Administration Quarterly, 52*(2), 221–258. https://doi.org/10.1177/0013161X15616863

Day, C., Stobart, G., Sammons, P., & Kington, A. (2006). Variations in the work and lives of teachers: Relative and relational effectiveness. *Teachers and Teaching, 12*(2), 169–192. https://doi.org/10.1080/13450600500467381

Eraut, M. (2011). Informal learning in the workplace: Evidence on the real value of work-based learning (WBL). *Development and Learning in Organizations: An International Journal, 25*(5), 8–12. https://doi.org/10.1108/14777281111159375

Gardner, W. L., Cogliser, C. C., Davis, K. M., & Dickens, M. P. (2011). Authentic leadership: A review of the literature and research agenda. *Leadership Quarterly, 22*(6), 1120–1145. https://doi.org/10.1016/j.leaqua.2011.09.007

Hallinger, P. (2018). Bringing context out of the shadows of leadership. *Educational Management Administration & Leadership, 46*(1), 5–24. https://doi.org/10.1177/1741143216670652

Leithwood, K., & Louis, K. S. (Eds.). (2012). *Linking leadership to student learning*. Jossey-Bass.

Murphy, J., Louis, K. S., & Smylie, M. (2017). Positive school leadership: How the Professional Standards for Educational Leaders can be brought to life. *Phi Delta Kappan, 99*(1), 21–24.

National Policy Board for Educational Administration. (2015). *Professional standards for educational leaders*. http://npbea.org/wp-content/uploads/2017/06/Professional-Standards-for-Educational-Leaders_2015.pdf

National Policy Board for Educational Administration. (2018). *National educational leadership preparation program recognition standards: Building level*. www.npbea.org/wp-content/uploads/2018/11/NELP-Building-Standards.pdf

Smylie, M. A., & Murphy, J. (2018). School leader standards from ISLLC to PSEL: Notes on their development and the work ahead. *University Council for Educational Administration Review, 59*(3), 24–28.

Ylimaki, R., & Jacobson, S. (2013). School leadership practice and preparation: Comparative perspectives on organizational learning (OL), instructional leadership (IL) and culturally responsive practices (CRP). *Journal of Educational Administration, 51*(1), 6–23. https://doi.org/10.1108/09578231311291404

Young, M. D., & Perrone, F. (2016). How are standards used, by whom, and to what end? *Journal of Research on Leadership Education, 11*(1), 3–11. https://doi.org/10.1177/1942775116647511

Standard 1
Mission, Vision, and Core Values
Robyn Conrad Hansen

> Effective educational leaders develop, advocate, and enact a shared mission, vision, and core values of high-quality education and academic success and well-being of *each* student.
>
> (PSEL, 2015, p. 9)

Extraordinary leaders have a well-developed **vision** that guides them in staying focused on their mission. This vision stretches the leader, both personally and professionally, as they strive for excellence in all aspects of their life. A leader's **vision** and **mission** are developed from a foundation of **core values** that resonate within them. Some of my personal core values include: honesty, integrity, loyalty, maintaining a healthy work/life balance, and ensuring family comes first. Reflect a moment: What are your core values?

John C. Gabriel and Paul C. Farmer (2009), authors of *How to Help Your School Thrive Without Breaking the Bank*, provide an insightful discussion on vision and mission. A vision is futuristic. It is your school's goals and aspiration, a look ahead to the future you envision. The mission is an overview of your organization's steps to accomplish this vision. It is the plan for the future. A vision should be succinct and easy to state, whereas a mission is extended and detailed in how to accomplish the vision (Gabriel & Farmer, 2009).

Bryson (2011, p. 204) defines a more advanced concept of creating a vision of success:

DOI: 10.4324/9781003145332-2

A description of what an organization will look like if it succeeds in implementing its strategies and achieves its full potential. Often, this statement includes the organization's mission, basic philosophy and core values, goals, basic strategies, performance criteria, important decision-making rules, and the ethical standards expected of all employees.

A vision of success helps all members of your team to be able to reflect clearly on their individual role and contributions to the overall accomplishments of the school and make the necessary corrections along the way.

Implementing Standard 1

What Should Effective Leaders Know and Be Able to Do to Implement Standard 1: Mission, Vision, and Core Values?

As administrators, we strive to be effective leaders. In the context of using the Professional Standards for Educational Leaders (PSEL), we will examine how the expectations of being an effective leader, outlined in the PSEL 2015, can be successfully implemented. In our current world of school choice, it is common for parents to review a school and/or district's vision and mission statement to see if it supports their family's core values. One of the most important tasks of a school/district leader is creating a comprehensive school vision and mission that is reflective of the core values of the school community. Expectation "a" for an effective leader under Standard 1 is to "Develop an educational mission for the school to promote the academic success and well-being of each student" (PSEL, 2015, p. 9). Likewise, the expectation "b" states that an effective leader should "In collaboration with members of the school and the community and using relevant data, develop and promote a vision for the school on the successful learning and development of each child and on instructional and organizational practices that promote such success" (PSEL, 2015, p. 9). This responsibility should not be performed in isolation but implemented with a team of well-informed stakeholders, including, students, parents, staff, teachers, and community. The contributors that are involved in establishing your vision and mission should be representative of the community's core values. These factors leading to uncovering your community's core values should be reflective of current data related to such things as student and staff attendance, academic performance, discipline referrals, graduation rates, staff turnover, socio-economic status, rural vs urban, diversity, and special considerations of the community, i.e., military families, immigrant families, and overseas families or tribal communities.

As Bamburg (1994, p. 23) observes, "Only when schools develop a shared understanding of current reality can a commitment to change be initiated and sustained." Stakeholders appreciate having a voice in the policies on campus. This openness improves buy-in and transparency, strengthens the overall vision and mission, ensures they are based on the community's core values, and decreases the fear of change. PSEL (2015, p. 9) expectation "e" says that as an effective leader you should "Review the school's mission and vision and adjust them to changing expectations and opportunities for the school and changing needs and situations of students." The vision and mission statements should be reviewed annually by the community and school staff to ensure they are representative of the ever-changing school culture and ensure the goals continue to be aligned with the vision and mission.

School leaders are powerful drivers for ongoing, never-ending school improvement and strategic planning focusing on academic excellence for all students. At the foundation of this work is a well-developed vision and mission based on shared core values. Often, we hear vision, mission, and core values listed as if they are one entity, when in fact they are three separate concepts working together to help shape an organization's future. According to PSEL (2015, p. 9) expectation "f," an effective leader will be able to "Develop shared understanding of and commitment to mission, vision, and core values within the school and the community." When developed in concert with one another, they form the basis for all decisions and actions. Here is a summary of each, beginning with how to identify your school/district's core values.

Core Values

In an article in the *Harvard Business Review* (July 2002), Patrick M. Lencioni defines core values as being unique principles that guide our actions. Core values are "ingrained" in all that we do. Core values are the "cultural cornerstones" within our organizations. PSEL (2015, p. 9) expectation "c" for Standard 1 states that an effective leader should "Articulate, advocate, and cultivate core values that define the school's culture and stress the imperative of child-centered education; high expectations and student support; equity, inclusiveness, and social justice; openness, caring, and trust; and continuous improvement."

How do you determine what your school's/district's core values are? First, you will need to decide which character traits should be emphasized and modeled. This can be a daunting task, but we will walk through some examples and best practices on how to identify the most agreed-upon core values for your school/district.

You should begin with defining or refining your core values by establishing a committee that is representative of your school community, including faculty, staff, parents, students, community, board members, and local business partners. One method you may choose is to start by identifying the core values reflective of the individuals on your committee to begin the conversation. To accomplish this, give each member a list of 20 core values that has been narrowed from a long list of values put together by the leadership team. The following table provides some ideas of different core values to consider, but it is recommended that you create your own list based on the culture of your school community:

faith	honor	service	responsibility	authenticity	caring	fairness
wisdom	justice	curiosity	leadership	understanding	creativity	growth
competency	balance	kindness	loyalty	determination	family	security
tradition	trust	honesty	citizenship	diversity	fun	happiness
recognition	peace	hope	freedom	knowledge	respect	patience
integrity	adventure	openness	wellness	benevolence	equity	love

Have each committee member, independently, choose their top five from the list, or they can share one of their own. You should document these into a comprehensive list. If time is short, you may want to make this a homework assignment prior to the general meeting, asking members to bring their top five core values list with them.

It is useful to utilize table teams (comprised of faculty, staff, parents, students, community, and business partners) to discuss their choices within

Standard 1: Mission, Vision, and Core Values

a safe, non-judgmental environment. The table teams come to consensus on their top five core values. A member of the team is the recorder and writes the top five core values on chart paper then places it on the wall (or easels) in a "parking lot" activity. (If your meeting is virtual, teams can be assigned a breakout room to discuss core values to be added to the full group's conversation with a tool like *JamBoard*™.) The parking lot activity gets everyone up and moving around the room. Together, teams walk the room seeing each group's top five core values. After a reasonable amount of time, usher the teams back to their original tables. Here, they further discuss and adjust their top five core values, if so desired. A *wordle*, a word cloud with the most common words or phrases highlighted, can be created on the computer with input from every group. This quickly illustrates graphically the consensus of the groups. For my school, the five most frequent core values listed were *Honesty, Integrity, Servant Leadership, Commitment to Students, and Teamwork*. These core values became our foundation in developing our school's vision, mission, goals, policies, practices, and vision of success.

This is a very personal, inclusive, and efficient process that involves the voices of all stakeholder groups. As a side benefit, it enables everyone to get to know each other better. At my school, it brought our school community closer—it bonded us with a greater depth of understanding and respect for one another.

Vision Statement

With your collective agreement of your community's core values, you and your school community are now ready to begin the essential work of creating the school's/district's shared vision and mission statements. These two statements serve as the guiding principles impacting behavior and decisions. A great place to start is with your vision statement, as it focuses on the future and describes what you want for your students and school community. For example, the vision statement of Arizona's largest public school district, Mesa Public Schools, is simply *Unprecedented Excellence in Education*.

It is beneficial to ask yourself several questions as you prepare to develop your vision statement. Think back to when you were an aspiring principal as you answer these questions:

- What was the vision you had of the school you wanted to lead?
- What did you think was the ideal educational environment?
- What was your standard for excellence?
- What were your expectations for students, adults, and yourself?

As a bright-eyed aspiring principal, I strived to be forward-looking, envisioning a future where all students reach their highest potential, educators are highly qualified and excel at the art and science of teaching, adults model core values, education focuses on the whole child, climate and culture ensures all are welcome and respected, and the uniqueness of the community is celebrated.

Your vision should be reflective of these ideals and offer a path to where you want your school to be in the future. The vision statement looks at least five years into the future. As with the establishment of the school's core values, the vision should be created with input from all stakeholders, representative of the core values that have been agreed upon. You may also need to consider if your district has a vision statement that they expect schools to align with. Typically, a school is able to adjust their vision statement to represent the uniqueness of their own campus.

The first step in creating your vision statement, after reviewing the core values, is to research several other already established vision statements, with the goal of narrowing the list to your top ten favorites, based on the ideals you have for the school as examples. Second, bring together a small, representative group of stakeholders, with diverse backgrounds and experience levels, to serve on the committee charged with drafting an inclusive vision statement. Consider limiting the committee to 10–15 people, depending on the size of your school. Have the school's core values visible around the room. It is nice to have healthy snacks and beverages for everyone to enjoy while working.

To begin, just as you did as an aspiring principal, seek input from the entire committee as to the ideal school/district they envision. Encourage thinking outside the box. Let the brainstorming continue until it seems that all ideas have been explored, documented, and clearly displayed. This will be the inspiration for drafting your school/district's vision. Next, working in smaller groups, allow each to become familiar with and "unpack" the example vision statements you provided. To unpack the statements, ask the groups to identify what are the key words or phrases that stand out

Standard 1: Mission, Vision, and Core Values

in these statements. Then, as a collective group, begin drafting a vision statement for your school/district. Encourage them to keep it concise and to the point, focusing on the ideal vision. A vision statement is just that, a statement. Your vision statement should be no longer than a sentence or two. Make sure the vision is something you are passionate about. As stated under PSEL Standard 1 (2015, p. 9), expectation "d" is that an effective leader should "Strategically develop, implement, and evaluate actions to achieve the vision for the school." As the leader, if you are not committed to the vision, if you lack conviction, others will know and not buy in to it. The vision statement shows the direction your school/district will be going, and the mission tells how. At the conclusion of this exercise, share your appreciation for the time and dedication of each person in attendance. Assure them that the next step will be to share the draft vision statement with all stakeholders, seeking input, giving opportunity for comment

Within the next week or two, bring the original vision statement committee back together, sharing the comments and recommendations for consideration. Ask the committee if they would like to alter the original draft to include any suggestions. Following a 30-minute time limit (the rich discussion could go on for hours), have the committee submit a final vision statement that will be shared with all stakeholders. Follow up with a sincere, well-written thank you note to each committee member. This sentiment will be appreciated and remembered.

At this point, it is time to have your vision statement visible around the campus, on the school's website, letterhead, marquee, in classrooms, etc. A parent at our school volunteered to paint the vision at the entrance of the school. A stencil was created so the vision could neatly be painted in prominent areas for all to see and serve as a reminder of the direction the school is headed. The advantage of creating an attainable vision statement is that it will rally the staff and increase engagement of the school community. At the district level, have the vision prominently displayed as a focal point guiding decision making for board and district leadership.

Mission Statement

According to Bryson (2011, p. 134), a mission statement should state the purpose of your organization. A mission statement outlines the expectations and motivation of your school/district. It defines the direction your school/

district is headed and should be focused on student growth and academic development. It should be based on your school's core values that promote a high-quality education with focus on academic success and the personal well-being of *each* student. It is from a well-formulated mission statement that the school/district's goals and priorities are captured.

The mission statement must be a clear and concise declaration about your strategy—it is the core of what you do. Within a school/district, the mission statement should drive the organization and help shape the culture (how we do things around here). Goals and priorities are developed in direct support of the mission. It is important for your mission statement to be aligned with the district's mission statement. For example, at Playa del Rey Elementary School in Gilbert, Arizona, our mission statement, aligned to the district's overall mission statement, was: *To provide a World-Class Education for all students, supported by World-Class Educators, preparing students to be World-Class contributing members of a global society.* Our mission drove our organization and kept us focused on our priorities. Each member of the school community, including students, set goals and school priorities that aligned with our mission statement. A thoughtful, well-written mission statement is intended to motivate the members of the school/district to achieve greater heights than they previously thought possible. All goals should be aligned to the mission of the organization, keeping you focused and on track to better serve your students, staff, and community.

In developing your mission statement, gather valuable data from a variety of sources showing the current complexity and diversity of your community, for example:

- Student achievement data from a variety of data points
- Student and faculty/staff attendance
- Staff/administrative turnover rates
- Students enrolled in honors/Advanced Placement (AP)/International Baccalaureate (IB) classes, including diversity of students
- Graduation rates
- Attendance at extra-curricular events
- Diversity in the classroom, English Language Learner (ELL) data
- Discipline rates and categories

Standard 1: Mission, Vision, and Core Values

- Open enrollment
- Socio-economic status of families
- Uniqueness of the community, i.e., military, tribal, rural, urban, immigrant families
- Special needs students
- Recent climate/culture surveys

While analyzing this type of data, purposefully examine what you discover about the school/district's uniqueness. Here are some things to consider:

- What are the social or political barriers that need addressing?
- What is the current mission?
- What are some changes to the current mission you would propose?
- What is the mission of the district/charter/or tribal council?
- What are your core values (as identified at the beginning of this chapter)?

After reflecting on the responses to these questions and others, draft a mission statement that aligns to the district, charter, or tribal mission. In Arizona's Mesa Public Schools, their mission statement reads: *The mission of the Mesa Public Schools is to develop a highly educated and productive community, one student at a time,* which supports their vision, *Unprecedented Excellence in Education.*

To create your mission statement, bring together a small representative group of stakeholders to draft the mission that is aligned to the vision and core values. Share the draft with the faculty and staff seeking input. Finalize the mission with your stakeholder group or your leadership team.

Continual Evaluation of Your Vision, Mission, and Core Values

As an effective leader, the responsibility of revisiting the vision and mission each year with the entire staff and stakeholders is very important. This process should not be rushed or forced; instead learn to enjoy execution of the process which yields rich and productive dialogue. This process helps develop trust and integrity within your community by giving others a voice and exhibiting transparency within this process. One of my favorite activities to do with stakeholder groups is a SWOC/T Analysis (Strengths, Weaknesses, Opportunities, Challenges or Threats). Completing a SWOC/T helps guide the organization to better identify the immediate and long-term desired outcomes. A leadership priority is to make sure you are current with the political, social, and economic trends of your state and community to assist in planning and making decisions related to opportunities and challenges. To have a balanced view and not concentrate heavily on threats or serious challenges, care should be taken to understand genuine opportunities for growth and achievement (Ackermann & Eden, 2011). To ensure all key groups are included in the discussion, create a stakeholder map highlighting all the stakeholders that contribute to your school/district. For example, parents, students, faculty, staff, board members, community members, businesses, and government agencies. For more information on SWOC/T Analysis refer to this website: www.c-concept.com/en/the-swot-analysis/

Here are a few actions to consider when developing your educational vision and mission for your school/district that promotes academic success and well-being of each student based on core values:

a) Find a mentor to help guide you through the process. The district level may choose to hire a vetted consultant.

b) Using the stakeholder map, develop a volunteer committee comprising stakeholders who are committed to the success of your school.

c) Gather data that casts light on the good, the bad, and the ugly of what is going on in your school, e.g., student and staff attendance, staff turnover, discipline referrals, graduation rates, standardized test scores, AP and IB numbers, participation in extra-curricular activities, mobility rate, special education population, ELL numbers, open enrollment, number of students bussed to school, etc.

d) Share exemplars of vision and mission statements with your committee to review.

e) Upon completing the vision and mission, set measurable goals with action steps that are time-bound, such as SMART (Specific, Measurable, Achievable, Relevant, Time bound) goals.

Standard 1: Mission, Vision, and Core Values

Each fall, it is good practice to share your personal SMART goals with faculty, staff, students, and parents and then ask them to create their own SMART goals that align with the school's vision and mission. To improve your ability to support all staff as their principal, meet with each person, privately, to review their goals (limit to three) and discuss what they need from you to achieve their goals. This would help guide professional development training to make sure it was personalized, and job embedded.

Developing your leadership skills and dispositions as an effective leader takes time and effort. The PSEL are designed to support and guide school leaders throughout their career. To help in developing your vision, mission, and core values, you should seek out a mentor as one of your first steps. The job of a principal can be very isolating and lonely at times. As stated under expectation "g," an effective leader is to "Model and pursue the school's mission, vision, and core values in all aspects of leadership" (PSEL, 2015, p. 9). In addition, if your district does not have an administrator professional learning community (PLC) already established, consider starting one so principals can gather together, set their own agenda, and talk openly about successes, concerns, and challenges, and make plans for moving forward. Throughout my career, it was very helpful to work with other administrators while establishing the vision and mission for my school and to learn about how they approached collaborating and consensus building with the entire school community (including district leadership).

Once you have established your school's vision and mission, based on core values, you need to routinely evaluate them and adjust as necessary; we recommend at least annually. Based on the expectations provided within the PSEL (2015, p 9), we provide a usable check list in Figure 2.1 to guide your progress in sustaining your educational vision and mission based on core values of your school to promote the academic success and well-being of each student:

The vision, mission, and core values statements should be prominently displayed around the school or district office, district buildings, on the website, letterhead, etc. We review them before meetings to help guide our decision making and we use them as the baseline for what is expected for every student. In alignment with our school's vision, mission, and core values, we adopted a school mantra. Each morning on the announcements the students recite this quote: "The future belongs to those who believe in the beauty of their dreams." This is credited to Eleanor Roosevelt from her July 4, 1957 syndicated newspaper column.

- ☐ Articulate, advocate, and cultivate the core values that define your school's culture and stress the imperative of student-centered education; high expectations and student support; equity, inclusiveness, and social justice; openness, caring, and trust; and continuous improvement.

- ☐ Develop an educational mission for the school to promote the academic success and well-being of each student.

- ☐ In collaboration with members of the school and the community and using relevant data, develop and promote a vision for the school on the successful learning and development of each student and on instructional and organizational practices that promote such success.

- ☐ Strategically develop, implement, and evaluate actions to continually achieve the vision for your school.

- ☐ Review your school's vision and mission and adjust to changing expectations and environment for the school, and the changing needs and situations of students.

- ☐ Develop shared understanding of and commitment to the mission, vision, and core values within your school and the community.

- ☐ Model and pursue your school's mission, vision, and core values in all aspects of your leadership.

Figure 2.1 Vision and Mission Progress Check List
Source: Adapted from PSEL (2015)

Voices from the Field

As a valuable contribution to this *Principal's Desk Reference*, we have collected vignettes shared by award-winning, proven leaders who are effective principals to help you better understand the "how" of implementing each standard. The two contributors to this chapter have valuable experience in establishing an effective vision, mission, and core values for schools in very diverse cultures in the US and globally. So often we only get the theory, but in this book we want to focus on the "how" of putting it into practice. These exemplar principals have learned many lessons over the years and are eager to share their thoughts and stories with you.

Standard 1: Mission, Vision, and Core Values

Vignette by Dr. Rachael George

You must know who you are and where you are going if you are ever going to get there. I believe that creating a common vision and mission while identifying core values is the most important thing you can do with staff, and it is my most favorite. While it is hard, emotional work, it is perhaps the most powerful work you can do as a leader when it comes to outcomes for kids. Through experience, I have found that establishing a common vision and mission unifies staff in a common direction while empowering them with a sense of purpose and belief that they can make a difference in the lives of students.

Growing all kids through academics, attitude, and attendance is important. This is the foundation that Sandy Grade School's success has been built on. Prior to the 2014–2015 school year, this was not the case. The school had just posted a record low when it came to their state assessment scores and the school's report card ranked them in the lowest 10 percent of Oregon elementary schools based on student achievement. As one could infer, if the achievement was this low, the growth of students was bound to be lower. Things were not going well.

That fall, as I stood before staff and went over the data and report card, feelings of disbelief and shock rippled through the staff. The team had no idea how they had reached this point. While we could not go back and change the year before, especially since I and a few others were not there, we did realize that we could change the future. As a team, we decided to dive deep and identify who we were, what we stood for, and how we were going to get there. Over the course of the fall months, there was a lot of talking, discussion, and listening as we worked to figure out our why. What was our purpose? What are we here for? What stake are we going to drive into the ground as a staff?

Through time, a common theme started to emerge. Growth. We knew that we could not control how students came to us, but we could control how the school day went. As a staff, we wanted to grow students regardless of where they came to us at. We wanted to take students to new heights and show them what they were capable of. Staff also made a point in sharing that it was essential that we grow all students, not just the students that were reading below grade level or needing some extra help in math. They wanted all students to grow, including our Talented and Gifted learners.

23

Once we knew that we were all about growing all students, we needed to figure out how we were going to get there. After many long and emotional conversations, we decided that if we could focus on academics, attitude, and attendance, we believed we could move the dial for kids when it came to growth. Let me tell you, it was incredibly hard to narrow it down to the three areas we were going to focus on, especially as the next step included us taking everything off the table that did not align with this work. You read that correctly, we took things off our plates and stopped doing things that we had been doing for years. If it was not connected back to academics, attitude, and attendance, we were going to set it off to the side, even if we had been doing it for years. As one could imagine, there were a lot of tears shed and emotionally charged conversations, but we got there. We had consensus and we were going to focus on academics, attitude, and attendance.

After the first year of having a common vision and mission, Sandy Grade went from the lowest 10 percent of elementary schools to outperforming 39 percent. The upward trend increased as the years went on, and within a four-year time span, Sandy Grade outperformed 80 percent of all Oregon elementary schools in academic achievement while maxing our growth scores set by the Oregon Department of Education.

So, what made the difference? Without a doubt, it was having a common understanding of who we were, where we were going, and how we were going to get there. While laying this foundation was hard and emotional, it was necessary work to move both staff and students forward to new heights. As the years go on, we constantly realign and recalibrate ourselves to our common vision and mission. This work is never done.

Vignette by Dr. Shannon Bruce Ramaka

In Prishtina, Kosovo, from 2015–2020, I had the opportunity to lead the American School of Kosovo (ASK) community in the process of revising our mission, vision, and values. ASK was founded by a passionate 23-year-old entrepreneur, Ardian Hoxha, who had a vision to build a great preK-grade 12 American-Albanian school that would foster students who would become leaders in the rebuilding of the country. In 2003, he had created the mission, vision, and values by himself, and by 2015, revising the mission, vision, and values was one of the nine school improvement

Standard 1: Mission, Vision, and Core Values

priorities recommended by the AdvancED (Cognia) accreditation team. I knew that the vision and mission needed to be "owned" by everyone, not just the founder of the school. I also knew that there was a lot of work to be done to bring the school up to international standards and that only a collaborative approach would be able to handle the quantity of work. Thus, my first goal was to encourage more involvement and motivation from all stakeholders. I began facilitating discussions about the mission of our school with teachers, parents, students, and school management in a variety of formats: in weekly newsletters, parent cafes, training and workshops, retreats, and staff meetings.

About 18 months later, in 2017, I felt that we had built enough of a foundation of communication from a variety of stakeholders, that we were ready to review our mission. I drafted nine different possibilities and presented them to the founder for his approval before sending them off in a form survey to teachers and parents. The end result was that we added the word "together" to the mission statement. Our mission statement evolved to: "Together, we are educating the leaders of tomorrow for a better future." From here, I intended to begin the next step of clarifying our vision; but we had already begun the process of designing and building a new campus that would combine our two schools into one. Fortunately, we had built the necessary foundation of communication with parents and students, and we were able to relocate in October of the 2018–2019 school year.

At the beginning of the 2019–2020 school year, I decided we were settled enough to begin the process of clarifying our vision. I also believed that the faculty had participated in enough common professional development that we had built a foundation of applied research that might help us articulate a new vision. For example, the US Embassy provided professional development by Dr. Robyn Hansen to a team of teachers in the use of formative assessments, how to use data to inform instruction, how to develop lesson plans using standards, and professional coaching. In turn, these teachers shared their knowledge in monthly staff meetings, lesson study experiences, and peer coaching experiences. As a staff, we also organized four international conferences called the "Kosovo Learning Summit" in which I designed the themes that might guide learning: "Engaging Learners" (2016), "Evolving Learners" (2017), "Learning Together" (2018), and "Designing Learning" (2020). During these conferences, teachers learned more about integration of technology, approaches to differentiation, needs of English as a Second Language (ESL) students, designing effective

25

project-based learning units, working with students who have special needs, and much more. By the time we came together in 2019 to review our vision and discuss what we believed about our school, we had taken a four-year professional learning journey together. As a result, new ideas emerged in our discussion: Teachers believed in project-based learning, service learning, and that the arts and world languages should be more of a priority in the school.

Using the ideas gathered from teachers, I created several draft vision statements and presented these to the principals to reflect on and add to. After a few weeks, I gathered a large leadership team that consisted of two principals, three teacher leaders, dean of students, HR manager, elementary and secondary coordinators, operations manager, finance manager, marketing manager, and admissions manager, and we worked over three one-hour sessions to revise and edit the drafts. After we had a draft that we all felt proud of, we shared it in a parent cafe and sent a survey to parents to gather their input. By January of 2020, we revised our vision statement; just in time before the disruptive and challenging time caused by the COVID-19 pandemic. Reaching this level of collaborative input was a highlight of my work at ASK. I hoped that the team would be able to refine the ASK core values with my successor as I moved on to accept a new position in the Netherlands.

The ASK vision at the beginning of 2019 was:

> To be a leading school in Europe by providing each student with a quality education in a safe and supportive environment in which a variety of learning experiences challenge all students to achieve self-discipline, self-motivation, and excellence in learning.

Our final ASK vision in January of 2020 became:

> Engaging all learners to think critically, creatively, and reflectively using an American curriculum that is integrated with technology so that each student may achieve academic excellence, make meaningful contributions to society, and become life-long learners and responsible global citizens.

The common denominator in each vision was the passion to make a difference and the clarity of picture that would allow my passion to be directed into it. I believe great visions start with great ideas, but they are realized by leaders who have the capacity to bring people together that have an unconscious appreciation of the vision and who can help flesh out the unique colors and details of the picture, to bring the vision to conscious reality. When the idea becomes visible others may also share their time and energy in the co creation of the vision. For me, the mission of the school or program shapes and describes the purpose succinctly. The mission is the "Why" of an organization. The vision explains the "What" as a picture others can understand and participate in. The "How" is represented by the values of the organization achieving the vision and mission. When all three, Mission, Vision, and Values, are in alignment, there is a synergy that creates powerful movement forward. Via the World Wide Web, in April 2020, the concept of VisionaryEd was created.

References

Ackermann, F., & Eden, C. (2011). Strategic management of stake holders: Theory and practice. *Long Range Planning, 44*(3), 179–196. www.sciepub.com/reference/174702

Bamburg, J. D. (1994). *Raising expectations to improve student learning. Urban Monograph Series.* North Central Regional Educational Laboratory.

Bryson, J. M. (2011). *Creating your strategic plan* (3rd ed.). Jossey-Bass/ Wiley.

Gabriel, J. C., & Farmer, P. C. (2009). *How to help your school thrive without breaking the bank.* ASCD. www.ascd.org/publications/books/107042/chapters/References.aspx

Lencioni, P. M. (2002, July). Making your values mean something. *Harvard Business Review* https://hbr.org/2002/07/make-your-values-mean-something

Mesa Public Schools: Mesa, Arizona. (n.d.). *Vision & Mission Statement.* www.mpsaz.org/

National Policy Board for Educational Administration. (2015). *Professional Standards for Educational Leaders.* www.npbea.org/psel/

Standard 2
Ethics and Professional Norms
Frank D. Davidson

> Effective educational leaders act ethically and according to professional norms to promote *each* student's academic success and well-being.
>
> (PSEL, 2015, p. 10)

Standard 2 of the Professional Standards for Educational Leaders (PSEL) includes an emphasis on professional norms reflecting democracy, integrity, fairness, equity, social awareness and justice, and respect for diversity. These values are visible in leaders' interactions with others, in the manner in which resources are managed, and in the care given to ensuring the success and well-being of each student. PSEL (2015, p. 10) expectation "f" states that an effective leader should "Provide moral direction for the school and promote ethical and professional behavior among faculty and staff" and expectation "d" states that an effective leader should "Safeguard and promote the values of democracy, individual freedom and responsibility, equity, social justice, community, and diversity." This standard's emphasis on ethics and professional norms forms the foundation of moral leadership, and their expression in the daily tasks of leading schools reflects the character of the leader. In this chapter, I refer to both moral leadership and ethical leadership. Consistent with the approach taken by theologians and ethicists, I use these terms interchangeably in the context of this discussion (Ciulla, 2004; Davidson & Hughes, 2020; Tillich, 2011).

Although the 2008 ISLLC standards included an emphasis on ethics in leadership, the PSEL reach beyond the earlier standards in two particular areas. First, the PSEL call upon leaders to be models of ethical conduct in virtually all aspects of their roles. PSEL (2015, p. 10) expectation "a" states that an effective leader should "Act ethically and professionally in personal conduct, relationships with others, decision-making, stewardship of the school's resources, and all aspects of school leadership." Second, the new standards include a focus on demonstrating a deep understanding of students' and staff members' social-emotional needs and cultural backgrounds (PSEL, 2015 and ISLLC Standards, 2008: A Crosswalk, 2016). Expectation "e" for Standard 2 says that an effective leader should "Lead with interpersonal and communication skill, social-emotional insight, and understanding of all students' and staff members' backgrounds and cultures." Murphy and colleagues comment on the increased attention to ethical leadership in the latest version of the professional standards, noting that

> Not only do the new standards emphasize the personal "virtues" associated with effective leaders (such as integrity and trustworthiness), they are careful also to highlight the social nature of the work, noting ways in which personal relationships and interactions make it possible to lead schools successfully.
>
> (Murphy et al., 2017, p. 22)

Leaders that are new to the principalship soon discover that one's character and ethical choices face the scrutiny of others on a daily basis, as decisions and dilemmas often become revealed to the school community in very public ways. Expectation "b" states they should "*Act according to and promote the professional norms of integrity, fairness, transparency, trust, collaboration, perseverance, learning, and continuous improvement.*" Greenfield states in his review of a quarter-century of scholarly thought on moral leadership that "school leadership is, by its nature and focus, a moral activity" (2004, p. 174). Davidson and Hughes assert that school leadership is a moral activity,

> because it requires minute-by-minute mindfulness and demonstration of the kinds of qualities that contribute to the well-being of the human community, such as love, honesty, fairmindedness, compassion, care for the vulnerable, equity, social justice, and respect for others. Parents entrust to educators that which is most precious to them, and educators assume the responsibility to care for students' health and well-being, to protect confidential information in

Frank D. Davidson

> the very public setting of a public school, to teach and model how to live in community, and to develop the capacity for critical thought.
>
> (2020, p. 4)

The world of a school leader is one that is rarely free of ethical dilemmas. I have certainly faced my share of such dilemmas. School leaders face difficult decisions related to a wide range of issues. Such decisions are not experienced as abstractions debated in the relatively safe confines of an academic setting (although educational leadership students should be exposed to such dilemmas and cases during graduate study), but they are instead often experienced as conflict-laden, emotionally charged, highly stressful, and quite consequential issues requiring immediate yet thoughtful action. Six decades of experience as school leaders has led us to the conclusion that the vast majority of leaders are well-intentioned and conscientious; however, there are factors that increase the potential for errors in judgment, including inexperience, competing demands on a leader's time and emotional resources, as well as the hard truth that many decisions simply have no solution, easy or otherwise.

One of the areas in which all school leaders will ultimately face ethical dilemmas are decisions having to do with student discipline. Finding the most ethical course of action can be incredibly challenging, particularly when parents or staff assert points of view that are in sharp conflict with one another. Principals must ultimately find a way to balance the need to provide a quality education to all students with the need to accommodate and effectively serve those who can be chronically disruptive. For an effective leader, PSEL (2015, p. 10) states in expectation "f" that they should *"Provide moral direction for the school and promote ethical and professional behavior among faculty and staff."*

Twenty-first-century realities including school choice and social media influences force schools to be ever conscious of their public image. A school that is not perceived as safe and orderly can be subject to hostile, inaccurate, and vicious social media firestorms that can lead to an exodus of families from the school. A school that fulfills its ethical and legal duty to serve all students, including those with severe emotional or cognitive difficulties, can be viewed by some as a school that is unsafe and poorly managed. School leaders must choose in a manner that is in the best interest of both the individual student and all other students who might be affected, even when reasonable people can disagree over what that "best interest" might be. Principals risk losing hard-earned trust if either party feels disregarded and must strive to remain in relationship with all parties while always acting ethically and morally.

 ## Setting the Foundation for Ethical Leadership

Graduate study is a time to introduce aspiring principals to the development of and commitment to a statement of one's personal beliefs, values, and vision. Those who hope to lead others must first have a fully formed view of why they wish to lead, whom they hope to serve, how they intend to model what they value, and what qualities they believe a school should embrace. Authentic leadership is based on the maxim "To thine own self be true" (Avolio & Gardner, 2005). In order to be in a position to act in a manner consistent with deeply held beliefs and principles, the authentic leader must first be able to effectively articulate such beliefs and principles. Starratt (2017) maintains that the development of a personal vision or mission ought to be the starting point in preparation for leadership:

> Most university preparation programs do not require its prospective administrators to come up with a vision statement that they are required to defend in some kind of public forum. But that is precisely one of the leadership skills needed by educational administrators.
>
> (Starratt, 2017, p. 49)

As previously noted, Shapiro and Stefkovich assert that "educational leaders should be given the opportunity to take the time to develop their own personal codes of ethics based on life stories and critical incidents and their own professional codes" (2016, p. 22). If those of us involved in the preparation of aspiring leaders fail to create opportunities for them to not only think deeply about their most closely held ideals and principles, but to also face the challenge of explaining them to others, then we fail in one of the most fundamental tasks in preparing future leaders. Those future leaders can be best served through a system that regularly requires, throughout the leadership preparation program, reflection on the development of such dispositions as professional ethics, empathy in one's relationships with

Frank D. Davidson

others, a commitment to equity and social justice, and openness to diverse cultures and individuals.

Building a Career on a Foundation of Ethical Leadership

Ethical leadership is not akin to a merit badge that, once achieved, signals to the world that *this* is an ethical leader. We are tested and retested throughout our lives and careers, and we will often be found wanting in this regard. To be an ethical leader requires acceptance of the notion that one is measured by the challenges of each new circumstance and the realization that a commitment to learning to lead ethically

> should be as much about the life-long personal struggle to be ethical, about failures to be ethical, the inconsistencies of ethical postures, the masquerading of self-interest and personal preference as ethical action, and the dilemmas which occur in everyday and professional life when one ethic trumps another.
>
> (Begley, 2006, p. 571)

Those qualities that distinguish leaders as ethical are the same qualities that earn the trust of others. Ethical leadership fosters trust, and trust leads to higher levels of learning. Trust is earned through daily evidence of integrity, competence, openness, benevolence, and reliability (Bryk & Schneider, 2002; Tschannen-Moran, 2014). As readers will note, these also reflect some of the core values of the authors of this book identified in the previous chapter—honesty, integrity, loyalty, maintaining a healthy work/life balance, and ensuring family comes first.

There will come a time in every leader's career—many times, in fact—when one must admit some type of failure. This could involve a poorly informed decision, a lack of effective oversight, inattention to critical details, or human stubbornness. In a study of school leaders' experiences with trust by Davidson and Hughes (2019), ethical leadership stood out as a critical factor in restoring trusting relationships after such a failure. Leaders in this study cited the importance of exhibiting moral leadership to recover from the inevitable loss of trust when a decision turns out badly:

Standard 2: Ethics and Professional Norms

While not all leaders enjoy the gift of time to recover from a loss of trust, the acknowledgement of missteps, gestures of openness to those with opposing views, and the passage of time appear to be essential for recovering from the loss of trust.

(Davidson & Hughes, 2019, p. 65)

The act of accepting and taking responsibility for failure serves as a model of norms of integrity, fairness, transparency, openness, trust, and continuous improvement. Leaders add to a reservoir of trust when they are willing to genuinely demonstrate humility and responsibility in admitting error, and, in doing so, they provide an essential example of ethical leadership to students, faculty, and parents.

Scholarly Work Related to Ethics

Scholarship related to the study of ethics includes a focus on the ethic of justice, the ethic of care, the ethic of critique, and the ethic of the profession (Begley, 2006; Begley & Johansson, 2003; Shapiro & Stefkovich, 2016; Starratt, 2017; Stefkovich & Hassinger, 2007; Stefkovich & O'Brien, 2004). The ethic of justice involves attention to the rule of law and to concepts of fairness and equity. The ethic of care reflects a focus on compassion, empathy, and relationships. The ethic of critique, grounded in critical theory, summons us to critically examine existing sources of power and privilege and the ways in which laws and policies empower and disempower certain groups and individuals. Finally, the ethic of the profession calls for school leaders to consider professional and personal ethical principles and codes, as well as standards of the profession and individual professional codes to create a dynamic model that places the "best interests of the student" as central (Shapiro & Stefkovich, 2016, p. 200). PSEL (2015, p. 10) expectation "c" states that an effective leader should *"Place children at the center of education and accept responsibility for each student's academic success and well-being."*

While each of these lenses is important for educational leaders to consider, Begley (2006) proposes that educational leaders sequence the application of these lenses by first considering the ethic of critique, next considering the ethic of care, then considering the ethic of justice. While cautioning that such an approach is "a stimulus for reflection,

Frank D. Davidson

not a prescription" (2006, p. 583), he argues that this sequence helps to ensure attention is given to the needs of underrepresented groups (through the ethic of critique), maintain focus on people rather than the organization (through the ethic of care), and balance organizational and individual needs.

One of the theses of this book is that effective school leadership requires ongoing self-reflection and growing self-knowledge concerning one's values and motivations, and how these influence attitudes, beliefs, and actions. Using the PSEL standards as a guide for self-reflection and engaging proven leaders in reflecting on their own practices and experiences, we believe that we can offer to aspiring and practicing leaders ways that they can engage in more authentic and ethical pathways of leading. Forming a habit of reflective practice does not depend upon having a specific time in one's calendar labeled "reflection time;" in fact, given the logistical and practical realities of schooling, it is difficult for an administrator to set aside time during the day for reflection. This habit can be accomplished through dialogue with professional colleagues or a trusted friend or mentor, and time for reflection may be more practical and meaningful in settings like your commute home, a walk in the woods, quiet time before bed, or a professional development session (Branson, 2007; Coombs, 2003). Begley concludes:

> It is not enough for school leaders to merely emulate the values of other principals currently viewed as experts. Leaders in schools must become reflective and authentic in their leadership practices. There is no reliable catalogue of correct values that school leaders can adopt as some sort of silver bullet solution for the dilemmas of administration. School leadership situations are much too context-bound to permit this kind of quick fix. School leaders need to be reflective practitioners.
>
> (2006, p. 584)

Voices from the Field

As a valuable contribution to this *Principal's Desk Reference*, we have collected vignettes shared by award-winning, proven leaders who are effective principals to help you better understand the "how" of implementing each standard. So often we only get the theory, but in this book we want to focus on the "how" of putting it into practice. The two contributors to this chapter have learned many lessons over the years and are willing to share their thoughts and stories with you on applying ethics and professional norms to your journey as a principal.

Vignette by Ms. Joanne Kramer

Provide moral direction for the school and promote ethical and professional behavior among faculty and staff.

(PSEL, 2015, p. 10)

As the daughter of a Foreign Service Officer, I grew up outside of the United States. Our family values were very strong and we lived in diverse communities and countries. We gained the trust and respect of those around us by acting professionally, promoting social justice, and being transparent and resilient when things didn't always go as expected. Every time we moved, we had to start all over again.

Morality, ethics, and professionalism aren't just sets of rules—they're behaviors. We do them or we don't. As an educational leader, I have always known that I need to lead by example in all situations. I have high expectations, but my staff always know that they'll find me in the trenches with them if they need me. I walk beside them. If they have duty on the playground when it's cold outside, I take a duty outside with them. If there is a flood in the restroom, I grab a mop and work with the custodian until the job is done. When teachers participate in training for new programs or new textbook adoptions, regardless of the length of the training, I learn right along with them. I always want to understand everything that my teachers are learning so that I can make sure it's put into practice in the classrooms. I take pride in my school—from the outcomes, to the band, to the flowers I plant out front. And if even a little bit of that rubs off on the staff, then it's working.

Being trustworthy and keeping my word and promises have demonstrated that building strong relationships with students, staff, and families is my number one priority. No one ever said it was going to be easy. Sometimes decisions are difficult because they are not popular and we must stand by them if we know it is the right thing to do. Treating everyone alike and not having favorites has influenced every action I take.

Frank D. Davidson

During the 2020 pandemic, our structures and practices in education had to be changed. What we thought was important and useful didn't matter any longer. Many staff members wanted to continue doing the same thing. Explaining the "why" or reason for the change helped them with the complex task of how we would return to school. As leaders, our job is to convene the right people where needed. Discussions and committee meetings were held in order to ensure every student's needs were taken into account and their potential could be developed. Our job is to review the practices and act with a sense of integrity and urgency. Whether we are new to our profession or have been working in education for a while, we must be courageous, do what is right and there will be no shame and no blame. We can then expect what we model from those that we lead.

Lead with interpersonal and communication skill, social-emotional insight, and understanding of all students' and staff members' backgrounds and cultures.

(PSEL, 2015, p. 10)

I learned from a young age that you have to meet people where they are in order to communicate effectively. In an educational setting, this is true for students, families, teachers, and staff. The most important skill of any leader is the ability to listen, and to understand what's being said, in context.

Emotions can run high in our profession. Teachers and staff members are overworked and underpaid. And they have lives outside of work. For these reasons, and for many more, it's important not only that they feel heard, but that they are heard.

Every student is unique. Their families vary culturally, and the intricate workings of their family dynamics can have an outsized influence on their child's success. While we can't know everything, we must listen in every way that we can, and be open to what we might hear.

Being fluent in Spanish has provided me with the opportunity to communicate effectively with Spanish-speaking parents throughout my career. It has been so valuable to see their faces light up when they learn that their child's teacher or principal will be able to meaningfully engage with them about their child's education in a language that they understand.

Place children at the center of education and accept responsibility for each student's academic success and well-being.

(PSEL, 2015, p. 10)

Standard 2: Ethics and Professional Norms

For the last 40 years I have worked in schools with the neediest of students. School cultures in communities with heavy poverty can sometimes be lackluster. It is not uncommon for staff to resolve that the status quo is permanent, and that positive change is impossible. I believe we have a moral obligation to give these students and the community the same opportunities that are provided to students whose parents pay tuition for them to attend school. We have to accept the lofty responsibility of making sure each student succeeds to the best of his or her ability—regardless of circumstance.

> *Safeguard and promote the values of democracy, individual freedom and responsibility, equity, social justice, community, and diversity.*
>
> (PSEL, 2015, p. 10)

Creating traditions that a school has, year after year, builds strong, caring, diverse communities that we can all be proud of. A leader's job is to help shape these traditions with the input of the neighborhood, the local businesses, parents, staff, and students. Asking for volunteers from the community has been one of the most rewarding decisions I made. Everyone loves students and will give time, talent, and treasure to help.

Some rituals such as Dia de los Muertos, Veteran's Day Assemblies, Engineering Day, and Leadership Day showcase the student body and the school in the eyes of the community. Spread the word using every type of communication available—newspaper, marquee, school news blasts, Facebook, Twitter, and other social media.

Vignette by Dr. Steven Jeras

One of the most important ethical obligations of an educational leader is to ensure that all students have equitable access to a high-quality educational experience. For many students, the chief obstacle to that access can be money. Students living in poverty often lack the resources to help them achieve in school, including home technology, proper and regular nutrition, and access to cultural experiences. Schools that service high rates of impoverished students confront this reality on a regular basis, trying to make the most of federal dollars, grant opportunities, and community partnerships to provide these resources and opportunities for their students.

Educators in affluent communities, however, should also be regularly engaged in these conversations as they, too, likely have students on any given day who struggle to meet the financial obligations of their school experience. I discovered this in my tenure as principal of a K-6 elementary school within an affluent community of Scottsdale, Arizona. When I arrived at the school, it appeared that we weren't lacking for much. Parents sent their students to school with whatever items the teacher required. Multiple notebooks, name brand markers, and personal headphones for the computer lab.

When looking around at the beautiful homes and luxury cars in the neighborhood, it was easy to assume that all families could readily meet the financial expectations associated with the school. As I built relationships within the community, I started to hear stories about families who had difficulty making these contributions. Some of these stories involved students who lived outside of the neighborhood but attended through open enrollment; others involved families facing hardships like a recent job loss. It was apparent to me that we needed systems in place to ensure that all students could benefit from all that we had to offer. Initially, not everyone saw the same need that I did. We had several school and community efforts to address equity for our students in financial need.

First, as a staff we re-evaluated our class supply lists and field trip opportunities. We didn't want to eliminate valuable field trip experiences, but we found ways to reduce costs. If a trip or activity was still too costly for many of our students to participate, we would pursue a different opportunity. We also examined the total additional fees throughout the year and placed a limit for each grade level. Second, we worked with our parent organization to establish a scholarship account to support families who needed it, and we utilized our tax credit account to offset the costs of these extracurricular events. We made these efforts very public, hoping to reduce the stigma for parents who might be too embarrassed to ask for help.

What I became most proud of was the collective mindset we developed about supporting each of our students and families. Even as the economy recovered, our parent leadership maintained a commitment to a scholarship account, and while we could ask for more money, we often asked, "Should we?" When we planned events and activities, we remained committed to ensuring that all students would be able to attend. In my current role supporting principals, when we talk about creating high-quality, engaging educational experiences, we also discuss how we can fulfill our ethical obligation to make sure each student can access them. As leaders, principals need to work to create a culture where teachers and parents are mindful of the needs of all of their students, even in affluent schools where those needs might not be readily apparent.

References

American Institutes for Research Center on Great Teachers and Leaders. (2016). *The Professional Standards for Educational Leaders (PSEL) 2015 and the Interstate Leaders Licensure Consortium (ISLLC) Standards 2008: A crosswalk.* https://gtlcenter.org/sites/default/files/PSEL_ISLLC_Crosswalk.pdf

Avolio, B. J., & Gardner, W. L. (2005). Authentic leadership development: Getting to the root of positive forms of leadership. *Leadership Quarterly, 16*(3), 315–338. https://doi.org/10.1016/j.leaqua.2005.03.001

Begley, P. T. (2006). Self-knowledge, capacity and sensitivity: Prerequisites to authentic leadership by school principals. *Journal of Educational Administration, 44*(6), 570–589. https://doi.org/10.1108/09578230610704792

Begley, P. T., & Johansson, O. (Eds.). (2003). *The ethical dimensions of school leadership.* Kluwer Academic Publishers.

Branson, C. (2007). Effects of structured self-reflection on the development of authentic leadership practices among Queensland primary school principals. *Educational Management Administration & Leadership, 35*(2), 225–246. https://doi.org/10.1177/1741143207075390

Bryk, A. S., & Schneider, B. L. (2002). *Trust in schools: A core resource for improvement.* Russell Sage Foundation.

Ciulla, J. B. (2004). Ethics and leadership effectiveness. In J. Antonakis, A. T. Cianciolo, & R. J. Sternberg (Eds.), *The nature of leadership* (pp. 302–327). Sage Publications, Inc.

Coombs, C. P. (2003). Reflective practice: Picturing ourselves. In P. T. Begley & O. Johansson (Eds.), *The ethical dimensions of school leadership* (pp. 49–65). Kluwer Academic Publishers.

Davidson, F. D., & Hughes, T. R. (2019). Exemplary superintendents' experiences with trust. *Education Leadership Review, 20*(1), 51–68.

Davidson, F. D., & Hughes, T. R. (2020). Moral dimensions of leadership. In R. Papa (Ed.), *Oxford Encyclopedia of educational administration*. Oxford University Press. https://doi.org/10.1093/acrefore/9780190264093.013.785

Greenfield, W. D. (2004). Moral leadership in schools. *Journal of Educational Administration, 42*(2), 174–196. https://doi.org/10.1108/09578230410525595

Murphy, J., Louis, K. S., & Smylie, M. (2017). Positive school leadership: How the Professional Standards for Educational Leaders can be brought to life. *Phi Delta Kappan, 99*(1), 21–24.

National Policy Board for Educational Administration. (2015). *Professional Standards for Educational Leaders.* www.npbea.org/psel/

Shapiro, J. P., & Stefkovich, J. A. (2016). *Ethical leadership and decision making in education: Applying theoretical perspectives to complex dilemmas* (4th ed.). Routledge.

Starratt, R. J. (2017). *Leading learning/learning leading: A retrospective on a life's work: The selected works of Robert J.* Starratt. Routledge.

Stefkovich, J. A., & Hassinger, R. E. (2007). Using case studies of ethical dilemmas for the development of moral literacy: Towards educating for social justice. *Journal of Educational Administration, 45*(4), 451–470. https://doi.org/10.1108/09578230710762454

Stefkovich, J. A., & O'Brien, G. M. (2004). Best interests of the student: An ethical model. *Journal of Educational Administration, 42*(2), 197–214.

Tillich, P. (2011). *Systematic theology* (Vol. 3). University of Chicago Press.

Tschannen-Moran, M. (2014). *Trust matters: Leadership for successful schools* (2nd ed.). Jossey-Bass.

Standard 3
Equity and Cultural Responsiveness
Frank D. Davidson

Effective educational leaders strive for equity of educational opportunity and culturally responsive practices to promote *each* student's academic success and well-being.

(PSEL, 2015, p. 11)

It has become increasingly evident that, in order for a diverse society to thrive, all institutions must more effectively make improvements toward the ideals of equity and social justice. As has been persuasively described by Gloria Ladson-Billings, "the cumulative effect of poor education, poor housing, poor health care, and poor government services create a bifurcated society that leaves more than its children behind" (2006, p. 10). Standard 3 of the PSEL recognizes this need. This standard emphasizes, to a greater extent than the ISLLC standards, values such as social justice, equity, equitable access to resources and opportunities, culturally responsive teaching, and fair treatment in school discipline policies (Farley et al., 2019). Expectation "b" of this standard says that an effective leader should "Ensure that each student has equitable access to effective teachers, learning opportunities, academic and social support, and other resources necessary for success" and expectation "g" states that an effective leader is expected to "Address matters of equity and cultural responsiveness in all aspects of leadership" (PSEL, 2015, p. 11).

As effective leaders, we often point to values and principles such as these that compelled us to pursue a career in education in the first place. For many leaders, our reasons for becoming educators were propelled by a desire to help those who have been systematically excluded from the benefits afforded by society's institutions and norms. Expectations "a" and "b" of this standard state that an effective leader should "Ensure that each student is treated fairly, respectfully, and with an understanding of each student's culture and context" and an effective leader should "Recognize, respect, and employ each student's strengths, diversity, and culture as assets for teaching and learning" (PSEL, 2015, p. 11). We can recall the idealism that inspired us to work toward making better lives for students, and we are grateful that we never lost that sense of idealism.

Despite leaders' oft-stated desires to employ education as a lever to overcome systemic injustices tied to race and ethnicity, as a profession, we are not especially well-prepared for this task (Skrla et al., 2004; Theoharis, 2007). As an example, according to preliminary findings from The School Superintendents Association's 2020 Decennial Study, even though nearly 90% of school superintendents reported that conversations about race and equity are either extremely or very important, just one in five said they were "very well prepared" for that responsibility (Arundel, 2020). Given this self-reported lack of preparation, as well as the underrepresentation of people of color in K-12 leadership roles, we all have much work to do in both reframing our perspectives and reforming our schools. Expectation "d" of PSEL (2015, p. 11) says an effective leader is expected to "Confront and alter institutional biases of student marginalization, deficit-based schooling, and low expectations associated with race, class, culture and language, gender and sexual orientation, and disability or special status." It also states that an effective leader should "Act with cultural competence and responsiveness in their interactions, decision making, and practice" (PSEL, 2015, p. 11).

I believe, as others do, that school leaders can "have a significant impact [on equity], despite educational policies, organizational cultures, and historic structures that contribute to a discriminatory educational system" (DeMatthews, 2015, p. 139). However, because of systemic and cultural barriers, including long-entrenched practices, norms, power dynamics, and resource distribution, this is not the work of a season or a year, but of an entire career. Maintaining a commitment to these values requires a deep and ongoing willingness on the part of school leaders to confront personal assumptions about the effects of schooling in America and about our own roles in furthering unjust practices. Admittedly, honestly recognizing, confronting, and admitting biases does not come easily. However, it is where we can begin to overcome systemic inequities in our schools. Expectation "d" states that an effective leader should "Develop

Standard 3: Cultural Responsiveness

student policies and address student misconduct in a positive, fair, and unbiased manner" (PSEL, 2015, p. 11).

The Challenges of Change

Committing to leadership that cultivates an inclusive, caring, and supportive school community involves a commitment to equity. It also must involve a recognition that all of the school's stakeholders may not deeply share that commitment. Upending existing practices that have favored some groups and disadvantaged others will not be universally welcomed. We remember well the challenges of, for example, opening access to advanced and gifted classes and programs. That increased access was not always welcome, but it was the right course of action. Leading a school to change its practices, particularly those related to issues of equity, is work that can be incredibly challenging, and can lead to both leaders and faculty experiencing mental, physical, and emotional anguish and exhaustion (Theoharis, 2007; Theoharis & Scanlan, 2021).

DeMatthews (2015) described the challenges faced by an elementary school principal in leading the school to be more inclusive and socially just. In that particular case, a novice principal faced difficult levels of resistance from groups of parents and teachers. DeMatthews notes that principals facing such challenges must draw upon "their skills, experiences, and personal strength" (2015, p. 159). When the pace of change is ultimately found to be too aggressive or out of step with the prevailing sentiments of teachers, parents, and senior leadership, the principal can be the focus of resentment and hostility. In the case of the subject of the DeMatthews study, the principal was forced to resign. As DeMatthews points out, "all students deserve committed, experienced, knowledgeable leaders who can manage the pressure of school administration, stay the course, and facilitate the development of inclusive, caring, high-performing, and amazing schools" (2015, p. 163). Farley and colleagues conclude that, under the conditions of competing interests and a polarized political landscape, it is understandable that "many acting school leaders struggle to maintain a focus on equity and inclusion" (2019, p. 9).

As leaders, each of us has faced decisions involving equitable access to effective teachers, opportunities, or other elements related to school

Frank D. Davidson

success. One of those decisions came to mind in the writing of this chapter. Some 30 years ago, as a first-year principal, just a week or so before the start of school, it came to light that one classroom in a particular grade level was filled with students whose parents had requested (or in some cases, demanded) placement in that particular class. The teacher was energetic, engaging, fun, caring, responsive, and inspiring. In contrast, another classroom in that grade level was populated by students whose parents were viewed as uncaring and unengaged. That particular teacher was struggling and was frequently absent because of failing health issues. The classroom was chaotic and disorganized, and expectations for students were low. The pattern of sorting students in this manner had been in place for some time. The prevailing view was that there was no price to be paid for inequitable access to effective teachers. As a political calculation, that may have been the case. Clearly, though, the price to be paid was substantial, given the effects of decisions such as these on the long-term prospects for students. Changing the situation required counseling the teacher into retirement at mid-year and frequent communication with faculty and parents about a more equitable approach toward student assignment to classes.

Equity Audits

In countless other ways, our decisions as leaders reflect the extent of our commitment to the equitable distribution of resources and the unbiased application of policies. Schools can begin to acknowledge where inequitable practices exist by initiating an equity audit (Skrla, McKenzie, & Scheurich, 2011; Skrla et al., 2004; Theoharis & Scanlan, 2021). Equity audits do not necessarily produce an obvious plan to increase equity within the school, nor will they make it any easier to overcome the resistance to change. Such audits are, however, a helpful tool for shedding light on teacher quality equity, programming equity, and achievement equity. The concept may be new to some practicing administrators, but the process of assessing a school in each of these areas is fairly straightforward, following the guidance of the authors named above. At our university, master's-level students are required to carry out an equity audit of their school during their course on instructional leadership, and the process can cause our students to look at their schools in a new way. An equity audit can help to critically examine decisions in areas such as the placement of students in gifted programs or advanced classes, the assignment of students to teachers, the implementation of discipline policies, professional development planning, and strategies for engaging parents. All of these are areas in which a commitment to equity can help to bring meaningful change to a school.

We are encouraged by the promise that the updated standards "have embraced a more assets-oriented understanding of students and schools" (Farley et al., 2019, p. 6). However, standards alone are insufficient; what is needed is leaders who can bring about meaningful action at the level of the classroom, the school, the district, the state, and the nation. Our teaching practices need to emphasize students' cultural assets and prior knowledge, rather than characterize students as lacking in "grit" (López, 2017). Expectation "e" states that an effective leader should "Promote the preparation of students to live productively in and contribute to the diverse cultural contexts of a global society" (PSEL, 2015, p. 11).

Voices from the Field

As a valuable contribution to this *Principal's Desk Reference*, we have collected vignettes shared by award-winning, proven leaders who are effective principals to help you better understand the "how" of implementing each standard. So often we only get the theory, but in this book we want to focus on the "how" of putting it into practice. The two leaders whose contributions follow provide examples of meaningful action that can create more inclusive and equitable schools. They also illustrate how effective uncomplicated acts of care, appreciation, and respect can be in building a healthy school culture where courageous conversations can begin (Skrla, McKenzie, & Scheurich, 2011). As these two leaders teach us, change of this magnitude requires genuine cultural awareness and an expansive embrace of caring, appreciating, and respecting others (Fowler & Jouganatos, 2020).

Vignette by Dr. Sarah Gentis Collins

As an elementary school principal for the past nine years, I have learned through successes and failures the critical importance of PSEL Standard 3: Equity and Cultural Responsiveness. I often tell my students that my job as their principal is to keep them safe and make sure they are learning, in that order. If they are not safe in our school, physically, emotionally, mentally, then any effort to reach and teach them could be in vain. To me, Standard 3 speaks to the safety of our students in schools to know they are being treated fairly, with respect and the recognition that students' strengths, diversity, and culture are assets to our teaching and learning.

Through my own research on culturally responsive teaching pedagogy, as well as my participation in equity work in my school district, my skill set in this area has evolved toward leadership that is more culturally competent and responsive. This is evident in my interactions with others, and in my decision making and professional and personal practices. One area that I have worked to transform my practice in is in the area of student behavioral supports. This standard refers to developing policies that address student misconduct in a positive, fair, and unbiased manner.

In my experiences, my district's use of Positive Behavioral Interventions and Supports (PBIS) has been an extremely effective way to use evidence-based systems to create structures that promote success for all students. It is also important to evaluate any unconscious biases that leaders may have and how these impact their response to student misconduct. An example of this in my own leadership journey is when I started paying attention to the different language registers that my students have been exposed to prior to coming to school. We automatically assume that students know the "rules" of an academic, or formal, registry. When they do not, we often view it as disrespectful and rude behavior, rather than acknowledging that all the student may know is an informal register when speaking to others.

It isn't enough to develop policies and procedures around equity and cultural responsiveness. This work does no good for children, families, and staff if it is not implemented, made a priority, and changed when data shows a need for improvement. Equity and cultural responsiveness is not a "set it and forget it" practice. As school leaders we have great influence on how others in our building, and oftentimes in our districts, confront, address, and promote equity and cultural responsiveness. This standard is one that I believe has not received as much attention in leadership development programs as the other nine standards and therefore it is our responsibility as school leaders to build our own competencies in this standard for the academic success and well-being of all our students.

Standard 3: Cultural Responsiveness

Vignette by Ms. Rosemary Agneessens

I was a principal in east central Phoenix (K-8, with a school population around 1,000) in an area with both poor social-economic condition and dangerous living conditions with drugs and gangs. The majority of the students had newly arrived from Mexico, lived in poverty, and were part of our free and reduced lunch (Title I) and English Language Learners (ELL) program. The school was considered underperforming based on state test results. I already had an understanding of the school's environment from my previous four years as Language Director of the Dual Language Program, so my question to myself and staff was: How do we best build a sense of a community at our school? Everyone needed to know deeply that they belonged.

My first action as principal was enhancing our outreach into the community. With staff on board, we began a series of "house meetings"—a term used in community organizing I did in Texas and in south Phoenix as an organizer with Valley Interfaith Project. Each grade had chosen several evenings where we invited grade-level parents to our school. What are their hopes and concerns for their children? What is their vision for the school? The turnout each night was encouraging, exciting, challenging, and the beginning of a new chapter for our school.

As a result of this outreach, several key issues surfaced: the speed of the traffic on the road at the front of the school; the crime, trash, and drugs along the canal that ran next to the school; and the crime in the neighborhood that families were afraid to report due to immigration status. Where to begin?

At our meetings, no one even mentioned test scores or the state's ratings. Parents were asked to sign up for the area of concern that most disturbed them. Through listening, building trust and confidence, and addressing their concerns, we knew we would be able to move forward, and academics would follow. First, however, a level of confidence in the process and willingness to work together was essential. We analyzed with parents the city structure, the departments to approach, the key individuals with whom to communicate to resolve these issues. City directors, council members, street department individuals, the local police department officials met with us. Parents were coached on how to run the meeting; meetings were conducted in Spanish. In organizing, we believe in the "iron

Frank D. Davidson

rule": never do for others what they can do for themselves. And the parents were learning the "how to do" for themselves.

Certainly nothing changed overnight but the players and stakeholders—those who could help us make change—collaborated with us. Our school succeeded in obtaining city funding for afterschool programs; the canal was cleaned up; new signage along the main road let drivers know a school was present and speed limits were better enforced. As all of these external changes happened, the school vibe—energy—and sense of community flourished and intensified. Students witnessed their parents taking active roles in creating something different at school; then students stepped up and began to take on their roles and responsibilities.

As the sense of parent/student ownership increased, as the school transformed into the center of the community—students developed a sense of pride in their school: This is our school, and we will help make it the best and will work diligently to succeed in our studies.

One meeting stands out as the solidification of our parent–student–school team. Some 350 parents attended. I asked for ten volunteers to step forward with a picture of one of their children. As I walked through the stats of academic success for Latinx students—the numbers that left school after eighth grade, those that didn't graduate from high school, the number that made it into college and who actually graduated—soon only one father was standing. I asked, "And what will we do about this?" That was a defining moment; there was a commitment to do whatever we needed to do for our school family.

In a series of meetings throughout the years, teachers and I met with parents to talk about their children's progress. Parents learned how to access the data to follow the hard work of their children. Parents, teachers, and students were part of a team for success.

The sense of ownership brought a feeling of pride and a level of confidence and competence of "si se puede"—"yes, you can." Our school motto: "Together We Can!" All of that work paid off as slowly state test scores rose. It did not take too long for our school to achieve Performing Plus; that school label took years to reach, especially since our student mobility was about 50% each year.

On the last day of school, a group of school parent leaders, the police chief, and several officers rode a school bus around the neighborhood so that parents could point out drug shops and houses of prostitution. The bus never slowed but police and parents were in conversation. The bus stopped for a time at the canal and together police and parents walked the newly cleaned-up area. As one parent commented: "We always see parents and children walking together and police patrolling. Today we saw police and parents walking together."

My years at this school were filled with the daily work of leading, organizing, building relationships, and working together. Those years were the toughest, most exhilarating, challenging, fulfilling, exhausting of my administrative career. The skills and strategies for creating change were left with parent and student leaders. For that, I am incredibly grateful.

References

Arundel, K. (2020, October 26). *Most superintendents say they're not "very well prepared" to lead race, equity conversations.* K-12 Dive. www.educationdive.com/news/superintendents-not--ready-to-lead-race-conversations/587717/?:%202020-10-26%20K-12%20Education%20Dive%20Newsletter%20%5Bissue:30460%5D&:%20K12

DeMatthews, D. (2015). Making sense of social justice leadership: A case study of a principal's experiences to create a more inclusive school. *Leadership and Policy in Schools, 14*(2), 139–166. https://doi.org/10.1080/15700763.2014.997939

Farley, A. N., Childs, J., & Johnson, O. (2019). Preparing leaders for wicked problems? How the revised PSEL and NELP standards address equity and justice. *Education Policy Analysis Archives, 27*(0), 115. https://doi.org/10.14507/epaa.27.4229

Fowler, D. J., & Jouganatos, S. M. (2020). Leadership practices for supporting equity in the prek-12 educational setting. In R. Papa (Ed.), *Handbook on promoting social justice in education* (pp. 399–211). Springer. https://doi.org/10.1007/978-3-030-14625-2_110-1

Ladson-Billings, G. (2006). From the achievement gap to the education debt: Understanding achievement in U.S. schools. *Educational Researcher, 35*(7), 3–12.

López, F. A. (2017). Altering the trajectory of the self-fulfilling prophecy: Asset-based pedagogy and classroom dynamics. *Journal of Teacher Education, 68*(2), 193–212. https://doi.org/10.1177/0022487116685751

National Policy Board for Educational Administration. (2015). *Professional Standards for Educational Leaders.* www.npbea.org/psel/

Skrla, L., McKenzie, K. B., & Scheurich, J. J. (2011). Becoming an equity-oriented change agent. In A. M. Blankstein & P. D. Houston (Eds.), *Leadership for social justice and democracy in our schools* (pp. 45–58). Corwin Press.

Skrla, L., Scheurich, J. J., Garcia, J., & Nolly, G. (2004). Equity audits: A practical leadership tool for developing equitable and excellent schools. *Educational Administration Quarterly, 40*(1), 133–161.

Theoharis, G. (2007). Navigating rough waters: A synthesis of the countervailing pressures against leading for social justice. *Journal of School Leadership, 17*(1), 4–27. https://doi.org/10.1177/105268460701700101

Theoharis, G., & Scanlan, M. (Eds.). (2021). *Leadership for increasingly diverse schools* (2nd ed.). Routledge.

Standard 4
Curriculum, Instruction, and Assessment

Robyn Conrad Hansen

> Effective educational leaders develop and support intellectually rigorous and coherent systems of curriculum, instruction, and assessment to promote each student's academic success and well-being.
>
> (PSEL, 2015, p. 12)

As an educational and instructional leader, developing a coherent system of curriculum, instruction, and assessment is challenging. This system must promote the vision, mission, and core values of the school (see Standard 1 in Chapter 2). It must have high expectations for student learning, aligned with academic standards, and be culturally responsive. Learning and achievement is at the center of what we do as principals. The most successful principals understand what it takes to be an exemplary leader. One of my favorite leadership books is by Kouzes and Posner, *The Leadership Challenge* (1995, p. 8), which offers these Five Fundamental Practices of Exemplary Leadership that provide guidance to help you develop your knowledge and skills as a dynamic instructional leader:

- Challenge the process
- Inspire a shared vision
- Enable others to act
- Model the way
- Encourage the heart

DOI: 10.4324/9781003145332-5

The driving force behind these five leadership practices came about after studying how ordinary individuals were able to accomplish extraordinary results. This chapter challenges you to venture out of your comfort zone and create a system of learning that is student-centered and provides a rigorous and relevant curriculum with aligned assessments. The purpose is to guide your teachers in their instructional practices whether in person, hybrid, or virtual that focuses on the development of the whole child, i.e., socially, emotionally, academically, physically, and psychologically. Let us explore each practice further:

Challenge the process: There will always be plenty of opportunities to challenge the status quo and plenty of obstacles for you to overcome along your leadership journey. The most successful leaders are those who know when and how to accept the challenge, take risks, be innovative, and make bold, courageous student-centered decisions.

Inspire a shared vision: Before you ever had your first administrative position, you had a dream, a vision what the future will look like, positively impacting student achievement. You were confident in your preparation, experiences, knowledge, and skills to make needed changes and accomplish extraordinary things. It is important to continually remind yourself of your vision. Discover a motto, phrase, verse, that speaks to you and inspires your vision. The motto echoed at our school every day on the announcements was, "The future belongs to those who believe in the beauty of their dreams." (Credited to Eleanor Roosevelt from her July 4, 1957 syndicated newspaper column.) Envision the future you want to create and then have the courage and confidence to do so.

Enabling others to act: Successful leaders know how to build a team based on trust, collaboration, and empowerment. PSEL Standard 6 (see Chapter 7 for more details) identifies what an effective leader must do to build the professional capacity of school personnel. A key element is to understand and utilize the characteristics of distributed leadership. "Distributed leadership is not something 'done' by an individual 'to' others, or a set of individual actions through which people contribute to a group or organization . . . [it] is a group activity that works through and within relationships, rather than individual action" (Bennett et al., 2003, p. 3). Hire the best, offer training and support, and then give your staff the autonomy to make key decisions that impact learning and align with the vision and mission of your school.

Standard 4: Curriculum, Instruction, and Assessment

Model the way: Truly understand your own beliefs, commitments, and core values. You need to model these daily, especially during challenging times. Adults and students are watching what you say and do, so act accordingly. Leaders are the first to act and they take on any task necessary to get the job done, i.e., wipe tables, answer phones, sweep the floor, cover duty schedules, chaperone events, cover a class, support a fellow administrator. I have even seen some driving buses. Successful principals should be quick to take the blame and freely offer compliments and acknowledge achievements by their team. Model to others how much you truly care—actions speak louder than words.

Encourage the heart: Celebrate the small wins which will build confidence and self-esteem in those seeking affirmation for a job well done, especially if a teacher's instructional or classroom management skills are at the novice level. Be present with your students, staff, and community on a daily basis. Smile, look people in the eye, bend down to the height of students, give authentic feedback, compliment genuinely, critique privately, and call people by name. Build a trusting climate where all feel welcome.

Relationships and Connectedness

To be an effective instructional leader, you must know and understand pedagogy, that is, the best approaches to teaching and learning in a variety of settings, i.e., in person, hybrid, or virtual. You should be addressing how family, social, and economic influences impact learning of your students. According to Linda Darling-Hammond et al. (2012), when evaluating teacher effectiveness, one of the largest influences on student learning is identifying and understanding the socio-economic conditions for each student. Educators need to connect with students by knowing them, their family, their backgrounds, likes, interests, and motivations. As Ruby Payne reminds us in her book *Emotional Poverty in All Demographics* (2018, p. 53), "When bonding and attachment is not secure and the inner self is weak, then the brain is not integrated and regulated. The result may be anger, anxiety, rage, revenge, and violence." Strong relationships are critical to student success. It is important to know your families and the circumstances in which they live. Walk home with groups of students after school. See who goes home to an empty place—are they safe? Ride the bus, so you see the dynamics of the bus environment and the neighborhoods in which your students live. These provide key insight into your students' environmental factors.

In order to support your teachers in their continuous improvement, it is important to visit their classrooms on a regular basis to see what skills and dispositions teachers show on a consistent basis. It is also a great way to get to know your students and determine the best professional development teachers need to reach their professional goals. Do not forget about your professional classified staff. Take time to walk with them, understand their roles and responsibilities they strive to achieve daily. What needs do they have to do their job better with greater satisfaction?

If you have not already learned about **Trauma Informed Teaching**, we would encourage you to take a deeper dive in this area. It is a mindset from where teachers begin planning for all students. Research by Abraham Maslow (1943; see McLeod, 2018) has shown that a safe learning environment with nurturing adult relationships fosters a sense of belonging that is critical for healing and learning to occur. Maslow used the terms physiological, safety, belonging and love, social needs, esteem, and self-actualization to develop a pattern people go through for motivation that leads to learning. A common phrase of late is: "We need to Maslow before we can Bloom." Referring to the need to establish a safe, loving environment where students and adults feel a sense of safety and belonging, before they will be able to climb Bloom's Taxonomy for critical thinking and learning.

ASCD published an article in *Educational Leadership* (October 2019) written by Jessica Minahan, where she writes about the importance of schools understanding how changes in the classroom can positively support students impacted by trauma (Minahan, 2019). Minahan shared in her paper that according to the Centers for Disease Control, schools can expect two-thirds of their students to have been impacted by at least one form of trauma, including being abused, witnessing violence, experiencing neglect, severe poverty, or a natural disaster. Of the public health concerns facing schools today, trauma may well be the most impactful. For this reason and others, educators and principals need to get to know their students, form trusting relationships, so they best know how to connect and plan for learning. Consider experiences your students may have had during the COVID-19 global crisis and the traumatic impact on their overall health and mental well-being.

Standard 4: Curriculum, Instruction, and Assessment

Time for Change

Education systems have a moral imperative to re-examine current practices and become the change agent needed to continually provide a robust, high-quality system of learning where administrators want to inspire, teachers want to galvanize student learning, families want to belong, and students want to excel.

Your primary responsibility as a principal is to the academic success, social-emotional welfare, and safety of students, staff, and community. Standard 4 states: "Effective educational leaders develop and support intellectually rigorous and coherent systems of curriculum, instruction, and assessment to promote each student's academic success and well-being" (PSEL, 2015, p. 12). At no time in our recent history have the world's education systems been more challenged than they were during the recent medical and social crisis. During this time our consideration for safety heightened to a greater proportion—sometimes at the expense of academic growth and achievement and the social-emotional health of students and staff. This caused many schools to close, students and teachers had to transition quickly to online learning without adequate technology, teaching strategies, or viable curriculum, and internet and technology access was limited, as was student learning. Teachers and students were forced into an educational system where distance learning was temporarily the only option. Parents, grandparents, or adult caregivers were largely responsible for supporting student learning in the home environment at a time where they, most often, were trying to manage the challenges of working from home or dealing with the effects of unemployment. Not only was the bandwidth of the internet stretched, so was people's patience and time. Through this period of crisis, families, schools, and communities learned to offer grace, kindness, and forgiveness to one another as teaching and learning made a sharp shift into a new paradigm where education became increasingly more complex.

In education, change is inevitable; however, at this period, contemplative change was critical to meet the growing demands of educators, parents, businesses, and society. Reflectively speaking, there has been a significant amount of good that has resulted due to the crisis related to education. For example, teachers have been incredibly innovative in how to teach with technology and meet the varying needs of students. Principals were

55

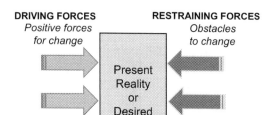

Figure 5.1 Force Field Analysis and the Three Stages of Change
Source: Adapted from Kurt Lewin (1948)

challenged with how best to support their teachers and staff, communicate effectively, and continue to be the leader they expect of themselves.

It may be easy to admit that change needs to happen, but how is it best implemented? Kurt Lewin is a change theorist dating back to 1947 whose research is still very relevant today. In the principal preparation courses at our university, future leaders are introduced to the basics of Lewin's three-stage change model, Force Field Analysis (Lewin, 1948). These three stages of change are shown in Figure 5.1:

The three stages include:

- **Stage 1: Unfreeze** the system—shake it up. Take time to understand the present reality or status quo. What are the needed initiatives to consider based on data? Who or what are the "restraining forces" or obstacles to change, and the "driving forces" or positive forces for change?
- **Stage 2: Implement Needed Change** based on your analysis of the issue(s)
- **Stage 3: Re-freeze** after the desired state of the system has been achieved. Give people time to adjust so as not to be in constant flux or in a state of motion. Begin collecting and analyzing data to track continuous improvements. Re-establish the equilibrium of the organization

Standard 4: Curriculum, Instruction, and Assessment

In the field of education, our system was **unfrozen** and shaken up due to the COVID-19 crisis. It was the catalyst to change current practices. Some students fell behind in academics and behavior or did not attend school at all. Teachers and administrators worried about the social-emotional well-being of students, families, and self. In this first stage of change, we identify the "restraining forces." Restraining forces might include personnel, budget, resources, skills, time, technology, community, new protocols, or district pressures. Take an honest look at current curriculum, instructional practices, and assessments. Are they meeting the needs of the classrooms? What changes should be made? Are your school's vision, mission, and core values still relevant? At the same time, identify the "driving forces." What is working well, who are your champions of change, what budget or resources do you have available? Now is a great time to come together as a faculty, staff, and community (include students as well, especially grades 5–12) to do a SWOT/C analysis. Identify the school/district's Strengths, Weaknesses, Opportunities, Threats, and Challenges. Seek facts to know where the organization is currently with socio-emotional risks, assessment data, enrollment, surveys, teacher evaluations, etc. to understand the "status quo" or present reality. As Lewin reports, "To bring about any change, the balance between the forces which maintain the social self-regulation at a given level has to be upset" (Lewin, 1948, p. 47).

The second stage is to **implement needed change**. After analyzing the SWOT/C analysis and other data you gathered, revisit your vision and mission statements, adjusting as required (see Chapter 2 for more details). Everyone in the system should create SMART goals (discussed later in this chapter). Members of your school team should focus on how they will support the vision and mission based on goals with a timeline and actionable steps. As the leader, look at what initiatives or actions you are pursuing based on the data. Evaluate your curriculum updates and the intentional use of professional learning communities (PLCs). You may want to consider increasing resources, providing professional development, updating technology, and making changes to the master schedule, classroom design, and safety protocols. I recommend the use of the updated *Understanding by Design* (Wiggins & McTighe, 2013) related to instructional planning and assessment. To support teacher development, you should increase the number of classroom walk-throughs that are authentic and provide timely feedback. This topic is discussed later in this chapter.

Lastly, stage three, we **re-freeze** the system by allowing everyone to settle into a routine with the implemented changes. Make sure to check in with individuals frequently to see what their "stages of concern" might be with the changes. More information can be obtained on "stages of concern" by reviewing the Concerns Based Adoption Model or CBAM, found in the book *Implementing Change: Patterns, Principles, and Potholes* by Hall and Hord (2015).

As the world continues to heal from this latest crisis, principals must focus on meeting Standard 4 expectation "a," which says an effective leader should "Implement coherent systems of curriculum, instruction, and assessment that promote the mission, vision, and core values of the school, incorporate high expectations for student learning, align with academic standards, and are culturally responsive" (PSEL, 2015, p. 12).

Education inequities became very apparent in many areas during the COVID crisis. Some students had adult support and supervision at home with computers and strong internet in a safe environment, where many others did not. The role of student, teacher, administrator, and parent must keep pace with these changing times so no child is left behind, at no fault of their own. It was encouraging to watch teachers, principals, and superintendents successfully adapt as they quickly became responsible for teaching and learning online, hybrid, or in person (sometimes all in the same day).

What do principals need to consider in the area of curriculum, instruction, and assessment? According to the expectations "b" and "c" of PSEL (2015, p. 12), effective leaders must be able to "Align and focus systems of curriculum, instruction, and assessment within and across grade levels to promote student academic success, love of learning, the identities and habits of learners, and healthy sense of self." They should "Promote instructional practice that is consistent with knowledge of child learning and development, effective pedagogy, and the needs of each student" (PSEL, 2015, p. 12).

As schools re-open for another year of learning, specific attention should be focused on considering where students are functioning academically and social-emotionally. Then you can design curriculum, instruction, and assessment that is future forward, meeting the needs of all learners, focusing on the Social Emotional Learning (SEL) and Tier I Instruction. The field of social-emotional learning has grown rapidly with many curricula products flooding the market to assist schools with approaches, research, resources, and tools to help educators develop social, emotional, and interpersonal

Standard 4: Curriculum, Instruction, and Assessment

skills to better support our students' varied developmental needs. Broadly speaking, SEL refers to the process through which individuals learn and apply a set of social, emotional, behavioral, and character skills required to succeed in a school setting, the workplace, relationships, and citizenship (Humphrey et al., 2011). Over the years, as a principal, we have employed several techniques and programs to support our students' growth and development in the areas of character development, self-regulation or executive function, conflict resolution, and anti-bullying efforts. It is important to be selective of the products and programs you choose so you can truly accomplish your goals of aiding the progressive development of children and adults.

Standard 4 expectation "d" describes what an effective leader should know and be able to provide in the area of rigor and relevance: "Promote instructional practice that is intellectually challenging, authentic to student experiences, recognizes student strengths, and is differentiated and personalized" (PSEL, 2015, p. 12). To better meet the academic needs of individual students, many schools have adopted the RTI—Response-To-Intervention instructional process model. All teachers and support staff in our school were trained on this model, with consistent and timely refresher courses to make sure a high degree of integrity of the model is maintained. Along with the training, follow-through and support by you, the principal, is critical to the success of the model. The best part of my day was time spent in classrooms working with groups of learners supporting math and reading development.

The RTI Action Network outlines the essential components in the Tiered Instructional Intervention to include Tier I—Core Instruction, Tier II—Group Interventions, and Tier III—Intensive Interventions, Ongoing Student Assessment, and Family Involvement. Tier I Instruction is aligned with State Standards and focuses on core reading and math. According to the RTI Action Network website (rtinetwork.org), "Many who advocate RTI models indicate that around 75%–80% of students should, theoretically, be expected to reach successful levels of competency through Tier 1 delivery" (RTI Action Network, n.d.). We were fortunate at our school to have great success with continuous student growth and development as evidenced through benchmark and state test scores with Tier I, II, and III Instruction and Interventions.

As a full Title I School, parent and family engagement was critical to this success. We established family nights that revolved around reading and math games and activities highlighting the work being done in the classrooms, so parents are knowledgeable and can reinforce learning at home. One of the favorite events was family math night focusing on the theme of Economics and Personal Finance. Arizona is one of the few states that includes Economics and Personal Finance in the Social Science Standards K-12. The comments from parents were very encouraging, including feedback statements like "This information will help get our family finances back on track." Or "I wish I had this information when I was in school; I may have made better choices."

Increasing teacher quality is the best offense for improving effective teaching with greater student achievement. By taking a closer look at how the PSEL describe an *Effective Leader* under Standard 4 (p. 12), you can better understand the interconnectedness of the Curriculum, Instruction, and Assessment triad. The school's learning system of curriculum, instruction, and assessment should promote the shared vision, mission, and core values (review Chapter 2) and high expectations for student learning by aligning with culturally responsive academic standards. Take a closer look at your curriculum, instruction, and assessment independently and you will be able to better understand their interconnectedness, as illustrated in Figure 5.2. It is counter-productive to try to unweave the curriculum, instruction, and assessment triad. They are tightly linked in so many ways.

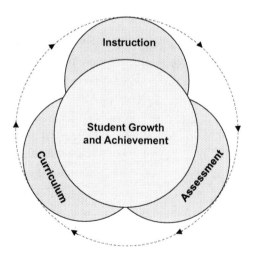

Figure 5.2 The Interdependency of the Curriculum, Instruction, and Assessment Triad
Source: Created by Dr. Robyn Hansen

Standard 4: Curriculum, Instruction, and Assessment

Curriculum

Another book that greatly impacted my leadership career has been Marzano's *What Works in Schools: Translating Research into Action* (2003). In it he implores schools and districts to focus the highest priority on raising student achievement. The question then is, how? According to Marzano and others, a school and district needs a guaranteed and viable curriculum. "A guaranteed and viable curriculum (GVC) ensures that all students have an equal opportunity to learn (OTL). Each student will have access to an effective or highly effective teacher, and access to the same content, knowledge and skills in each section or class" (Marzano, 2003, p. 22). With a GVC every student is guaranteed access to materials and teaching to learn a core curriculum with time available to meet their learning needs while acquiring knowledge in the guaranteed curriculum. Marzano (2003, p. 7) states, "The schools that are highly effective produce results that almost entirely overcome the effects of student background."

Curriculum is based on standards, not textbooks. It is the scope and sequence of information students are to learn. In most states, there are too many standards to cover in a single year so you should work with your teachers collaboratively to create a curriculum map for each grade level/ subject. A curriculum map is paramount to structuring the curriculum to provide rigorous, relevant courses that offer students and teachers time to study and apply knowledge at a greater depth. The map shows teachers and parents what students need to learn. Curriculum should be scaffolded so standards are taught in a logical sequence with enough overlap to avoid gaps, especially in locations of high mobility or following a crisis. Marzano (2003) reminds us that curriculum must be viewed from a horizontal and vertical lens demonstrating the sequence of what is to be learned.

The use of vertical articulation, discussing academic standards and outcomes from grade to grade or course to course, is vital. The most effective use of a curriculum map is when teachers are given time to create a map on their own and not just use one created by someone else. Teachers benefit from the collaborative conversation with others. They truly understand the vertical and horizontal alignment of the standards and are more likely to adhere to the curriculum map when they are part of its development. By "unpacking" the academic standards, teachers identify what is essential

61

to be taught and learned. Students are hungry for and capable of doing rigorous work. Schools must implement the curriculum to be challenging and support effective instruction. This is particularly true at the secondary level in order to have the content areas map of all courses in math, science, English, and the social sciences.

Your curriculum and instruction should be reflective of the surrounding culture. For example, when visiting schools on the Navajo Nation in northern Arizona, I immediately saw how the native language and customs of the Navajo people are woven throughout the curriculum in a variety of subjects, including language arts, music, physical education, and the social sciences. Likewise, when visiting schools in Hawaii, I saw how the native culture and language was visible throughout their curriculum and daily activities. When teachers and principals come together, with support from the district, to work collaboratively and adding to their collective capacity, they maximize learning for all students while keeping the cultures and traditions alive for current and future generations.

 Instruction

What should principals know and be able to do in the area of instructional leadership? According to Leithwood et al. (2004), "Leadership is second only to classroom instruction among all school-related factors that contribute to what students learn at school." A more recent Wallace Foundation report, *How Principals Affect Students and Schools*, cites new empirical evidence that says:

> We find that a 1 standard deviation increase in principal effectiveness increases the typical student's achievement by 0.13 standard deviations in math and 0.09 standard deviations in reading. To translate this result, we estimate that the impact of replacing a below-average elementary school principal (i.e., one at the 25th percentile of effectiveness) with an above-average principal (i.e., at the 75th percentile) would result in an additional 2.9 months of math learning and 2.7 months of reading learning each year for students in that school. Effects of this replacement in math would be larger than more than two-thirds of educational interventions compiled in a recent review, and the effects in reading would be larger than about half of interventions.
>
> (Kraft, 2020, cited in Grissom et al., 2021, p. xiii)

Standard 4: Curriculum, Instruction, and Assessment

As the Wallace Report points out, a teacher's influence is within the classroom, based on the number of students they instruct each year (approximately 25–150). A principal's influence is far reaching when considering the effect on all students enrolled in the school for multiple years. With this being said, principals need to be strong, confident instructional leaders—leadership does matter in the success of our students.

The PSEL expectation "c" for this standard defines an effective leader as someone who is able to "Promote instructional practice that is consistent with knowledge of child learning and development, effective pedagogy, and the needs of each student" and expectation "d" states an effective leader should "Ensure instructional practice that is intellectually challenging, authentic to student experiences, recognizes student strengths, and is differentiated and personalized" (PSEL, 2015, p. 12).

The big question becomes: How am I supposed to accomplish these expectations? Reflecting on my extensive career in PK-12 school leadership, here are a few of the most impactful initiatives and skills we used to become and remain a highly rated school of choice:

- Know and understand pedagogy and the curriculum. Be able to unpack academic standards to have an intellectual conversation with your teachers
- Increase your proficiency in the use of pertinent data and technology
- Be knowledgeable of the many facets of education, i.e., child development, social-emotional learning, and neuroscience
- Be excited about classroom observations and understand how this positively impacts instruction
- Keep life fun and energized at school
- Build strong relationships with students, faculty, staff, parents, and community
- Model a healthy work–life balance
- Have mentors to support your professional growth and development throughout your career. Get a mentor, be a mentor
- Participate actively in professional organizations at both state and national levels

One of the best-practice initiatives used in our school and district included developing PLCs for teachers. A team of teacher volunteers and myself attended a three-day summit sponsored by Solution Tree™ where we learned from Richard and Rebecca Dufour, Robert Eaker, and others about the value and benefit of establishing PLCs within our school. We found time in our school's master schedule for common planning. Our professional development was meaningfully focused on data analysis and its use in unit and lesson design. We established teacher-led instructional teams that were laser focused on individual student growth and achievement, data analysis, developing common formative and summative assessments, unit planning, collegial support, and goal setting.

It should be noted that principals also benefit greatly from being part of a principal-led PLC. The job of a principal can be very isolating. Having dedicated time to meet with other principals is not a luxury, but a necessity. Our district principals would rotate school meeting locations to provide time for classroom walk-throughs, increase the inter-rater reliability of teacher evaluations, and "walk the halls" to get ideas of fundraisers, parent engagement, student work, data walls, etc. Following the implementation of PLCs at the teacher and principal levels, further professional development was provided in McTighe and Wiggins' *Understanding by Design: Professional Development Workbook* (2004) to highlight the interconnectedness of curriculum, assessment, and instruction. If your district/charter does not currently have Principal PLCs, speak to your colleagues about starting one. You will all benefit greatly from the rich conversations, sharing of ideas, and collegiality, resulting in increased productivity and decreased stress.

By using Understanding by Design in planning instructional units, teachers began with the end in mind: what are the **desired results**? All too often, consideration for how teachers will assess if students truly understand the concepts of the standards, goals, and objectives comes too late in the planning process. With Understanding by Design, assessments are designed in Stage 2 as part of Assessment Evidence and Performance Tasks. Teachers plan performance assessments together, as well as other types of evidence of learning such as formative assessments, quizzes, summative exams, performance tasks, or reflection. During Stage 3: Learning Plan, teachers decide what learning experiences students will need to achieve the desired results. Understanding by Design encourages teachers to adhere to the PSEL expectation of an effective leader as stated in Standard 4 expectation

64

Standard 4: Curriculum, Instruction, and Assessment

"g," which states: "Use assessment data appropriately… to monitor student progress and improve instruction" (PSEL, 2015, p. 12).

Teachers are the architects of the learning experiences. Differentiation, engagement, innovation, and collaborative learning is planned to support the learning needs of individual students. We have also used the Understanding by Design framework in planning school field trips to ensure the desired outcomes were achieved. You can even try it with your next family vacation as a place to begin!

At the recommendation of our leadership team, we added a Stage 4: Reflection to the Understanding by Design process. Reflection is an active process our school community uses in all aspects of our daily practices to support continuous improvement. The dialogues teachers have in their PLCs is rich and focused on student success based on timely data.

Simultaneously, while we were implementing Understanding by Design, I began reading more about brain research and brain plasticity. Brain plasticity means the brain continues to develop pathways to permit lifelong learning. The brain does not have a limited capacity. I was particularly interested in how to develop and challenge the learning capacity for our students in Special Education and the Gifted and Talented students. This goal aligns with Standard 4, expectation "c," which says, "Promote instructional practice that is consistent with knowledge of child learning and development, effective pedagogy, and the needs of each student" (PSEL, 2015, p. 12). While attending a conference, Dr. Pat Wolfe, author of *Brain Matters: Translating Research into Classroom Practice* (2010), was a keynote and breakout session speaker. She related neuroscience research to improved classroom practice that was fascinating and practical. The BrainWare group interviewed Dr. Wolfe in 2020 and that interview can be found at:

https://mybrainware.com/blog/interview-with-patricia-wolfe-author-brain-matters/

Her talk was enlightening and impacted my leadership for the rest of my career. She highlighted several areas that all educators (and parents) should know:

1. Experiences shape the brain, and it is the only organ in the body that sculpts itself from outside experiences. A reason to support field trips and family vacations and outings

2. Memory is not stored in just one area of the brain, but across interconnected areas

3. Memory is not static; it decays naturally over time, but there is a lot to be done to slow the deterioration

4. Emotion is a primary catalyst in the learning process—we know this and encourage positive classroom environments promoting learning

5. The environment must be physically and psychologically safe for learning to occur—Maslow introduced safety and a sense of belonging in 1943

In her 2020 interview, Dr. Wolfe recommends we begin to incorporate this data in our classrooms and schools. She encourages all educators to become knowledgeable in the basics of how the brain works. Brain-compatible instruction adds to higher achievement, but the goal is more than high test scores. Our students need to be able to transfer knowledge in a variety of applications, including real-world predictable and unpredictable settings. Marzano (2003, p. 109) also affirms, "Learning requires engagement in tasks that are structured or are sufficiently similar to allow for effective transfer of knowledge." Wolfe also conducted additional research and trainings in the areas of brain and addiction, early brain development, the aging brain, and reading and the brain.

A friend whom I respect and value, Dr. Lisa Strohman, has a TED Talk entitled *Empowering Kids to Rise Above Technology Addition* (September 30, 2017) which is required viewing for graduate students in one of my principal preparation courses, *Critical Issues in Educational Leadership*. She has also created a TED Talk in March 2021 on *How Do You Find Self Worth* that talks about how social media is influencing our self-worth. She has written two books to accompany her research, called *Unplug: Raising Kids In a Technology Addicted World* (Strohman & Westendorf, 2015) and *Digital Distress: Growing Up Online* (Strohman & Westendorf, in press). She reminds us, as with any addiction, you must first admit there is a problem. Adults and children are on their devices a vast majority of the day. Much of the learning modality in our schools is now focused on the use of technology. Parents and educators need to understand the effects and unintended consequences that prolonged screen time may have on brain development, executive function (self-regulatory skills), eye movement,

Standard 4: Curriculum, Instruction, and Assessment

and reading. Not to mention lack of exercise, play, social interaction, and internet predators stalking our children and those who are vulnerable. Dr. Strohman shares effective strategies parents and educators should use which offer hope for those who are concerned that technology is negatively impacting their children. Dr. Strohman is a world-renowned psychologist and a staunch advocate for youth, bringing awareness of the dangers of technology abuse and mental health. Technology is an integral part of our daily lives; however, understanding unintended consequences or abuse of technology is vital for parents and educators alike.

Dr. Wolfe's and Dr. Strohman's work, and that of other notable brain researchers, brings us to the research of William Daggett, and the Rigor/Relevance Framework (2016). Use of this framework by our district to support improved curriculum, instruction, and assessment was instrumental in academic growth and achievement of many of our schools. If you or your district are looking for an impactful model, you may want to consider additional research on Daggett's model to increase student performance and improve instruction based on strong student relationships. Daggett's work aligns with Standard 4 expectation "d," which states: "Ensure instructional practice that is intellectually challenging, authentic to student experiences, recognizes student strengths, and is differentiated and personalized" (PSEL, 2015, p. 12). Here is a link to a white paper with a synopsis of his work:

https://leadered.com/wp-content/uploads/Rigor-Relevance-Framework-White-Paper-2016.pdf

When first implemented, I would conduct classroom walk-throughs based on Daggett's A, B, C, D quadrants and tally, in each quadrant, the number of questions a teacher would ask as we focused on critical thinking questioning as a part of a complete lesson. The data showed that 83% of questions the teachers asked of students were in quadrants A and C. These results indicated that more professional development was needed on how best to apply the learning to real-world predictable and unpredictable situations. An example of my sample data within the four quadrants of Dr. Daggett's Rigor, Relevance, and Relationships is provided in Figure 5.3.

As our teachers continued to learn and develop skills following McTighe and Wiggins' *Understanding by Design*, we then explored more deeply the area of Dr. Daggett's Rigor, Relevance, and Relationships. All the research works we reviewed complemented each other very well and were immediately useful; therefore the teachers did not feel the professional development was "one more thing added to their already full plate." The

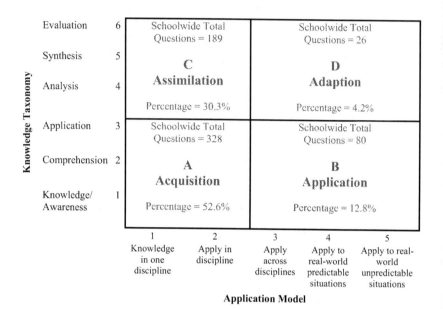

Figure 5.3 Sample Walk-Through Results by Quadrant
Source: Adapted from William Daggett (2016), Copyright Houghton Mifflin Harcourt

work was well orchestrated and tied together perfectly to enhance student achievement through improved curriculum, assessment, and instruction. PSEL Standard 4 expectation "d" states that effective leaders are expected to "Ensure instructional practice that is intellectually challenging, authentic to student experiences, recognizes student strengths, and is differentiated and personalized" (PSEL, 2015, p. 12). As the instructional leader, it is imperative that you and your administrative team are visiting classrooms on a regular basis. Gathering valuable data to inform professional development, both school-wide and individually, to inform best practices and support improvement planning.

To be an effective instructional leader, you must know and understand pedagogy, that is, the best approaches to teaching and learning in a variety of settings, i.e., in person, hybrid, or virtual. One of the graduate courses I teach at the university is *Supervision of Instruction*. I truly believe this is one of the most important course offerings in the preparation of principals. The philosophy studied is that of Clinical Supervision. "Clinical supervision is a complex enterprise, but its essential elements—planning conference,

Standard 4: Curriculum, Instruction, and Assessment

classroom observation, feedback conference—are simple" (Gall & Acheson, 2011, p. 62). Teacher observations should be safe, supportive, and informative, leading to improved practice. Peer observations also lead to better teaching. I recommend that you encourage teachers to visit other teachers' classrooms for short 10-to-15-minute periods, focusing on one aspect that is being practiced by the single teacher or the school, i.e., differentiating, classroom management, engagement, critical thinking questioning techniques, use of technology, etc.

We began this practice several years ago when the idea of peer visits was discussed in a faculty meeting but there was not much voluntary involvement until my school photography company gave me an e-reader to give away. To generate some enthusiasm for peer visits, each time a teacher visited another's classroom they would email me to share a couple positive take-aways from the experience. They did not share who they visited, as this was not at all part of anyone's evaluation. At the end of the semester, the participating teachers' names were put into a "hat" based on the number of times they visited classrooms. One name was drawn to win the device. The first semester 48% of the faculty visited at least one classroom with 25% visiting at least three different classrooms. We were given another device second semester and this time 96% of faculty visited at least one classroom and 83% of the faculty visited at least three different classrooms. This simple activity helped increase collaboration, communication, and support of teachers throughout the school. Teachers became accustomed to and looked forward to colleagues joining them in their classrooms. Doors remained open and professional relationships flourished. This might be an activity you would like to try at your school.

Continuing with our conversation on supporting teacher instructional practices, there are several reasons why clinical supervision is used in our principal preparation program at the university. Here are a few highlights on planning conferences, observations, and feedback conferences:

1. The teacher-driven planning conference allows the teacher and administrator time for discussion about the upcoming formal observation. The administrator and teacher discuss classroom observation techniques that will be used to inform the continuous improvement of the teacher. Ideally, prior to a formal observation the administrator has been in the classroom several times offering feedback and recommendations

69

2. During the observation, the administrator is busy taking notes based on the discussion from the planning conference using seating chart data collection techniques. Several observational data collection techniques are outlined in the Gall and Acheson book *Clinical Supervision and Teacher Development* (2011) to support teacher development. Although script-taping is one of the techniques, there are better ways that give valuable feedback to the teacher based on seating charts. An observer can easily, with practice, use three to four techniques in a single class setting

3. Third, the feedback conference, preferably within 24 hours of the observation, is teacher-driven, just as in the planning conference. The teacher reviews the data and reflects on how well the lesson went. The conversation focuses on improvements to instruction, assessment data, and movement toward professional goal (SMART) attainment. Effective supervision is cyclical in nature— the feedback conference sets the stage for the next planning conference in a never-ending cycle of improvement

SMART (Specific, Measurable, Attainable, Relevant, Time-based) goals are used extensively within our school. This type of goal adds clarity and focus, while defining action steps greatly increase levels of job performance and success as they relate to the school's vision and mission. Everyone in our school writes goals based on our school's vision and mission statements and data and personal outlook for the future. I always include certified and classified staff, students, and administration in this process. The goals are reviewed by each individual at least quarterly with refinement as needed. SMART templates are available on many internet locations with examples for teachers, students, and administrators.

Culturally Responsive Teaching

Culturally responsive teaching is not a new concept, but it has received greater attention in the past few years and provides a more well-rounded educational environment. Geneva Gay from the University of Washington, Seattle, wrote the book *Culturally Responsive Teaching: Theory, Research, and Practice* in 2018. She discusses how culturally responsive teaching

Standard 4: Curriculum, Instruction, and Assessment

uses cultural qualities, insights, experiences, history, and viewpoints of ethnically diverse students as a means for teaching more effectively (Gay, 2018). She highlights five essential elements of culturally responsive teaching, which are summarized here:

1. Be mindful of your knowledge of different cultures and ethnicities within your community

2. Review curriculum and library sources to be inclusive of ethnic and cultural diversity content

3. Build caring, safe classrooms and school

4. Know the best ways to communicate with ethnically diverse families and students

5. Be reflective of classroom practices making sure instruction is delivered responsively to ethnic diversity

This chapter is focused on developing better practices in the areas of curriculum, instruction, and assessment. Instructional leaders and teachers agree that effective teaching requires high-level knowledge in content areas and pedagogy. To truly be effective in our teaching and meet the needs of all students, we must also understand the make-up of our student population: their beliefs, perspectives, and experiences. Too many teachers are not prepared to teach an ethnically and culturally diverse student population. I know this first-hand. As a new principal, I was not initially prepared to lead a diverse school community. In a few short years, the demographics of our school community changed considerably, and we went from primarily English- and Spanish-speaking families to families that spoke 17 different languages as the main language at home. To begin to welcome our new families, flags of their country adorned the main hallway so they would feel included. As other families joined our community, they too felt welcome and knew that others from their country were enrolled. Our school developed partnerships with the nearby high school, community colleges, and university to have our welcome letters, brochures, registration material, health cards, student handbook, newsletters, etc. translated into all the languages. And, if needed, have someone come to our school to translate for the student and family.

Students were given opportunities to share special memories of their prior home country, i.e., language, holidays, traditions, values, foods,

71

dress, religion, government, music, topography, sports, family, and friends. Our school already had Student Ambassadors in place to give tours and welcome new students, but we found this program to be even more valuable now with the rapid change in school culture. We invited parents/grandparents to participate in parent groups, after-school events, and musical programs. The vision and mission were revisited as our core values were re-examined, making sure we were inclusive and meeting the needs of our students. Our curriculum was reviewed to see what updates could be made to the formal curriculum (district adopted and approved) and informal curricula (adaptions made to differentiate at our school while still following the standards).

Teachers and staff participated in professional development focusing on the strengths of our diverse community and changes we could make to be more understanding and culturally responsive. We evaluated our hiring practices to ensure we were still being diverse on campus. Culturally responsive teachers embed instructional materials and make adjustments to improve the quality of education for all students. The librarian increased reading choices and authors, teachers used more culturally diverse literacy in the classroom to introduce concepts and lessons, the music teacher chose more diverse songs, dances, and performances, the physical education teacher learned games from students' native countries. Our sixth-grade teachers expanded the culminating World's Fair social science unit where students took our school community on a world tour showcasing their home country or nationality. The art teacher, along with student and parent volunteers, painted murals representing the different cultures at the school.

Faculty and staff positively embraced our students establishing an inclusive learning environment where families felt welcome. Our students easily accepted and wanted to learn more about the different cultures and traditions. Results from surveys and positive statements, reinforced our knowledge of promoting a welcoming environment. This type of inclusion became contagious and new curricula ideas, clubs, pen pal program, events, and performances sprang up at all levels. Our school community, the learning experiences, and friendships became richer because of the level of diversity we enjoyed. Evidence of our school theme, "One World, One Dream," was seen throughout the school. Upon entering the school, you see a world map showing all the countries that are represented by the staff, faculty, and students.

Standard 4: Curriculum, Instruction, and Assessment

Assessment

Even though assessment is the third component of this triad, it should not be mistaken as less important. All three components are interconnected and work in concert with one another. Quality assessments allow educators to identify skills already acquired, gaps in learning, and a student's misunderstanding of prior materials. Thus, better enabling the teacher to plan for and meet the individual needs of each learner. According to the PSEL expectation "f," effective leaders "Employ valid assessments that are consistent with knowledge of child learning and development and technical standards of measurement" and expectation "g" states "Use assessment data appropriately and within technical limitations to monitor student progress and improve instruction" (PSEL, 2015, p. 12). Looking at schools today, time allocated to assessing students could be better spent having them engaged in more discovery and application of knowledge. Too much time is spent preparing for high-stakes tests.

The use of authentic assessments, such as lab experiments, project-based learning, and capstone projects and other performance tasks, as discussed in *Understanding by Design*, are preferred to true/false and question and answer assessments. The more teachers can make assessments a regular part of the daily routine and then use the data in designing challenging classroom learning the more engaged students will be, and teachers. It is important that, as the principal, you encourage teachers to develop common formative and summative assessments within their PLCs. With the use of formative or diagnostic assessments, teachers will know where all the students are in the learning process based on academic standards. This informs teachers of where they need to make learning more rigorous and which students need interventions. Approximately 75%–80% of all students should be receiving Tier I instruction, with Tier II and Tier III instruction for those who need interventions to close learning gaps. Lessons should be differentiated and meaningful.

Some of the formative assessments you may want to consider using are reflective journal entries, graphic organizers, "short" quizzes, bell work, ticket-out-the-door, or class discussion. Formative assessments (assessment "for" learning) can also be used at the end of a lesson or unit as a summative assessment showing the growth of learning, i.e., pre–post-test. Summative assessments (assessment "of" learning) provide data for the teacher and administration showing student growth and achievement. Summative assessments are usually grade bound; however, that should not preclude teachers from making assessments engaging, differentiated, hands on, and performance task oriented. Encourage your teachers to consider the use of technology for summative assessments to be real-world and relevant by having students create a video, podcast, website, pamphlet, create a game, or develop software. According to the PSEL expectation "e," effective leaders "Promote the effective use of technology in the service of teaching and learning" (2015, p. 12). If this is a gap in learning for your teachers, plan to add technology training to your professional development. As with all assessments, you should provide the learner with a rubric, so students know the requirements ahead of time.

A conversation related to curriculum, instruction, and assessment would not be complete without a discussion about grading. Does your school promote mastery learning where students have multiple opportunities to fail and grow before the final grade is recorded? We implemented a grading philosophy in our school that was motivational and positive, which took some time and conversation. Some teachers believe students get one chance to show what they have learned. Feedback is minimal and often students do not feel good about their performance. Others believe students should have several opportunities to improve their grade, representing more of an ipsative philosophy.

Ipsative assessment compares a student's performance with his or her pre-existing performance. With feedback, coaching, and practice students are motivated to continue to improve, working toward their personal best, as in sports. This is where the student SMART goals come in to play. Students track their own progress toward their goals. Gwyneth Hughes' research is highlighted in an article entitled *Ipsative Assessment: Motivation Through Making Progress* (Chapman et al., 2015). Hughes suggests assessments are demotivating for students and outlines how ipsative assessment can be motivating for learners. She points out that assessments can become very competitive. The purpose of assessment should be to offer feedback on performance and learning and help guide instructional planning. Assessments should focus on comparing results from past performance to results on current performance and providing feedback to the learner and teacher. Chapman et al. (2015, p. 248) conclude that "in order to successfully support students' learning, institutions need to adopt a dual system approach that combines traditional purposes of assessments (e.g., competition) with processes that support scaffolded learning (i.e., ipsative assessment)."

Follow-Through Is Critical for Successful Implementation of Initiatives

Several initiatives have been discussed in this chapter, including PLCs, Understanding by Design, the value in understanding neuroscience and brain research, rigor and relevance within curriculum design and instruction, assessment, use of SMART goals, clinical supervision, and the importance of establishing collegial and student relationships. Unfortunately, the best intentions can fail or waste away because of lack of follow-through on the part of the principal/superintendent. Progress toward the vision must be monitored by the principal and the district. With the use of principal PLCs, school leaders resolve challenges together, adding to the principal's collective capacity. Providing first- and second-year principals with an experienced mentor is critical.

The district should be explicit with the expectations for principals related to student achievement and they need to provide personalized, job-embedded professional development maximizing the principal's effectiveness. The use of Title I and II dollars for principal professional development is money well spent. A principal evaluation system (developed by and for principals) should be in place and aligned with the PSEL to guide principals on a continuum of growth throughout their career. The development of principals' self-efficacy is necessary to achieve the vision and mission efficiently.

John Hattie is not only known for his exceptional research on teacher self-efficacy, but also principal self-efficacy. In an article titled "School Principals' Self-Efficacy and Its Measurement in a Context of Re-structuring" (Dimmock & Hattie, 1996), Hattie and Clive Dimmock conclude that leadership self-efficacy is a catalyst for change and decreasing the principal's stress level. With increased self-efficacy of the leader, skill shown in completing performance tasks also increases with greater school reform and management. To be a viable change agent and capable instructional leader, principals need to possess confidence in their abilities. Efficacious principals tend to be more persistent in goal attainment and are more adaptable to change (Osterman & Sullivan, 1996). Not surprising then, Licklider and Niska (1993) report a principal's self-efficacy is directly related to the quality of teacher supervision. The more confident a principal is in their knowledge and skills, the more support teachers will have to improve curriculum, instruction, and assessment practices. A principal's self-efficacy has a positive correlation with quality teaching and improved student learning.

If you are like me, I was asking how, as an administrator, can I accomplish all that is involved in being an effective instructional leader as outlined in the PSEL, while finding time to do other required tasks in a reasonable work week? A few years ago, I discovered that the best professional development for maintaining a work–life balance is *BreakThrough Coaching* (www.the-breakthrough-coach.com). This two-day training will be life changing—truly! Your secretary (you will hear why being a secretary is an honor) and you will learn how to work efficiently and effectively as a team. You will schedule your week with "office" and "coaching" days, setting your priorities, making it easy to get into classrooms, being visible around the school, attending meetings, completing reports, tending to student discipline, supporting staff, meeting with parents and community, staying current with professional reading, while reaching or exceeding all your goals without taking work home. Time is scheduled for family, friends, and exercise, helping to make sure you get and stay healthy—mentally, emotionally, spiritually, and physically. Your family and school community need you around for a long time—you owe it to yourself, and those you love and who love you, to check out BreakThrough Coaching.

Summary

In conclusion, this chapter contained a robust discussion of many complex topics, including curriculum, instruction, assessment, pedagogy, brain research, child development, PLCs, and instructional leadership. Now is the time to review and update the design and implementation of the curriculum, instruction, and assessment at your school to meet the demands of a challenging future where all students succeed and thrive.

It is recommended that you take the PSEL Self-Assessment found in Appendix B at the end of this book. It is important for you to be honest with the evaluation of your current reality related to the standards and

Standard 4: Curriculum, Instruction, and Assessment

expectations. Seek quality professional development to improve your leadership knowledge and skills. Have a clear vision of increased student achievement in a system of high performance. After reflecting on your strengths and gaps in these areas, consider enhancing your professional library with research, books, or articles by some of my favorite authors and researchers:

- Linda Darling-Hammond
- The Wallace Foundation
- Ruby Payne
- McRel
- Robert Marzano
- George Couros
- Charlotte Danielson
- Lee Jenkins
- John Hattie
- Pat Wolfe
- Lisa Strohman
- Michael Fullan
- Michael Schmoker
- William Daggett
- Shawn Smith
- Todd Whitaker

We highly recommend membership of professional organizations, i.e., National Association of Elementary School Principals (NAESP), National Association of Secondary School Principals (NASSP), ASCD, AASA, ISTE, among many others. These organizations provide timely and up-to-date principal-related research articles with relevant information to inform your practice, not to mention the inspiring national conferences.

One of the main reasons the PSEL were developed was due to the role of the principal becoming more complex. Principals and district leaders need standards to guide their practice to provide the best educational environment for developing the whole child, increasing student achievement, faculty performance, and community engagement.

77

Principals with greater self-efficacy adapt to changing conditions, motivate faculty, and provide exceptional learning opportunities for students. The PSEL direct principals and other instructional leaders to have collaborative discussions related to current reality of practice— knowing how best to develop instructional excellence in teachers and staff. The standards help guide principals to focus their energy on ongoing, desired professional development for teachers and staff that is personalized and job-embedded to improve instruction, learning, and student achievement, as found in Standard 4, expectation "a," which states that instructional leaders should "Implement coherent systems of curriculum, instruction, and assessment that promote the mission, vision, and core values of the school, high expectations for student learning, align with academic standards, and are culturally responsive" (PSEL, 2015, p. 12).

Voices From the Field

As a valuable contribution to this *Principal's Desk Reference*, we have collected vignettes shared by award-winning, proven leaders who are effective principals to help you better understand the "how" of implementing each standard. So often we only get the theory, but in this book we want to focus on the "how" of putting it into practice. Following, you will hear from an exemplar Blue Ribbon Principal, who has learned many lessons over the years and is eager to share her thoughts and stories with you.

Vignette by Dr. Marianne Lescher

A principal has many roles, wears many hats, and has tremendous responsibilities. The job is extremely complex and demanding. However, when you get to the very core, you will find curriculum, instruction, and assessment, because most everything starts there. What you teach, how you teach it, where your priorities land, and how you ascertain if you were successful in these endeavors all rests here.

It starts with the vision—where your school is and where you are heading. I had the incredible opportunity to "transform" a typical K-5

Standard 4: Curriculum, Instruction, and Assessment

neighborhood school into a flagship "school of choice" within my district, taking it to a "traditional model" school. The school was a good school but had declining enrollment and changing demographics, such that it was identified to be the first traditional K-8 school in our district. I was tasked with this exciting and daunting project and given a year to envision and design what this new school would be (all while keeping my "day job" at another district K-5 school!).

It all started with the vision... what would this new school "be," what would it look like and feel like when you walked in? What would our priorities be for instructional practices and methodologies? What curriculum materials would we use? What training would the staff need? It all started with visioning. We solicited volunteers for this year-long envisioning journey, and we had teachers from across the district sign on... some were currently on staff of the existing school to be transformed and others were at other district schools. We visited many schools across our geographic area... spending days soaking it all in from several different districts and charters. These other schools were extremely gracious with their time and knowledge, and it gave us the opportunity to see what "traditional models" looked like and felt like.

Throughout this journey, we identified the key components of what would be our core beliefs and values for what teaching and learning would look like for students, staff, and families. We landed on specific curriculum materials and on the methodologies for instruction that would form the cornerstone of our practices. We designed our professional development plans and clearly agreed on what instruction would look like each day. We met as grade-level teams and cross-grade-level teams to vertically articulate and map the progressions for instruction and learning. As staff were added to our team, these priorities were clearly identified and reinforced so that the consistency of application of our core curriculum and instructional components were rock-solid. By the end of our year-long journey, we were confident in our plan and strategies.

Fast forward three years... I received an email that our school was nominated to be a National Blue Ribbon School of Excellence, for our efforts and achievements in "closing the achievement gaps" for our students with exceptional results. We had to compile a profile, submit achievement test results, send in descriptive narratives. It was a comprehensive process and after all was submitted... we waited. A few months later... I received the call... we were a National Blue Ribbon School of Excellence, the first in our district's history! I must admit, the proudest day of my entire career as an educator. Many asked… how did you do it? How did it happen in those first three years in our newly developed and implemented model? As I have reflected many times over, we can trace it back to those first decisions made by our planning and transformation team, where we clearly identified what our priorities would be in the core areas of curriculum, instruction, and assessment. We stood our ground and ensured consistency of implementation. We ensured that 100% of our teachers had the required and essential trainings and we recalibrated each year so that we were sure we were spot on in each classroom.

Fast forward to the ten-year anniversary of our transformational journey. I have the tremendous honor of continuing as the principal of this amazing school. Many staff who began this journey ten years ago continue to be on staff today. We have been recognized as an A+ School of Excellence twice along the way and are a Nationally Accredited School for Spalding (one of only 13 across the US recognized by Spalding Education International). Along the way, we have had our share of challenges and celebrations. We experienced the unimaginable challenges all schools faced with the COVID pandemic and share the concerns across the globe for students who have experienced learning loss such that it could take years to eradicate. When our school reopens again in a "normal" manner, and our teachers and staff return to "normal" schedules… I know that we will have our work cut out for us.

We have learned a great deal during these many months, and we have developed many new skill sets in technology and distance education that will serve us well as we move forward. In our planning process, I will be returning to some key components and principles that have served us well since our school transformed over ten years ago. We must recommit to the core instructional decisions and principles for consistency of implementation of curriculum and standards. We must ensure that teachers recalibrate their methodologies and techniques so that students have seamless opportunities for learning, class-to-class, and grade-to-grade. We will utilize our new learning in technology to enhance the experiences for students, teachers, and families. We will continue to refine, enhance, and re-imagine our vision for students such that they are receiving the best possible opportunities for academic excellence.

References

Bennett, N., Wise, C., Woods, P. A., & Harvey, J. A. (2003). Distributed leadership. *International Journal of Management Reviews, 13*, 251–269, https://doi.org/10.1111/j.1468-2370.2011. 00306.x

BrainWare. (2020). *An interview with Dr. Patricia Wolfe, author of Brain Matters.* [Audio]. https://mybrainware.com/blog/interview-with-patricia-wolfe-author-brain-matters/

Chapman, A., Luhanga, U., & DeLuca, C. (2015). Ipsative assessment: Motivation through marking progress. By Gwyneth Hughes. *British Journal of Educational Studies, 63*(2), 246–248. https://doi.org/10.1080/00071005.2015.1035906

Daggett, W. R. (2016). *Rigor/Relevance Framework®: A guide to focusing resources to increase student performance.* International Center for Leadership in Education. Houghton Mifflin Harcourt. www.daggett.com/pdf/Rigor%20Relevance%20Framework%20White%20Paper%202016.pdf

Darling-Hammond, L., Amrein-Beardsley, A., Haertel, E., & Rothstein, J. (2012). Evaluating teacher evaluation. *Standard Center for Opportunity Policy in Education (SCOPE), 93*(6), 8–15. https://doi.org/10.1177/003172171209300603

Dimmock, C., & Hattie, J. (1996). School principals' self-efficacy and its measurement in a context of restructuring. *School Effectiveness and School Improvement, 7*, 62–75.

Gall, M. D., & Acheson, K. A. (2011). *Clinical supervision and teacher development: Preservice and inservice applications.* John Wiley and Sons, Inc. https://eric.ed.gov/?id=ED476151

Gay, G. (2018). *Culturally responsive teaching: Theory, Research, and Practice* (3rd ed.). Teachers College Press. https://books.google.com/books?id=0ZlNDwAAQBAJ&dq=gay+culturally+responsive+teaching&lr=

Grissom, J. A., Egalite, A. J., & Lindsay, C. A. (2021, February). *How principals affect students and schools: A systematic synthesis of two decades of research.* The Wallace Foundation. www.wallacefoundation.org/principalsynthesis

Hall, G. E., & Hord, S., M. (2015). *Implementing change: Patterns, principles, and potholes.* Pearson. www.worldcat.org/title/implementing-change-patterns-principles-and-potholes/oclc/859579935?referer=di&ht=edition

Humphrey, N., Kalambouka, A., Wigelsworth, M., Lendrum, A., Deighton, J., & Wolpert, M. (2011). Measure of social and emotional skills for children and young people: A systematic review. *Educational and Psychological Measurement, 71*(4), 617–637. https://doi.org/10.1177/0013164410382896

Kouzes, J. M., & Posner, B. Z. (1995). *The leadership challenge: How to keep getting extraordinary things done in organizations* (2nd ed.). Jossey-Bass.

Leithwood, K., Seashore, K., Anderson, S., & Wahlstrom, K. (2004). *Review of research: How leadership influences student learning.* Wallace Foundation. www.wallacefoundation.org/knowledge-center/documents/how-leadership-influences-student-learning.pdf

Lewin, K. (1948). *Resolving social conflicts.* Harper & Brothers.

Licklider, B. L., & Niska, J. M. (1993). Improving supervision of cooperative learning: A new approach to staff development for principals. *Journal of Personnel Evaluation in Education, 6,* 367–378. https://doi.org/10.1007/BF00122136

Marzano, R. J. (2003). *What works in schools: Translating research into action.* ASCD. www.ascd.org/Publications/Books/Overview/What-Works-in-Schools.aspx

McLeod, S. A. (2018, May 21). *Maslow's hierarchy of needs.* Simply Psychology. www.simplypsychology.org/maslow.html

McTighe, J., & Wiggins, G. P. (2004). *Understanding by design: Professional development workbook.* ASCD. www.ascd.org/books/the-understanding-by-design-professional-development-workbook

Minahan, J. (2019). Trauma-informed teaching strategies. *Educational Leadership, 77*(2), 30–35.

National Policy Board for Educational Administration. (2015). *Professional standards for educational leaders.* www.npbea.org/psel/

Osterman, K., & Sullivan, S. (1996). New principals in an urban bureaucracy: A sense of efficacy. *Journal of School Leadership, 6,* 661–690. https://doi.org/10.1177/105268469600600605

Payne, R. K. (2018). *Emotional poverty in all demographics: How to reduce anger, anxiety, and violence in the classroom.* Aha! Process, Inc. www.ahaprocess.com

RTI Action Network: A Program of the National Center for Learning Disabilities. (n.d.). www.rtinetwork.org/essential/tieredinstruction/tiered-instruction-and-intervention-rti-model

Standard 4: Curriculum, Instruction, and Assessment

Strohman, L. K. (2017, September 30). *Empowering kids to rise above technology addiction* [Video]. TED Conferences. www.ted.com/talks/lisa_strohman_empowering_kids_to_rise_above_technology_addiction

Strohman, L. K. (2021, March). *How do you find self worth?* [Video]. TED Conferences. www.ted.com/talks/dr_lisa_strohman_how_do_you_find_self_worth_lisa_strohman_tedxgrandcanyonuniversity?utm_campaign=tedspread&utm_medium=referral&utm_source=tedcomshare

Strohman, L. K., & Westendorf, M. J. (2015). *Unplug: Raising kids in a technology addicted world*. Lulu Publishing Services. www.lulu.com/en/us/shop/melissa-j-westendorf-jd-phd-and-lisa-k-strohman-jd-phd/unplug-raising-kids-in-a-technology-addicted-world/paperback/product-1km986rk.html?page=1&pageSize=4

Strohman, L. K., & Westendorf, M. J. (in press). *Digital distress: Growing up online*. Lulu Publishing Services.

Wiggins, G. P., & McTighe, J. (2013). *Understanding by design* (2nd ed.). ASCD www.ascd.org/Publications/Books/Overview/Understanding-by-Design-Expanded-2nd-Edition.aspx

Wolfe, P. (2010). *Brain matters: Translating research into classroom practice* (2nd ed.). ASCD. https://shop.ascd.org/PersonifyEbusiness/Store/Product-Details/productId/264215877

Standard 5
Community of Care and Support for Students
Frank D. Davidson

> Effective educational leaders cultivate an inclusive, caring, and supportive school community that promotes the academic success and well-being of *each* student.
>
> (PSEL, 2015, p. 13)

Standard 5 emphasizes behaviors of effective leaders that foster a culture of inclusion and acceptance, honor the school community's languages and cultures, address students' social and emotional needs, and create a safe and healthy school environment with a balanced approach to students' academic, social, emotional, and physical needs (PSEL, 2015, p. 13).

One of the consequences of the standards and accountability movement that gained momentum in the 1990s and early 2000s was a substantial focus on students' standardized test scores, generally to the exclusion of other valued aims of schooling. The move in recent years to incorporate more social and emotional learning reflects a desire of school leaders to see students as more than just input–output devices programmed to produce test outcomes, but as living, breathing, thinking organisms with needs, interests, and challenges that are all their own. Citing the insufficiency of a narrow approach toward academic achievement, Murphy suggests that professional standards should involve "weaving the wisdom, needs, concerns, interests, and worries of students deeply into the 'doing of schooling' without sacrificing academic success" (2015, p. 725). Standard 5 of PSEL states that effective educational leaders have a responsibility to "cultivate an inclusive, caring, and supportive school community that promotes the academic success and well-being of each student" (2015, p. 13).

Standard 5: Community of Care

Inclusion

Until recently, inclusion and inclusive education has largely been associated with special education. Young and Arnold describe a broader perspective of inclusion to include all student groups. They assert that leaders cannot meet stakeholders' expectations for educational outcomes without an "intentional focus on inclusion" (2020, p. 2), the goal of which (stated in expectation "a") is to "Build and maintain a safe, caring, and healthy school environment that meets the academic, social, emotional, and physical needs of each student" (PSEL, 2015, p. 13). The two authors call on leaders to produce more inclusive schools by "treating others as human beings, no matter their state, condition or behavior" (Young & Arnold, 2020, p. 11), and by "being deeply mindful of others' identities; fostering understanding, respect, and dignity; and working to build a sense of mutual responsibility for and commitment to cultivating an inclusive, supportive, and rigorous educational experience for each student" (2020, p. 12). Their advocacy for this approach toward leadership is consistent with that described by Skrla and colleagues as grounded in care, appreciation, and respect for others (Skrla et al., 2011). Expectation "b" of this standard states that an effective leader should "Create and sustain a school environment in which each student is known, accepted and valued, trusted and respected, cared for, and encouraged to be an active and responsible member of the school community" (PSEL, 2015, p. 13).

Improving School Safety Through Caring Relationships

The PSEL expects an effective leader to "Build and maintain a safe, caring, and healthy school environment that meets the academic, social, emotional, and physical needs of each student," as described in expectation "a" (2015, p. 13). Educators across the US react with frustration, anger, and despair at the unwillingness of policymakers at various levels to confront the dangers that too often have spilled over into schools. Just as has been the case with the global crisis of 2020–2021, educators can take meaningful and significant steps to keep children safe at school. Educators can and must take steps such as controlling access to a campus, protecting front office

Frank D. Davidson

staff, maintaining and updating emergency operations plans, practicing lockdowns, increasing vigilance and visibility during student arrival and dismissal, and conducting threat assessments with law enforcement professionals.

The above are all important and vital steps. However, as we strive to develop improved security on our campuses, we must recognize that improving safety cannot depend solely on such measures as these. Bill Bond, who was principal of Heath High School in Paducah, Kentucky, where a tragic school shooting took place in 1997, has noted that students have a basic need to have a caring adult as part of their educational experience. In testimony to the US House of Representatives in 2013, Bond stated that

> The most effective way to prevent acts of violence targeted at schools is by building trusting relationships with students and others in the community so that threats come to light and can be investigated as appropriate. The solution is a matter of school culture. It's a matter of community engagement.
>
> (National Association of Secondary School Principals, 2013)

Steps for Creating a Supportive School Environment

In creating a supportive school environment, PSEL in their expectations "c" through "f" require effective leaders to be able to

> c) Provide coherent systems of academic and social supports, services, extracurricular activities, and accommodations to meet the range of learning needs of each student, d) Promote adult-student, student-peer, and school-community relationships that value and support academic learning and positive social and emotional development, e) Cultivate and reinforce student engagement in school and positive student conduct, and d) Infuse the school's learning environment with the cultures and languages of the school's community.
>
> (PSEL, 2015, p. 13)

In a longitudinal study of 200 elementary schools in Chicago, Bryk and colleagues identified five supports that were effective in advancing

Standard 5: Community of Care

school improvement (Bryk, 2010; Bryk et al., 2018; Bryk & Schneider, 2002). These organizational features can serve as a helpful guide to all school leaders for creating a supportive school community, and they strike a needed balance between academic demands, the school's sense of community, and students' social and emotional needs. Those features are:

- A coherent system of instructional planning
- The quality of the school's professional capacity
- Strong parent–community–school ties
- A learning climate centered on support for each student
- Leadership that drives change

This research team found that a core, yet often untapped source of support for school improvement was evident in the social capital of a school's neighborhood. Those neighborhoods with a history of working together and with strong institutions, particularly religious institutions, can help to create connections supportive of school improvement. Leaders who reach out to local leaders can also help a school to become more attentive to and respectful of the cultures found in the school's community. As Shirley notes, school leaders will increasingly need new ways to

> network not only with one another but also to reach out to community members to confront common problems, to share expertise, and to slowly but surely transform schools from islands of bureaucracy to centers of civic engagement. The interdependent relationship between democracy and education may remain fractious and demanding, but it also remains indispensable.
>
> (2009, p. 183)

A practical example of this type of outreach can be found in Ms. Rosemary Agneessens' recollections of her community outreach efforts at her elementary school in Chapter 4 of this book.

Notably, the research by Bryk and his colleagues also lead to conclusions about the role of relational trust in creating conditions supportive of meaningful change. Four traits—respect, competence, personal regard for others' ideas and influence, and integrity—were found to be of such importance that a deficit in one or more areas would be sufficient to weaken trust. Regarding trust, Bryk concluded that, "Absent such trust, schools find it nearly impossible to strengthen parent-community ties, build professional capacity, and enable a student-centered learning climate" (2010, p. 27). Practical steps that leaders can take to create more inclusive, caring, and supportive school communities that will benefit each child, both academically and in terms of their well-being, include the following:

1. Develop an outreach plan to draw from the strength of the existing social capital in your community. In collaboration with your faculty and staff and with recognized community leaders, identify religious institutions, neighborhood associations, or community organizations that have a stake in the well-being of the community. Hearing about their needs and concerns, while sharing those of the school, can help to create or strengthen ties that could be of benefit to the school and community. Moreover, as Khalifa and colleagues note, engagement of the community in culturally responsive ways "often occurs through the promotion of overlapping school–community spaces—bringing the community into the school and establishing a school presence in the community" (2016, p. 1297)

2. If this is not already a practice, set aside time to regularly journal, and use this time to critically reflect on your leadership in relation to the competencies related to Standard 5. This is also a time to come to grips with personal biases, assumptions, and values from one's cultural background, and to recognize that we are all "cultural being[s] influenced by multidimensional aspects of cultural identity" (Khalifa et al., 2016, p. 1285)

3. Seek out professional development opportunities for school staff on inclusion and the implementation of culturally responsive teaching. In light of evidence that "teachers' instructional behaviors are strongly influenced by their attitudes and beliefs about various dimensions of student diversity" (Gay, 2013, p. 56), such training could serve to surface, challenge, and shape teachers' perspective

4. Develop a network of colleagues where you can mentor others and be mentored as you navigate the inevitable challenges and struggles that leaders face. It is essential to cultivate a network of support with others who understand the pressures and stresses of leading

Voices from the Field

As a valuable contribution to this *Principal's Desk Reference*, we have collected vignettes shared by award-winning, proven leaders who are effective principals to help you better understand the "how" of implementing each standard. So often we only get the theory, but in this book we want to focus on the "how" of putting it into practice. The following contributors have learned many lessons over the years and are willing to share their thoughts and stories with you.

Vignette by Dr. Howard C. Carlson

Standard 5 of PSEL (2015, p. 13), Community of Care and Support for Students, encourages school leaders to look deeply at their context and to study the "why" behind how students perform academically. Once the unique challenges and dispositions of the students have been assessed, school leaders then aspire to cultivate a community which cares for each student and supports their academic success.

In the Wickenburg Unified School District, located in the state of Arizona, we addressed Standard 5 in several ways, but in this writing, I would like to outline one which was particularly helpful in creating a community of caring and success for all students. The example I provide focuses on infusing into the learning environment the cultures of the community and the world at large. To the extent we can know our students and the cultures and subcultures they represent, we can then build a bridge to who they are as individuals, which creates an environment for establishing relationship.

Wickenburg is one of the oldest towns in the state of Arizona and has a rich history which includes German immigrants, Native American influences, and a noteworthy Latino culture. Although the different groups in the community maintain individual identities, they coalesce around the cowboy culture which dates to the community's inception. To create a caring environment for all students within the school system, which we know is a precursor to learning, each of these cultures and subcultures must be embraced and celebrated. To do this the schools partner with the local Desert Caballeros Western Museum, the Chamber of Commerce, and

Del E. Webb Center for the Performing Arts to offer a variety of events and activities.

In the fall of the year the chamber celebrates Fiesta de Septiembre, an event to honor Wickenburg's Latino heritage. The celebration is brought into the schools through activities like the high school culinary students participating in the salsa-making contest. During the month of December, the museum conducts a cowboy poetry event, which draws poets and crowds from across the US. The event is brought into the schools through elementary and middle school students meeting with professional poets and then writing their own cowboy poetry. The best student poetry is then displayed, and the students are provided an opportunity to read their writings to the event's audience. To introduce students to the arts and more specifically community-themed genres, the Del E. Webb Center for the Performing Arts provides free events for school students of all ages. Schools take a field trip to the theater and students enjoy attending an event in a professional setting.

Standard 5 also encourages us to think beyond what we understand as our current school community to a larger context. Schools are becoming increasingly ethnically and culturally diverse and therefore to create a community of care and support for all students the school population must be exposed to ethnicities and cultures from around the world.

In Wickenburg, the way this is accomplished is through providing what was initially called "Festival Fridays." Students thoroughly enjoy these events which bring in speakers and performers from around the world. Students are introduced to parts of the world they did not know and may represent the home of a future classmate. Introducing students to a broader context promotes understanding and acceptance, which ultimately prepares them to be more caring as time develops. Increasing awareness on the part of the existing school population also encourages a more caring and supportive learning environment for new students entering the system, which hastens their path to academic success.

If school leaders truly desire to infuse Standard 5, "Effective educational leaders cultivate an inclusive, caring, and supportive school community that promotes the academic success and well-being of each student" (PSEL, 2015, p. 13) in their schools they must be prepared to not only bring in the community, but also the world. Doing so creates understanding and understanding leads to acceptance; acceptance reduces stress in the learning environment and provides opportunity for relationship.

Standard 5: Community of Care

Relationship, once established, is foundational for student learning and academic success. Standard 5 of PSEL challenges us to embrace this type of thinking: moving our schools from conceptual ideas related to creating community and support for students to a successful shift in school culture.

Vignette by Dr. Michael L. Wright

Fundamental to any influential leadership endeavor is the responsibility to cultivate a sense of community and belonging for all. In educational settings, doing so is especially critical for students. Nothing significant or enduring occurs in the absence of a common purpose and shared values. More often than not, each school's climate and culture represent stakeholder attitudes regarding the importance of student learning and total support, or in some cases, the absence thereof. This sentiment applies to how schools view their responsibilities connected to each student's sense of belonging and well-being. Hence, the immense importance of creating and successfully implementing meaningful mission and vision statements capable of directing the staff's focus and behaviors. Moreover, purposefully crafted and successfully incorporated institutional declarations serve as guideposts to inform and direct organizational culture and norms. For example, in part, our district's vision statement reads: Our school "is the heart of our community; a family of diverse members committed to ensuring a purposeful, creative learning environment within a caring, collaborative culture for all."

Notably, when we decided to create a vision statement, every effort was made to ensure representation from every part of our school community. Participants included students (from middle and high school), parents, school board, community members, faculty, administration, and support staff, each playing an essential role throughout the process. To maximize institutional acceptance, an all-hands-on deck approach is required. Our meetings and activities advanced over almost nine months involving 75 people. Eventually, our efforts produced a concise statement encapsulating the most critical elements of creating a student-centered culture. Despite the apparent challenges of organizing and effectively facilitating a diverse group of stakeholders of such a large size, the outcome was far greater than anticipated. As stakeholders met, over time, artificial walls that long separated people came tumbling down, replaced with bridges of understanding, fostering a strong sense of community. By the end of that school year, over 60 people of the original 75 continued right to the end. Since that time, our vision statement has served as a sacred compass to inform our district's decision-making. It also, among other things, instructs stakeholder behavioral and performance expectations.

Eventually, purposeful proclamations must evolve into something significantly more than mere aspirational declarations. Instead, an organizational vision and mission statement must direct energies that lead daily school activities, actions, and strengths. Evidence indicating the importance of fostering a sense of student acceptance and how belonging ties to achievement is easy to find. Importantly, each school must foster an environment capable of fully embracing students' emotional, social, intellectual, and physical interests. In such educational settings, students were put in the best position to learn, grow, and progress personally and academically. What's more, a well-conceived vision possesses the power to create a vivid view of the organization's desired future state and ultimate destination. This is accomplished through carefully crafted language designed to help all visualize outcomes. This final destination inspires stakeholders to fulfill specific duties and actions connected to achieving the wanted future state.

In due course, organizational vision provides schools a forum to create aspirations and standards for students and all other stakeholders they seek to serve. Foremost are the health, safety, and welfare, which produce both the context and primary force of effective educational leadership.

Finally, students and staff must feel safe, secure, and welcomed before they are prepared to fully participate. These are also vital components of equity. States and communities unwilling to adequately fund programs and supports designed expressly to enhance equity are shortsighted and misguided. Recently, long-overlooked issues associated with equity have resurfaced in a time when the divide between socioeconomic classes has never been wider. What will happen to the current generation of children and youth of our most vulnerable populations is mostly an outgrowth of the quality of support provided.

In summary, student learning is directly correlated to the degree to which basic learner requirements are met. Such needs include access to a stable food source; safe, suitable housing and living conditions; and the extent to which all experience a sense of unconditional acceptance and belonging at school.

References

Bryk, A. S. (2010). Organizing schools for improvement. *Phi Delta Kappan, 91*(7), 23–30.

Bryk, A. S., & Schneider, B. L. (2002). *Trust in schools: A core resource for improvement.* Russell Sage Foundation.

Bryk, A. S., Sebring, P. B., Kerbow, D., Rollow, S., & Easton, J. Q. (2018). *Charting Chicago school reform: Democratic localism as a lever for change.* Routledge.

Gay, G. (2013). Teaching to and through cultural diversity. *Curriculum Inquiry, 43*(1), 48–70. https://doi.org/10.1111/curi.12002

Khalifa, M. A., Gooden, M. A., & Davis, J. E. (2016). Culturally responsive school leadership: A synthesis of the literature. *Review of Educational Research, 86*(4), 1272–1311. https://doi.org/10.3102/0034654316630383

Murphy, J. (2015). The empirical and moral foundations of the ISLLC standards. *Journal of Educational Administration, 53*(6), 718–734.

National Association of Secondary School Principals. (2013). *Statement to the US House Education and Labor Committee* (testimony of Bill Bond). US House of Representatives. https://edlabor.house.gov/imo/media/doc/documents/2.27.13-BondTestimony.pdf

National Policy Board for Educational Administration. (2015). *Professional standards for educational leaders.* www.npbea.org/psel/

Shirley, D. (2009). Community organizing and educational change. In A. Hargreaves, A. Lieberman, M. Fullan, & D. Hopkins (Eds.), *Second international handbook of educational change* (pp. 169–186). Springer Netherlands. https://doi.org/10.1007/978-90-481-2660-6_10

Skrla, L., McKenzie, K. B., & Scheurich, J. J. (2011). Becoming an equity-oriented change agent. In A. M. Blankstein & P. D. Houston (Eds.), *Leadership for social justice and democracy in our schools* (pp. 45–58). Corwin Press.

Young, M. D., & Arnold, N. W. (2020). An emerging framework for inclusive educational leadership. In R. Papa (Ed.), *Oxford research encyclopedia of education.* Oxford University Press. https://doi.org/10.1093/acrefore/9780190264093.013.987

Standard 6
Professional Capacity of School Personnel

Robyn Conrad Hansen

> Effective educational leaders develop the professional capacity and practice of school personnel to promote *each* student's academic success and well-being.
> (PSEL, 2015, p. 14)

Educational leadership plays a key role in improving school outcomes by building the capacity of school personnel, influencing the motivations and capacities of teachers, and establishing the school climate and learning environment. Leadership has become a priority in education policy agendas throughout the world. We discussed that **quality leadership does matter** in Chapter 5 (Standard 4: Curriculum, Instruction, and Assessment). The Wallace Report (Grissom et al., 2021), *How Principals Affect Students and Schools*, indicates that a principal's effect is far reaching when considering the influence principals have on hiring staff, fostering continuous improvement, motivation of staff, and the development of teacher leadership. In this chapter, we explore some of my favorite leadership practices that you can implement to develop the professional capacity of all school personnel to benefit student growth and development in alignment with the expectations of an effective leader associated with Standard 6. Effective school leadership is essential for improving the efficiency and academic and social-emotional equity of school.

School leaders need time, capacity, and support to concentrate on the practices known to improve student learning that focus on the whole child. Greater degrees of autonomy should be coupled with models of distributed leadership, as well as new types of accountability systems with training and development for school leadership. This formula will aid in attracting high-quality educators to the field of school administration (Pont et al., 2008).

Effective educational leaders purposefully focus attention on supporting the continuous development of teachers and staff, and concentrate on their own, ongoing, professional development throughout their career. Standard 6 of PSEL: Professional Capacity of School Personnel (PSEL, 2015), and associated expectations of effective leaders, focuses attention on developing successful and caring teachers and other professional staff into an educationally effective faculty. Quality leaders foster continuous improvement of individuals and collective instructional capacity to achieve greatness for each student. It is important that you, as the principal, gain skills in varying methods to motivate teachers and staff to the highest levels of professional practice by sharing actionable feedback for continuous learning and improvement. In essence, you as an effective leader need to know the value of and how to distribute leadership. Finally, you must know how to promote the personal and professional health, well-being, and work–life balance of faculty and staff while attending to your own health and wellness as a model to others. This chapter is divided into four distinct, yet connected components related to Standard 6:

a. Leadership styles (transformational and distributed)
b. Change theory
c. Culture of continuous learning
d. Healthy work–life balance

Leadership Style: Transformational Leadership

Transformational leadership is a popular leadership theory that began in 1973. Even though this chapter focuses more on distributed leadership, we explore how combining these two leadership styles can aid you in becoming an effective leader. Transformational leadership gained popularity in the early 1970s when James V. Downton first introduced the theory. Later, in 1985, researcher Bernard Bass expanded the ideas to include ways of measuring its success. Those ideas suggest that if principals are authentic strong leaders, then employees will be inspired to follow them.

Authentic leadership is valued by faculty and staff. A transformational leader motivates others to achieve their highest potential. The concept is that a leader works to develop and create a vision and then inspires employees to perform at higher levels (Burns, 1978). In this leadership style, leaders work to build and transform their organization toward fulfilling its mission. If a solid foundation is set, this work should be sustainable, even after the current leader is gone (Davidson, 2015). According to Bass (1985), a transformational leader:

- Encourages the motivation and positive development of followers
- Exemplifies moral standards within the organization and encourages the same of others
- Fosters an ethical work environment with clear values, priorities, and standards
- Builds school culture by encouraging employees to move from an attitude of self-interest to a mindset where they are working for the common good
- Holds an emphasis on authenticity, cooperation, and open communication
- Provides coaching and mentoring but allows employees to make decisions and take ownership of tasks

Transformational leaders create a mission, based on a vision, that is inspiring and represents the school community and is challenging to those who follow with lofty expectations and goals. (See Chapter 2 for more information on how to create a vision and mission based on core values.) Transformational leaders are charismatic, enthusiastic, and optimistic. The leader has high moral and ethical standards and others strive to assimilate their actions (Bass & Riggio, 2006).

Leadership Style: Distributed Leadership

In comparison, distributed leadership takes transformational leadership and shared leadership to a deeper level, contextualizing the theory

Standard 6: Professional Capacity

by building leadership capacity in faculty and staff. It flattens the more traditional hierarchical approach seen in organizations and elevates personnel to a higher level of authority and decision making. Most teachers do not want to become school administrators; however, they do want a voice in decisions and actions. Leading from the front of the classroom is the preferred approach to school leadership for many talented educators. When asked, the best teachers want an opportunity to lead. They are more likely to remain long term at schools where their voices are heard and valued, as well as being respected for their opinions and actions. In top-performing countries, teachers are prepared as leaders and then given time in their schedule to lead. Effective leaders should provide opportunities for professional growth which makes it easier to "recruit, hire, support, develop, and retain effective and caring teachers and other professional staff and form them into an educationally effective faculty," as stated in expectation "a" of the PSEL (2015, p. 14). Expectation "b" for this standard says that effective leaders need to "Plan for and manage staff turnover and succession, providing opportunities for effective induction and mentoring of new personnel" (PSEL, 2015, p. 14).

Within distributed leadership, teachers exercise their intellect, personality, and experience. They become part of developing the colleagues around them in the school and the organization (Leithwood et al., 2004). Distributed leadership provides the idea that professional development is organically applied through common proficiencies and mutual ways of working; it creates an influential learning atmosphere (Harris, 2005).

> Distributed leadership is not something "done" by an individual "to" others, or a set of individual actions through which people contribute to a group or organization . . . [it] is a group activity that works through and within relationships, rather than individual action.
>
> (Bennett et al., 2003, p. 3)

Figure 7.1 illustrates the key differences between distributive and transformational leadership models.

As stated under Standard 6 expectation "g," an effective leader should "Develop the capacity, opportunities, and support for teacher leadership and leadership from other members of the school community" (PSEL, 2015, p. 14). You, as a principal, should build relationships and leadership capacity among your staff. Distributed leadership is about creating

Distributed Leadership vs. Transformational Leadership

- ❏ It takes shared leadership to a deeper level
- ❏ Leadership is a property of a group of interacting people
- ❏ There is openness to the boundaries of leadership
- ❏ Expertise is distributed across many areas

- ❏ Changes the complexity of an organization
- ❏ Emotionally charged
- ❏ Leaders and followers raise each other up to higher level of morality and motivation
- ❏ Stimulates people to think in new ways
- ❏ Develops leadership capacity in others

Figure 7.1 Comparison of Distributive and Transformational Leadership Models
Source: Created by Dr. Robyn Hansen

leadership density and building and sustaining leadership capacity throughout the organization. People in many different roles can lead and confidently affect the performance of their schools in different ways while increasing a positive climate and culture.

As a newly assigned principal to my school, I learned early that I could not do my job effectively and enjoy a long, healthy career by taking on all the leadership roles myself. The school was home to 1,200 students and nearly 100 faculty and staff. An assistant principal was not provided, so I relied on a wonderful social worker for support with some administrative duties. The school was relatively new, only in its fourth year, with many forces of change occurring due to rapid growth and changing demographics in our community.

Due to this type of complicated contextual environment, we established a **distributive leadership cabinet**. Staff members contributed in an advisory role assisting the principal as a cabinet member, like that of the President of the United States. The cabinet positions were decided upon by a committee comprising the entire school community, including parents, teachers, staff, business leaders, and student representation. We performed a needs assessment and SWOT/C (strengths, weaknesses, opportunities, threats, and challenges) analysis to be used by the committee to discuss school priorities and the need for decision-making leadership positions on the cabinet. The committee then outlined the roles and responsibilities for each cabinet seat.

Each cabinet member is responsible for developing and supporting their team member's capacity for a continuous succession plan for

Standard 6: Professional Capacity

leadership related to that seat. To add consistency in leadership and avoid having too many leaders rolling off the cabinet at the same time, we established a system where a third of the positions initially started as a one-year term, another third of the seats were initially for two years, and the final third fulfilled a full three-year term. Those replacing outgoing members were all given a full three-year term. The cabinet met monthly to report progress toward their goals which aligned to the school's vision and mission. Cabinet leaders met with their team as often as needed to make progress toward their goals and action steps, and with the principal as needed. Distributed leadership became a very efficient leadership model, encouraging teachers and staff to share their voice and leadership skills in decisions impacting the greater good of the school community. Highly qualified teachers and staff desire a position in a school where they have an active voice in the decision making process. Our school became a school of choice for teachers, staff, and families.

It is beneficial to evaluate your distributive leadership cabinet annually to ensure you are including all key stakeholders. Figure 7.2 shows an example of the various cabinet seats our school established as part of our distributed leadership model. The diagram illustrates that the principal is part of the leadership cabinet but assumes a lower hierarchical position than in a contemporary organizational chart. We used non-traditional leadership

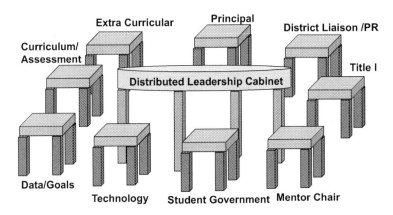

- Cabinet members are chosen by school needs
- Members sit at the table as part of their leadership role within the school

Figure 7.2 Example of a Distributive Leadership Cabinet
Source: Created by Dr. Robyn Hansen

roles, i.e., culture, mentor chair, parent involvement, as compared to more traditional leadership roles of department or grade-level chair. Limit your cabinet seats to be reflective of your school population. A good working team of 7–11 members with distinct roles and responsibilities.

This model is sustainable and can quickly become teacher and staff led; thankfully, the next principal also believed in distributed leadership, making the transition very smooth. Working with the district office, the cabinet members earned a stipend (extra pay) for their leadership and extra time spent supporting the vision and mission of the school community.

An effective leader, as stated in expectation "c," should also "Develop teachers' and staff members' professional knowledge, skills, and practice through differentiated opportunities for learning and growth, guided by understanding of professional and adult learning and development" (PSEL, 2015, p. 14). This expectation is referring to andragogy, which is the art and science of teaching adult learners in a way that gives them new learning opportunities with the ability to problem solve. In contrast, pedagogy is the art and science of teaching school-aged learners.

Distributed leadership does not mean that no one is responsible for the overall performance of the organization. It means, rather, that the job of administrative leaders is primarily about enhancing the skills and knowledge of people in the organization, creating a common culture of expectations around the use of those skills and knowledge, holding the various pieces of the organization together in a productive relationship with each other, and holding individuals accountable for their contributions to the collective result (Elmore, 2000).

Change Theory

Never in our nation's history and around the world has the need for embracing change and understanding change theory been more prevalent. During the end of the 2020 school year and through the 2020–2021 and 2021–2022 school years, educators had to change direction at a moment's notice as schools and districts globally closed their doors and re-opened to a virtual world of teaching and learning. Those leaders, who were well versed and skilled in change theory, appeared to have the smoothest transition to online or hybrid teaching and learning. They were visionary

Standard 6: Professional Capacity

leaders with systems and training in place to implement change quickly, while continuing to support students and staff.

Effective leaders understand when and how to use change theory. Organizations tend to maintain themselves and it is only through leadership that they can identify where change is needed and make it happen. The leader is often the catalyst for necessary change within the system. A must read for all leaders is Jim Collins' *Good to Great* (2001) book. In it he says good is the enemy of great. Meaning, good schools or organizations often do not see a reason for change. Like the thought, "If it's not broken, don't fix it," visionary leaders understand that change is inevitable and becomes necessary for continuous growth and achievement. Expectation "f" for Standard 6 states that educational leaders should "Empower and motivate teachers and staff to the highest levels of professional practice and to continuous learning and improvement" (PSEL, 2015, p. 14). Effective leaders understand the value of systems thinking to foster leadership development that is systemic, where personnel solve complex problems together, better supporting the system (school or district). There is limited need to implement quick fixes to solve an issue if you have a quality ongoing school improvement plan.

Leaders establish a rich culture of continuous improvement. In Michael Fullan's book, *Leading in a Culture of Change* (2020), he writes that exceptional leadership is the ability to take the lead and foresee the need for change before circumstances dictate forced change. Outstanding schools are poised and ready for unforeseen, outside forces of change. They have developed a culture of learning that is flexible and poised for change, even during unprecedented times. The effective leader (expectation "g") will "Develop the capacity, opportunities, and support for teacher leadership and leadership from other members of the school community" (PSEL, 2015, p. 14).

Culture of Respect and Continuous Learning

As a principal (especially if new to your building), you will need time to meet with your staff and community, to disaggregate and analyze data and other evidence to see what the strengths and weaknesses of the school/

district are. After attending a *StrengthFinders 2.0* training developed by Tom Rath and Gallup, my thoughts of personal, professional, and school improvement moved from focusing on a deficit model of improvement (focusing on the weaknesses or deficiencies) to one of discovering our strengths (Rath & Gallup, 2018). In examining Standard 6, expectation "d," an effective leader will "Foster continuous improvement of individual and collective instructional capacity to achieve outcomes envisioned for each student" (PSEL, 2015, p. 14). Teachers are encouraged to look at their instructional strengths and the learning strengths of students to plan the best course of action for growth and development. If you think back to when you were deciding on a career, I imagine you went with your strengths, not weaknesses. I believe all students need to be minimally proficient in all subject areas to be a well-educated, contributing member of society; however, spending too much time working on a student's weaknesses could be better spent concentrating on their strengths. They, too, will choose a career based on their strengths.

Spending the time to recruit, hire, support, develop, and retain effective and caring teachers and other professional staff and form them into an educationally effective faculty (PSEL, 2015, p. 14, expectation "a") is a crucial role of principals. As Jim Collins (2001) says in his book *Good to Great*, you first get the right people on the bus, then in the right seats. Developing a school culture where everyone feels safe, welcome, and valued will be communicated in the community and beyond, which enhances your ability to attract high-quality professional candidates who desire the opportunity to contribute and make a difference.

In preparation for new staff interviews, you are encouraged to form a diverse team representing your school community, including experience, ethnicity, gender, and roles within the school. Have a well-developed job description outlining the characteristics and strengths your school needs in this candidate. Work with your mentor to have well-prepared questions and scenarios representing the vision, mission, core values, and strengths of your school to see who is the best fit for your school community. Your team will be interviewing the candidate and the candidate will also be interviewing you and your team. One of the questions often asked by the candidate is, "Please share with me if there is an orientation process prior to beginning my job and will I have a mentor?" Todd Whitaker in his book *What Great Principals Do Differently: Fifteen Things that Matter Most* (2003) recommends starting the induction of a new teacher at the

Standard 6: Professional Capacity

interview. He indicates that when you realize that the candidate you are interviewing is a great hire, then you should start right away to make your expectations of their performance very clear. He continues to suggest that effective principals establish expectations for all staff at the first faculty meeting of the year and provide follow-through throughout the coming months. To exceed your school goals, you should surround yourself with outstanding teachers and professional staff.

Just as it is expected that administrators have a thorough onboarding process and quality mentoring for the first year or two, teachers and staff are looking forward to this as well. Standard 6, expectation "b," says an effective leader should "Plan for and manage staff turnover and succession, providing opportunities for effective induction and mentoring of new personnel" (PSEL, 2015, p. 14). Building positive, respectful relationships with your school team is helpful in so many ways. For example, if a teacher or staff member plans to leave your school, it is important for them to share this information with you as soon as possible, so you can plan for filling the vacancy. Succession planning is important not only for the principal or superintendent, but for your valued staff as well. Consider the institutional knowledge and skills that walk out the door with one of your best, most well-respected team members. You may need time to plan for and train someone or a team to assume their role and responsibilities. Having classified personnel members cross-trained in at least one other position is valuable for their professional growth and development, as well as a safety and security measure of the system. For example, as a principal, you may be off campus for a meeting, professional training, or a personal day. Who has been trained to assume the lead during a safety event, like a fire or lockdown drill? It is advised to have a chain of command for all major roles in your school in case of absence or an emergency, ensuring that someone well trained will be able to actively step in to cover a lead role.

Welcoming new teachers and staff to your school should be a sense of pride. Classified employees may start at a variety of times during the school year. Having a colleague responsible for greeting them on the first day, showing them around the school, introducing them to others, sharing their schedule and responsibilities, as well as a simple thing like where they put personal items or their lunch. An employee handbook is a valuable tool and should be created by an internal team to answer policy and procedure questions, establish safety protocols, and set expectations. It should be available online and printed as requested. Providing a certified and classified staff member as a mentor to each new employee is a sign of a well-organized and caring school. The trained mentor should meet with the mentee on a regular basis for the first few months, then as needed. These small steps go a long way in establishing a respectful, professional culture promoting continuous learning.

Another aspect of continuous learning involves expectation "d," where an effective leader is able to "Foster continuous improvement of individual and collective instructional capacity to achieve outcomes envisioned for each student" (PSEL, 2015, p. 14). The goal is to know your teachers and staff well and develop a comprehensive professional development plan that is personalized, ongoing, and job-embedded for each person. A one-size-fits-all staff in service often misses the mark of truly impacting continuous improvement. It is recommended to plan your academic year's professional development aligned with assessment and personnel evaluation evidence. Each member of your school team should be encouraged to write SMART goals at the beginning of each year based on data. At the first faculty meeting of the year, share your goals with the team and ask each person to write their goals (typically three) based on their job and expectations for student learning. Later, meet privately with each of them to review their plan.

A SMART goal is **s**pecific, **m**easurable, **a**ction oriented, **r**elevant, and **t**ime bound. SMART goals are discussed in greater depth under Standard 4 (Chapter 5). According to expectation "c" for this standard, as an instructional leader, it is your responsibility to "Develop teachers' and staff members' professional knowledge, skills, and practice through differentiated opportunities for learning and growth, guided by understanding of professional and adult learning and development" (PSEL, 2015, p. 14). The focus is to improve the practice of all teachers and staff. With a comprehensive evaluation system, aligned with each person's job responsibilities, an effective principal (according to expectation "e") will be able to "Deliver actionable feedback about instruction and other professional practice through valid, research-anchored systems of supervision and evaluation to support the development of teachers' and staff members' knowledge, skills, and practice" (PSEL, 2015, p. 14).

In Chapter 5, under Standard 4, we examined a great deal of information related to teacher supervision with the use of classroom observation data collection techniques and feedback conferences from clinical supervision and teacher development (Gall & Acheson, 2011). You, as the principal,

Standard 6: Professional Capacity

are accountable to the school community for continuous improvement in teacher and staff practices leading to increases in student growth and achievement. Principals must redesign how teachers and staff are supported, not just supervised. As discussed in Chapter 5, clinical supervision utilizes a three-step approach:

1. Planning conference to discuss the observation to take place within 24 hours. The teacher supplies a seating chart for the principal to use in data collection techniques
2. Formal observation, supported by walk-throughs, both formal and informal
3. Feedback conferences, held within 48 hours of the observation, that form the foundation of ongoing continuous improvement

Clinical supervision helps provide a cycle of professional, differentiated learning to build teacher and staff instructional capacity to promote greater student overall success.

Healthy Work–Life Balance

During my first year as a principal, I learned a hard lesson when I gained 15 pounds, mostly from enjoying the multitude of sweets shared by the children for their birthday celebration. Remember, I had 1,200 children attending my school—that is a lot of cupcakes! For most of the year, my stress level was off the charts trying to exceed the expectations of my district and community, while learning the elementary curriculum (secondary was my life for most of my career at that point). I was getting to know and form valuable relationships with staff, students, parents, and community, and working long hours, all while being a mother, wife, and daughter. It started to take its toll on my health and sustainability, and I knew my work–life balance needed to change.

Earlier in my life, after graduating with my bachelor's degree in education, I chose to enroll in nursing school. Upon entering the classroom one day, our nursing professor had written something on the board that helped us re-evaluate the stress we were putting ourselves under. A robust discussion pursued in our class related to the causes of stress and the inherent negative effects it puts on our immune system, decreasing our ability to

Dis + Ease = Disease	
Concerns for Balanced Health & Wellness	
Warning Signs of Stress	**Stress-Related Diseases**
• Trouble sleeping	❋ Colds—decreased immunity
• Weight gain or loss	❋ Headaches—migraines
• Irritable	❋ Obesity—diabetes
• Depressed—mood swings	❋ Cancers
• High blood pressure	❋ Heart disease
• Trouble concentrating	❋ Skin conditions—acne, rashes
• Anxiety	❋ Premature aging
	❋ Asthma

Figure 7.3 Concerns for a Balanced Health and Wellness
Source: Created by Dr. Robyn Hansen

fight diseases. You have heard of "flight or fight" as a reaction to a threat. When you feel this, there is a chemical reaction in your body allowing you to act so you can avoid injury. The hair on the back of your neck stands up, heart rate increases, muscles tighten, blood pressure increases, and you breathe faster. Small amounts of stress can be handled well by most people. What causes stress for one person may not cause stress in another. However, the danger arises with prolonged, chronic stress. Figure 7.3 illustrates some diseases that are associated with chronic stress. A healthy life balance includes getting enough sleep. Studies have shown that sleep-deprived people also are prone to the same chronic diseases as chronic stress. The value of creating a positive work–life balance is immeasurable for sustained happiness, longevity at work and life, and an overall healthy mind and body.

Worldwide, the school district's office of talent management (HR) are changing the expectations of job roles and responsibilities. They are updating the benefit packages offered to teachers and staff and modernizing the methods used to recruit new employees by addressing the priority placed upon work–life balance. This is especially true for the current members of the millennial generation, those born between 1980 and 1999 (Alton, 2019; Rook, 2019; University of California Berkeley, 2019). Expectation "h" says an effective principal should "Promote the personal and professional health, well-being, and work-life balance of faculty and staff" (PSEL, 2015, p. 14). In addition, expectation "i" states that they should "Tend to their own learning and effectiveness through reflection,

Standard 6: Professional Capacity

study, and improvement, maintaining a healthy work-life balance" (PSEL, 2015, p. 14).

As the leader, you will need to "model the way." One day at a faculty meeting, although 15 pounds is hard to hide, I shared with my staff the unhealthy lifestyle I was living. It included increased stress from my job and trying to live up to all the expectations that I thought others had of me, working too many hours, taking work home, not eating or sleeping well, and lack of exercise and fun. Several staff members were nodding their heads in agreement, as they, too, were working very hard. One teacher asked, "What can we do about it?" The agenda for the current meeting was put on hold while we brainstormed several ideas to support each other to align to a healthier work–life balance. This may be a beneficial exercise in your staff meeting. Some of the ideas we came up with were:

- Changing "Fat Friday" shared lunches to "Virtuous Friday" lunches where recipes for healthy meals were shared, eventually creating a cookbook to use as a fundraiser
- Starting a Marathon Club: Friday mornings, students, families, and community members were welcome to join the staff in running/ walking a mile with the goal of reaching 26.2 miles (length of a marathon) by spring break
- Our school nurse brought in a nutritionist, on a professional development day, to educate us on a healthy lifestyle, which included realistic weight goals, life-long diet, nutrition, and exercise. She recommended keeping a journal and being reflective of our eating, exercise, and feelings as we were on this healthy work–life balance journey
- Our physical education teacher worked with those interested in creating a workout schedule
- We hired a parent who was a yoga instructor and she offered sessions after school twice a week
- To add to the camaraderie and stress relief of the office team, we brought a dining room table into the front office. This provided a location where we would sit and eat (after students were back in classrooms) and share events of the day (taking turns to answer the phone and/or greet guests). Teachers and staff also took the time to slow down and eat together during lunch

- Walking the school grounds with the students during breaks several times a week and interacting with different groups of students—always having tennis shoes in the office

Through our healthy lifestyle journey, I was very happy to learn that play should be an essential part of a healthy lifestyle. In Brene Brown's book *The Gifts of Imperfection* (2010, p. 3), she defines Wholehearted living as

> When we dig down past the feel-good words (love, belonging, and authenticity) and excavate the daily activities and experiences that put *heart* in Wholehearted living, we can see how people define the concepts that drive their actions, beliefs, and emotions.

She introduces the reader to the work of Dr. Stuart Brown, founder of the National Institute for Play. Dr. Brown, along with Christopher Vaughan (2009) authored a book titled, *Play, How It Shapes the Brain, Opens the Imagination, and Invigorates the Soul*. The contents of the book explain why children and adults need play in their lives, and typically this does not include the use of technology. Play helps to form our brain pathways, fosters empathy, supports development of executive function or self-regulatory skills, develops social skills, and supports social-emotional learning. Play is the basis of creativity and innovation. Play is not only essential for your students, but for the adults on campus as well—including you!

By the end of the school year, with support and encouragement from family and colleagues, most everyone on the staff either reached their health goals or made significant progress toward them. Attendance of faculty and staff improved, as well as overall energy, as observed by increased participation in school events, teamwork, innovative ideas, and smiles. Allowing us to develop the professional capacity and practice to promote our own and each student's academic success and well-being. Beware: *Stressed reversed = Desserts*!

 ## Voices from the Field

As a valuable contribution to this *Principal's Desk Reference*, we have collected vignettes shared by award-winning, proven leaders who are effective principals to help you better understand the "how" of implementing

Standard 6: Professional Capacity

each standard. So often we only get the theory, but in this book we want to focus on the "how" of putting it into practice. This exemplar principal has learned many lessons over the years and is eager to share her thoughts and stories with you.

Vignette by Dr. Liza Caraballo-Suarez

When Teachers and Principals Share Leadership in a School, Both the Adults and Students Win

When you have a school culture that has a positive spirit of collaboration, you build a community which invests in each person that then leads to each person investing in their community. You build trust and create an environment that gives space for everyone to have a voice and be the best of themselves. When teachers have an increased sense of collective responsibility the results are increased sense of professionalism.

I am the proud principal of a 3K-5 Title I school in Williamsburg, Brooklyn with 340 students. All students have access to free breakfast and lunch. We are a two-time magnet school and a Leader in Me Lighthouse school. We believe that trust and distributed leadership helps produce equitable student achievement. It has helped us support student success while at the same time promoting strong relationships and partnerships with members of the school community. Key factors for our success include:

- Developing a culture of trust where teachers' strengths and knowledge are honored and recognized
- Providing students, parents, and members of the community with voice
- Using a data team process to measure the impact of instruction on student learning
- Providing teachers with professional development on evidence-based teaching/student learning strategies with time for teachers to collaborate and plan instruction together
- Monitoring student learning and celebrating every success
- Regularly communicating updates on our school improvement story with our community

109

As a principal for over 20 years, I believe the key to improving student learning is to allow teachers to share their expertise and create a collective responsibility for improving student learning by inviting teachers and staff into leadership. The challenges of leadership for learning are not just the responsibility of one leader. Principals benefit from the support of teachers and others to serve as additional instructional leaders. This does not take the responsibility of leading the school away from me, it enhances the relationships, skills, and knowledge of all staff and creates a school culture that is mutually interdependent and holds all accountable for their contributions to the collective result.

When I first became the school principal, I recognized the importance of building a strong culture. I knew it would only happen through dialogue and collaborative inquiry and I began by assessing the population and needs of my school community at all levels, not just academically. I was visible and transparent so the community could get to know me. It was important to understand who and what type of audience I was serving and working with throughout the years. One of my initiatives was to speak to different stakeholders to get a sense of their thoughts, concerns, and strengths that could be an asset to the students. These stakeholders included parents, teachers, politicians, students, and community members as well as central office personnel, as I truly believe that it takes a village to raise a child. I learned about the values of my community and the struggles they had. I learned that many community members had rarely traveled outside the immediate neighborhood, nor had they visited museums or other cultural institutions in NYC. We immediately incorporated trips at the end of every unit and invited parents to chaperone.

I also recognized how to use internal and external resources, including experiential resources. The school had many vacancies and I wanted to ensure that new staff members looked like my students and reflected the community. A diverse hiring group was created who would review resumes and then interview all potential candidates at the first level. They would then recommend a second-level interview and I would have a conversation with the applicant to finalize the selected decision. If teachers on the committee recommended them to the second level, it was because the applicant believed that all students could learn, regardless of race, ability, color, or religion. In addition, the team members could actually see themselves working with the applicant they had interviewed.

Standard 6: Professional Capacity

We then focused on reviewing the history of the school performance over the past several years. We understood that this data had to be the lens to evaluate students' learning as it spoke to instruction and best practices and provided different allocation memorandums for the school. It was critical to understand how the students performed. The strengths of the staff were tapped into, as well as their knowledge on data and their input on the trends that had occurred with subgroups that were considered struggling. During our biweekly inquiry committee meeting, we began to ask ourselves: Why was there an achievement gap? Was it the way we were addressing their needs? How often did we focus only on their needs and not their strengths? In other words, why did teachers continue to teach a standard or strategy that we took for granted students needed to be taught? Therefore, through the recommendations of the committee, they were able to work with their colleagues to make necessary changes resulting in increased student achievement. Some of these suggestions included: a variety of personalized, job-embedded professional development activities, classroom inter-visitation with lead teachers, and the assessment of the teaching strategies used at the end of the week or unit.

Distributive leadership builds capacity, and it is an effective and economical resource for principals. In taking time to know my staff's strengths and weaknesses I have also learned their interests, personal and professional, goals, hobbies, and family members. I use this information to place them in positions and highlight the different teaching and learning styles among the staff. As a principal of 20 years, I am very proud of my school's high teacher retention. When staff move on it is due to retirement or a promotion to a leadership position. I have mentored 12 teachers in attaining their administrative degree. Eight have become assistant principals, three became principals, and one is a district supervisor. I also make sure we nurture staff to be mentors. We have a teacher on my staff who loves mathematical and business administration. In speaking with her, I asked her if she would like to know how the school budget operates. She was shocked that I had acknowledged her interests. I asked my current assistant principal to mentor her and now she is on the budgeting committee managing, creating, and certifying purchase orders. It is a common practice to have my assistant principals or lead teachers from my school model classroom instruction, provide professional development, or become part of the school safety emergency response building team. As a two-time Magnet award recipient, two different teachers have become the magnet specialists and plan with their colleagues to implement the mission of the magnet theme into their curriculum. In addition, they research different vendors or community-based organizations to enhance different students' learning styles.

I value what parents bring and recognize how they can advocate and support school initiatives. For example, our parents have participated in NYC's participatory budgeting. They attended several meetings with our council representative to elaborate on how we needed to upgrade our technology. We received funding to purchase a 21st-century technology center for upper grades. The following year, we received funding for an early childhood technology center. Their advocacy provided a state-of-the-art library that can be used by all in the building.

It is crucial that you share your vision, mission, and goals with central staff. Social and emotional learning (SEL) has always been the top of my concern with the concept that students in elementary must have a solid and strong foundation. Students need to have opportunities to master some of these skills or strategies before transitioning into middle school. Central staff knew that I was an advocate of SEL as I had spoken at several meetings on this topic. As a result, when they had grants for SEL our school benefitted from a Leader In Me (LIM) grant that was provided to our students and staff. The LIM process created by Stephen Covey, "*The Seven Habits of Highly Effective People*," promoted another level of confidence throughout the school community. After having several conversations with staff members, the Parent Teachers Association (PTA) executive board and the school leadership team agreed that the process should be given a chance. The significance outcome of this process was that it gave students a voice. Students were able to apply for certain positions throughout the building and become leaders to other students. There was one English Language student who was very shy and decided to join the chorus. We were all able to hear her beautiful voice and she even agreed to do a solo stanza during the fifth grade moving-on ceremony. During leadership day, students performed for the middle school principals through a variety of performances highlighting ways the LIM process impacted them. We were all amazed at the level of confidence and leadership abilities students had developed.

Distributive leadership is powerful when principals do not micromanage and allow others to share decision making and grow into leaders. The purpose of joining forces is to enhance student learning,

Standard 6: Professional Capacity

create a friendly and safe environment, and promote leadership to a level at which all stakeholders feel validated. Each person plays an important role and has specific goals, as I have mentioned earlier. Equity should not only apply to students but to staff members as well. As principals, being able to provide support in different capacities can contribute to success for all. Favoritism should not exist in the building. If one grade or department receives materials, supplies, and allocations, then all should get them as well.

Our school is focused on building a culture of trust with positive relationships. Through distributive leadership, we have developed a shared ownership in a learning environment that demonstrates commitment, collaboration, and celebration of equitable student growth and achievement. We focus on implementation and impact of our instruction and assessment practices and engage in ongoing evidence-informed decisions to measure our effectiveness and next steps. As a result **both the adults and students win**. Teachers know they are part of a community that values them and is inclusive. We have created a sense of community that has strong collaborative professional learning communities and teams with a common goal.

Our students and parents are appreciated and valued for their strengths and individual qualities. Students are learning to be mindful of making positive choices for themselves and others and engaging and developing ownership of their learning to demonstrate new knowledge and skills. Parents are empowered and participate as purposeful collaborators toward school success. We have noted that student performance is increasing school-wide, and evidence-based instructional practices are being implemented consistently towards an equitable and viable curriculum so that all students get and have access to these strategies.

Together we all are continuing to be innovators in our teaching and learning journey.

References

Alton, L. (2019, September 10). *Work-life integration: The evolution of work-life balance*. ADP. www.adp.com/spark/articles/2018/10/the-evolution-from-work-life-balance-to-work-life-integration.aspx

Bass, B. (1985). *Leadership and performance beyond expectations*. Free Press: Collier Macmillan. www.worldcat.org/title/leadership-and-performance-beyond-expectations/oclc/1150215692?referer=di&ht=edition

Bass, B., & Riggio, R. (2006). *Transformational leadership* (2nd ed.). L. Erlbaum Associates. www.taylorfrancis.com/books/mono/10.4324/9781410617095/transformational-leadership-bernard-bass-ronald-riggio

Bennett, N., Wise, C., Woods, P.A., & Harvey, J.A. (2003). *Distributed leadership*. National College of School Leadership.

Brown, B. (2010). *The gifts of imperfection: Let go of who you think you're supposed to be and embrace who you are*. Hazelden Publishing. www.hazelden.org/store/item/15924

Brown, S., & Vaughan, C. (2009). *Play: How it shapes the brain, opens the imagination, and invigorates the soul*. Penguin Group. www.penguinrandomhouse.com/books/303738/play-by-stuart-brown/

Burns, J. M. (1978). *Leadership*. Harper & Row.

Collins, J. (2001). *Good to great*. HarperCollins Publishers Inc. www.harpercollins.com/products/good-to-great-jim-collins

Covey, S. R. (1989). *The 7 habits of highly effective people*. Free Press.

Davidson, F. (2015). Secrets of creating positive work cultures: The work lives of teachers. In F. W. English (Ed.), *The SAGE guide to educational leadership and management* (pp. 401–415). SAGE Publications, Inc. https://doi.org/10.4135/9781483346649.n39

Elmore, R. F. (2000). *Building a new structure for school leadership*. Albert Shanker Institute. www.shankerinstitute.org

Fullan, M. (2020). *Leading in a culture of change* (2nd ed). Jossey-Bass. https://michaelfullan.ca/books/leading-in-a-culture-of-change-second-edition

Gall, M. D., & Acheson, K. A. (2011). *Clinical supervision and teacher development: Preservice and inservice application*. John Wiley and Sons, Inc. https://eric.ed.gov/?id=ED476151

Grissom, J. A., Egalite, A. J., & Lindsay, C. A. (2021). *How principals affect students and schools: A systematic synthesis of two decades of research*. The Wallace Foundation. www.wallacefoundation.org/knowledge-center/pages/how-principals-affect-students-and-schools-a-systematic-synthesis-of-two-decades-of-research.aspx

Harris, A. (2005). Reflections on distributed leadership. *Management in Education, 19*(2), 10–12. https://doi.org/10.1177/08920206050190020301

Leithwood, K., Seashore, K., Anderson, S., & Wahlstrom, K. (2004). *Review of research: How leadership influences student learning.* Wallace Foundation. www.wallacefoundation.org/knowledge-center/documents/how-leadership-influences-student-learning.pdf

National Policy Board for Educational Administration. (2015). *Professional standards for educational leaders.* www.npbea.org/wp-content/uploads/2017/06/Professional-Standards-for-Educational-Leaders_2015.pdf

Pont, B., Nusche, D., & Moorman, H. (2008). *Improving school leadership. Volume 1: Policy and practice.* OECD.

Rath, T., & Gallup. (2018). *StrengthsFinder 2.0.* Gallop Press. www.gallup.com/cliftonstrengths/en/strengthsfinder.aspx

Rook, D. (2019, November 7). *The multi-generational definition of work-life balance.* JP Griffin Group. www.griffinbenefits.com/blog/changing-definition-work-life-balance

University of California Berkeley, Haas School of Business. (2019). *Why work/life integration instead of work/life balance?* https://haas.berkeley.edu/human-resources/work-life-integration/

Whitaker, T. (2003). *What great principals do differently: Fifteen things that matter most.* Eye on Education.

Standard 7
Professional Community for Teachers and Staff

Robyn Conrad Hansen

> Effective educational leaders foster a professional community of teachers and other professional staff to promote *each* student's academic success and well-being.
>
> (PSEL, 2015, p. 15)

As a principal and an effective educational leader, to achieve the vision of your school, you must attend to the ongoing professional development needs of all faculty and staff. Teachers and other professional staff desire to work in a place where they are valued, where it is safe and supportive with a professional learning community that is focused on student success. Taking time to build strong, working relationships where peers feel comfortable sharing ideas and being reflective of their practice as it contributes to a collaborative learning environment. Creating a shared vision and mission based on your school's core values allows everyone to feel like they are an integral part of the plan. The day of the one-room schoolhouse is nearly gone; however, some schools are still working on this premise where teachers work in isolation. Professional learning communities offer teachers and staff the chance to learn from one another in shared visioning and planning, examining what works and what does not to afford students a greater opportunity for success. Leadership is critical to the success of a well-functioning professional community. The *Education Leadership Capability Framework* (Education Council of Aotearoa New Zealand, 2018) emphasizes that it is the responsibility of leadership to make sure the conditions and practices are in place to build a strong sense of an engaging, active, and high-achieving community that is sustainable.

Standard 7: Professional Community

Ongoing professional learning, innovation, and continuous improvement on the part of the faculty and staff are key elements leading to the success of learners.

Collaborative Culture and Mutual Accountability

In Chapter 2, we discussed the role effective educational leaders play in the development, advocacy, and enactment of a shared mission and vision based on core values. In this chapter, our focus is on the knowledge and skills needed by leaders to foster a professional community of teachers and other professional staff to achieve the vision. It is mainly through a collaborative culture where members of the school community feel committed to the success of all students. Collaboration takes time and cannot be forced or mandated. Principals help professionals build trusting relationships, encourage self-reflection, and understand their role in accomplishing the mission. According to expectation "b" for this standard, an effective leader will "Empower and entrust teachers and staff with collective responsibility for meeting the academic, social, emotional, and physical needs of each student, pursuant to the mission, vision, and core values of the school" (PSEL, 2015, p. 15).

According to Kruse and Seashore Louis (2009), a school culture should be created to ensure positive outcomes for all students, which requires everyone doing their part every day. These authors encourage helping all members of the school community feel like an integral part of the team, instilling a sense of pride and ownership in goals for the benefit of all students. They have five recommended tips for building a collaborative school culture:

1. **Focus on a clear outcome**: The best collaborative projects focus on improving student success and making the school a better place for all students to learn

2. **Expand leadership opportunities**: Expanding leadership opportunities develops a critical mass of school members who have leadership skills. As more members become adept at helping the school achieve its goals, more work can be accomplished. Expanding leadership opportunities also reinforces a core tenet of collaboration: equality among all parties (supporting the distributive leadership model that we discuss in Chapter 7)

3. **Create meaningful opportunities for work**: People are more willing to collaborate on work that has a significant personal meaning for them. Organizing people around projects in which they feel personally invested creates more synergy for the project, energizing faculty, staff, and parents and advancing a collaborative culture

4. **Coordinate efforts**: Managing collaborative work is vital to success. You can coordinate and manage efforts in several ways, including online through chat rooms and blogs or at committee meetings during which members regularly report on their progress. Capitalize on work across teams

5. **Celebrate the work of others**: Absolutely celebrate your successes! Find ways to publicize your ongoing collaborative work, giving credit to those who have taken on new roles

Collaborative cultures are more successful when there is common time for groups to meet during the school day. Use of group norms is important, as norms establish a set of expectations for all to follow, increasing dialogue and efficiency. Some norms that we use for meetings include:

- Meetings start and end on time
- Devices are silenced
- Everyone is encouraged to share ideas and thoughts
- Everyone will be respectful of others

Success also occurs with a sense of mutual or reciprocal accountability: a common belief in continuous improvement happening as a collaborative team with everyone responsible for doing their part. Expectation "c" tells us that an effective leader will,

> Establish and sustain a professional culture of engagement and commitment to shared vision, goals, and objectives pertaining to the education of the whole child; high expectations for professional work; ethical and equitable practice; trust and open communication; collaboration, collective efficacy, and continuous individual and organizational learning and improvement.
>
> (PSEL, 2015, p. 15)

Standard 7: Professional Community

This expectation may seem daunting, so let us break it down to more actionable items.

First thing to remember is to avoid "quick fixes." Long-term systemic school improvement takes time and a plan. You have your vision and mission, so work to support the goals with every action. Michael Fullan (2013) recommends concentrating on increasing the leadership capacity of faculty and staff, not just those in formal leadership roles. Spend time on establishing and cultivating collaborative teams with shared leadership among the members. Model this practice with your distributed leadership team (see Chapter 7) and show that you are committed to a shared vision of educating the whole child. Set high expectations of professional work, ensure you are ethical with equitable practices, and that you display a trusting and open communication style that is collaborative. This will enhance continuous individual and organizational learning and improvement. Be true to your beliefs and core values. Live your wholehearted life as described by Brene Brown (2010) in Chapter 7, where she indicates that we should look beyond the feel-good words like love, belonging, and authenticity. We should try to understand what drives a person's actions, beliefs, and emotions.

Mutual accountability suggests a commitment by all members to do their part in accomplishing the mission of the organization. Expectation "d" states that an effective leader should "Promote mutual accountability among teachers and other professional staff for each student's success and the effectiveness of the school as a whole" (PSEL, 2015, p. 15). To establish mutual accountability, principals must set clear roles and outline associated responsibilities with these roles. Begin with the end in mind: What are the expected outcomes? What evidence will be expected to demonstrate progress is being made toward the goals? Celebrate benchmark gains and be reflective of what worked well and what did not. Empower and trust others with collective responsibility to meet the goal.

In this context, mutual accountability refers to how team members support and hold each other accountable for accomplishing tasks at or above expected levels of success. It is not performance pressure that is externally enforced on the team, i.e., district office or state pressure to perform at or above a threshold, but the internal pressure coming from a group of professionals with the same shared vision and mission. An integral part of the team are the classified staff members. They are your classroom paraprofessionals, who support some of our more fragile students with encouragement, accountability, and respect. The cafeteria staff, who prepares nutritious meals to feed the brains and bodies of our students allowing them to feel nourished and cared for. The bus drivers, who are the first and last team members to see the students each day. They know their homes, neighborhoods, and if they are having a good start to the day. The health care workers and social workers, who take care of the physical, psychological, and emotional needs, allowing students to be in the classroom where they learn best. The custodial crew, who maintains the school inside and out providing a clean, well-run environment that is safe and a source of pride. Finally, the front office team; their job responsibilities seem endless. They welcome everyone into the building greeting them by name, limit classroom disruptions, make sure absent students are safe, compile reports to support funding sources, and take care of the day-to-day activities of running a school.

Team mutual accountability provides a safety net for new members as they learn the curriculum and what is expected; at the same time, experienced members take the lead in setting goals and expectations. As in team sports, each member has a job to do, they understand their performance task and work together to achieve a common goal. Each member holds themselves and then each other accountable for delivering specific actions and attitudes. As the team grows in strength and maturity, the collective efficacy also improves. Team members should learn other positions via cross training, in the case of an absence, ensuring the functions of the school will proceed efficiently.

An expectation "h" of an effective leader supporting a professional community for teachers and staff requires them to "Encourage faculty-initiated improvement of programs and practices" (PSEL, 2015, p. 15). Teachers and staff are encouraged to bring forward problems they see in curriculum, policies, procedures, or day-to-day activities of the school; however, they are also tasked with being a problem solver and presenting one or more viable solutions to be discussed. It is our belief that each school should have a strong moral imperative that all students can learn and improving teacher and staff capacity is the most effective way to improve student achievement.

Culture of Professional Learning and Continuous Improvement

An environment of professional learning and continuous improvement is focused on improving outcomes, i.e., graduation rates, closing the

Standard 7: Professional Community

achievement gaps, increased learning in all subjects, and of course, test scores. Principals know "what" is expected, but the "how" is more elusive and harder to understand. According to the expectations "a", "e", "f", and "g" for PSEL (2015, p. 15) Standard 7, an effective leader should know and be able to:

"a" – *Develop workplace conditions for teachers and other professional staff that promote effective professional development, practice, and student learning.*

"e" – *Develop and support open, productive, caring and trusting working relationships among leaders, faculty, and staff to promote professional capacity and the improvement of practice.*

"f" – *Design and implement job-embedded and other opportunities for professional learning collaboratively with faculty and staff.*

"g" – *Provide opportunities for collaborative examination of practice, collegial feedback, and collective learning.*

Taking a closer look at each of these expectations allows us to discover some specific actions effective leaders may employ to be successful. Beginning with expectation "a" as well as "f". As the principal, one of your important roles is the establishment of trust. The professional community must trust each other, as well as you, the principal. One of the ways to start building trust is to schedule time to meet with each teacher and staff member individually. If you are a first-year principal, you may want to start this even before you are given the keys to the building. This practice should be continued as new staff members are hired. This time can be spent getting to know each other, using discussion topics such as: who we are as a person, our hobbies, what drives us, our professional goals, what are our likes and dislikes, and is there anything we would change about our responsibilities or the school? The time spent cultivating relationships earns dividends throughout your career—it's all about relationships.

After you get to know the individuals, it is time for some team building activities. At a faculty retreat, prior to the school year beginning, it was time to have some fun getting to know everyone better. In partnership with our town's Parks and Recreation Department, a staff member came to lead us in some team building activities that were suitable for all ages and physicality. If you are near a community college, university, or recreation center, they may be a good source of information and facilitation of team

121

building activities. Otherwise, there are plenty of sources online to choose from. As we learned in Chapter 7 under Healthy Work–Life Balance, Dr. Stuart Brown, founder of the National Institute for Play, encourages not only children, but also adults to enjoy the art of play. Dr. Brown, along with Christopher Vaughan, authored a book titled, *Play: How It Shapes the Brain, Opens the Imagination, and Invigorates the Soul* (2009). The contents of the book explain how play helps to form our brain pathways, fosters empathy, supports development of executive function or self-regulatory skills, develops social skills enhancing social-emotional learning, and is the basis of creativity and innovation. Our team building activity went so well that the leadership team recommended continuing the practice once a month for the rest of the year. At that point, teacher and staff teams took responsibility for leading the activity for a particular month. Examples of some of the team building activities we enjoyed:

- Water balloon volleyball with a bed sheet outside over a net
- Line or square dancing
- Minute to Win It type games
- Indoor whiffle ball, with more "athletic" members riding tricycles around the bases and when playing in the field
- Food Network's Chopped™ baskets where teams create a dessert or appetizer in a short period of time with basket ingredients for all to enjoy
- Door decorating contests during the year
- Posing a fictional problem that must be solved—Escape Room
- Building a skyscraper with toothpicks and tiny marshmallows: Who can build the tallest or most structurally sound in a limited amount of time?

For team building, we begin with working teams, those who work together most of the time such as grade or subject area teams. Then, mix up the groups later in the year. This causes a bit of creative tension; however, soon everyone sees their conceptual view of team expanding. The increased collaborative work ethic will positively impact the performance of the professional community.

Standard 7: Professional Community

Teachers genuinely enjoy having colleagues visit their classroom. There is so much good teaching and learning happening in schools, but only a few administrators, coaches, or mentors have the privilege of experiencing this great work. High-performing systems integrate both adult learning and student outcomes to drive their professional learning design. Think about a system that provides learning leaders or coaches with time to visit classrooms regularly and provide timely and actionable feedback. School districts must develop evaluation systems that support continuous learning and accountability and find time and resources for teachers and staff to develop professionally through a personalized, job-embedded professional development plan. Likewise, districts are responsible for providing necessary training for principals in the use of the teacher and staff evaluation system. Principals have similar professional development needs as teachers. Principals must have personalized, job-embedded professional development that aligns to their goals and supports their continuous learning throughout their career. Principal evaluation systems should be tightly aligned to the PSEL expectations for each standard. You may want to investigate the use of district funds or Title monies to pay for membership of professional organizations that provide timely and relevant research, podcasts, webinars, and state or national conferences to enhance the professional network of colleagues. District office and superintendents need to continue learning throughout their career as well.

Another consideration in meeting expectations "a" and "f" is the classroom assignments at your school. Are teaching teams near each other? Are the classrooms in the same hallway, pod, or floor? If not, consider a bold and courageous decision to move teachers' classrooms for a more conducive arrangement promoting collaboration. For example, the school where I became principal had the same grade levels scattered around the building, making it difficult to have students attend another class and making it harder to support a new teacher or perform team planning. We had five sixth-grade classrooms, all located in a different part of the building. Yes, it was uncomfortable and somewhat disruptive to move classrooms, but at the end of the first year, 39 teachers moved their classroom location to provide better teaming and working with students. There was some conversation and concessions as to who was moving where, but all in all the moves went well. Everyone pitched in to help with the sorting, packing, moving, and set up in the new room. It brought the staff closer together and was seen as the best course of action to support collaboration and student achievement.

As a principal, you can use vertical and horizontal articulation to enhance your implementation of expectation "g", which says, "Provide opportunities for collaborative examination of practice, collegial feedback, and collective learning," and expectation "e", which says, "Develop and support open, productive, caring and trusting working relationships among leaders, faculty, and staff to promote professional capacity and the improvement of practice" (PSEL, 2015, p. 15). Time is a valuable resource that must be used wisely. Vertical and horizontal articulation are ongoing events that lead to professional learning, collaboration, innovation, productive work relationships, and increased student learning that support the use of this valuable resource. Vertical and horizontal articulation work well in large and small districts. Now with the use of virtual conferencing, distance is not an issue even for the most rural communities with internet. The premise behind vertical articulation is to have teachers in grade levels or subjects (both elementary and secondary) come together to share the alignment of instruction. Most curricula are scaffolded, meaning a standard is introduced in one course, reinforced in the next, and mastered in the upper grade/course. Teachers discuss student data, find gaps in learning, work together to better align the curriculum to standards, and support each other's lesson design and teaching. On a vertical articulation day at school, we all meet in a large area like the media center, cafeteria, or gymnasium, which makes it efficient for teams to meet and the principal to move among teams. A schedule is created showing which grades/subjects meet at what time and then rotate after the allotted time. For elementary level, middle grade teachers are invited to join the conversation, as well as the reverse for secondary. With horizontal articulation, it is beneficial to bring teachers who teach like grades or subjects together from different schools to review the alignment of standards. It is also beneficial to have teachers collaborate and share unit designs, including project-based learning, proven teaching practices, and authentic assessments. Of particular interest is the sharing of literature alignment with lessons and culturally responsive teaching practices.

As teachers have more time to learn together and develop individual competencies, the mindset of working as an individual shifts to working as a team. Members understand how collective performance outshines that of the individual. You start hearing more "we" phrases than "I" statements.

The team comes together to rally support for one another without pointing to a weakest link. You start to hear terms like "our kids" or "our goals." With a culture of professional learning and continuous improvement the professional learning communities become truly focused on the whole child by helping each student succeed. The teams become intrinsically motivated to do well and enjoy discovering innovative teaching methods while trusting one another's knowledge and expertise.

Just as teachers build strong community within the classroom based on rules and expectations developed in collaboration with the students, principals build strong professional community of teachers and staff that is valued by all for enhancing accountability and teamwork, as well as social and emotional support. Many schools feel like a family. In fact, we are with our co-workers and students more waking hours then we are with our own families. Time, resources, and energy spent on building professional learning communities will benefit students and adults alike.

Voices from the Field

As a valuable contribution to this *Principal's Desk Reference*, we have collected vignettes shared by award-winning, proven leaders who are effective principals to help you better understand the "how" of implementing each standard. So often we only get the theory, but in this book we want to focus on the "how" of putting it into practice. This exemplar principal has learned many lessons over the years and is eager to share their thoughts and stories with you.

Vignette by Ms. Ines Schreiner

The dream of being an effective leader, having plans and processes theoretically in place, is a beautiful thing. It is the basic equipment every leader needs to bring, to even dare to engage in the adventure of being a school leader. The richer, the bolder the dream, the better! Leaders bring the vision; leaders bring the **WHY**. The more personal the WHY, the harder the leader will work to achieve the goal. An interesting and demanding task, when integrating an international school curriculum into a local system that is very conservative and bureaucratic. Now how do we make the personal goal of the leader the common goal of the community?

> What _characteristics_ should be identified when leaders observe their teams and what _processes_ do we have to put in place in order for the community to care for each other with one shared treasure in mind—the student?

Being a first-time head of a secondary school in Austria, I have big dreams. My dreams are all inclusive, all consuming, and always revolve around the same questions: How can I help make this school a better place for our students? How can I make the teaching team care as much as I care? Finally, how do I make the community in which our school was founded care about our ambitions and how can I implement change in the community? First, I thought with purely my compassion for each and every individual in the school community, I cannot go wrong, this must be the answer. If I just show what it means to give 150% every single day, the team will follow and do the same. And yes, that is a good start, but it is not enough. I must define exactly what _characteristics_ I want to see. Almost as if I am designing an assessment rubric for my classes. **A rubric for a successful learning community**. As our school is an International Baccalaureate® (IB) continuum school, I looked into our Middle Years Program (MYP) rubrics and concluded that they are too subject specific and one teacher might be more intrigued by it, depending on how familiar he or she is with it or not. So, I decided to go with the Primary Years Program (PYP) terminology of Developing – Emerging – Achieving – Excelling. What are the characteristics that I want to see?

The WHAT

Shared values and vision are the number one characteristic of a successful learning community and the most difficult one. Finding the common denominator in an international school, with over 30 different cultural backgrounds, is a difficult endeavor. Bringing it back to the student and learning—regardless of your culture and ethnicity, it needs to be helpful and self-explanatory, reassuringly simple. Bringing together teacher communities in an international school is an extraordinary task and if they are not completely open-minded individuals—don't even try. Catching the

Standard 7: Professional Community

nuances of language and personalities takes a special leader, who has to be extremely sensitive and inclusive in nature and yet define the school's bottom line in terms of values and regulations.

The collective accountability and shared responsibility are tricky characteristics as well. I have this vision of running a school like a jazz band versus an orchestra. This works well with distributed leadership like department heads, yet you must understand everyone's **WHY** and be ready to take over and perform your solo. In an ideal distributed leadership school, the trust amongst staff members is high enough that the players easily lean back and let each other's members lead. As an administrator I like to hand over the baton occasionally, to a trusted band member, but I realize now that I always need to be aware of the wand being handed back to me sooner than expected.

An exercise I did at the extended leadership team's retreat was to ask the heads of departments to collect situations in which they would rather play in an orchestra than a jazz band. When is the need for strong conduct necessary and when can/should school leaders let the extended leadership team, department heads, teacher leaders, students, and parents take the lead? Interesting conversations and discussions arise from such activities. An outstanding musical performance does not just happen overnight. The right combination between creativity, passion, knowledge, and determination, skillfully combined, will create something magical. The next segment is a prerequisite for a well-performed sonnet.

Mutual trust, respect, and support should be the base for every relationship in a community; however, I am observing that positive outcomes of critical conversations depend very much on the amount of personal engagement, the amount of vulnerability and honesty the members are willing to give. The more tasks focused the better, but without personal engagement, even the most task-focused person cannot always succeed in a school full of individuals. Schools are not factories, and that makes the members so emotional, so personal. I would venture to say that the teaching and learning business is probably the most emotional business in the world, because the most precious human being of our lives is involved, our children.

Nevertheless, I observed and experienced that conflicts, regardless of whether the students or teachers are involved, are best handled with extreme care not to attack the self-worth of your counterpart. Try to stick with the task at hand and never cross the line of the basic rules of respectful behavior. Friendships amongst staff members can also be a barrier for a professional learning community, because members do not always share the same opinion and views on items but are biased when their friends are involved. "It is lonely at the top" is not just a saying.

Be careful when offering support; it might be taken as a hidden criticism. Formulate your opinion. Sometimes I practice in front of the mirror to get a feeling for what the other person sees. It is an interesting and valuable practice; so much goes into body language and the message you send needs to be clear and focused.

The promotion of professional collaboration and reflective practice can be provided in a fun and entertaining way. My colleagues from primary school have established a very engaging routine. They call it five-minute sharing. The activity is run like speed dating and teachers get together in groups and share their favorite practice for five minutes and then move on to the next colleague. After the initial sharing, teams for observations are formed and the dates continue. The positive aspect of this type of lesson observation/feedback is that teachers do not feel threatened by a superior coming to watch their classes, but rather engage with their peers in an informal way.

HOW—Procedures in Place

As an experienced teacher leader, I understand how important it is to put measurable benchmarks in place, so you can observe the progress or just make an inventory on your current situation. For this purpose, a rubric is the best way of assessing your professional learning community. You might use it in a range of ways. For example: Individual staff members complete the rubric privately and give it to a designated person or team who collates responses and feeds these back to the staff for discussion.

Individual staff members complete the rubric before sharing and discussing their responses with each other. Small groups complete the rubric together and then compare and summarize their responses.

I have experienced the importance of clearly set guidelines, goals, and boundaries this year as a first-time principal. It is impossible to please everyone; not every issue is worth fighting for. Letting go of things that are minor and understanding the core values of your school are essential!

Leave some gas in the tank for the way home!

References

Brown, B. (2010). *The gifts of imperfection: Let go of who you think you're supposed to be and embrace who you are.* Hazelden Publishing. www.hazelden.org/store/item/15924

Brown, S., & Vaughan, C. (2009). *Play: How it shapes the brain, opens the imagination, and invigorates the soul.* Penguin Group. www.penguinrandomhouse.com/books/303738/play-by-stuart-brown/

Education Council of Aotearoa New Zealand. (2018). *Education leadership capability framework.* https://teachingcouncil.nz/assets/Files/Leadership-Strategy/Leadership_Capability_Framework.pdf

Fullan, M. (2013). *Motion leadership in action: More skinny on becoming change savvy.* Corwin Press. https://us.corwin.com/en-us/nam/book/motion-leadership-action

Kruse, S., & Seashore Louis, K. (2009). *Building strong school cultures: A leader's guide to change.* Corwin Press. https://us.corwin.com/en-us/nam/book/building-strong-school-cultures

National Policy Board for Educational Administration. (2015). *Professional standards for educational leaders.* www.npbea.org/psel/

Standard 8
Meaningful Engagement of Families and Community

Robyn Conrad Hansen

> Effective educational leaders engage families and the community in meaningful, reciprocal, and mutually beneficial ways to promote *each* student's academic success and well-being.
>
> (PSEL, 2015, p. 16)

Substantial research shows when there is a strong bond among parents, school, and community, all coming together for the benefit of student growth and development, children are more successful. The school principal is responsible for forming this bond by creating lasting relationships, being visible, developing effective two-way communication. It is very important to educate your faculty and staff on the importance of supporting meaningful engagement with families and community, while advocating on behalf of all children. An aspect of the principalship that I truly enjoyed was creating an environment that fostered the coming together of community to form a family atmosphere with the school at the center. At our school, a "Hall of Memories" is created by students nearing the end of sixth grade, where they could reflect on their time at the school, listing their favorite memories they will carry with them. Without question, most memories listed are of times spent with classmates, teachers, and parents in extra-curricular events, like athletic competitions, dances, concerts, plays, field trips, school carnivals, movie nights, the Talent Show, Water Day, Track & Field Day, Fine Dining, cultural events, and special community guests visiting the school. We have a rich and diverse list of invitees to special events, including the Mountain Man, Native American Chief, Oneida, dignitaries from China and Northern Ireland, sports figures, and even

Standard 8: Families and Community

astronaut LeRoy Chiao. Meaningful engagement of students and families enhances the learning experience and broadens the real-life adventures for students. These events take a great deal of planning and preparation. None of these events would have been as successful without the support of our teachers, parents, student groups, and community. Research tells us that even more than use of technology, young people want to spend time with adults they care about. Parents may think their children do not want them around at school, but they really do. This chapter addresses three themes of meaningful engagement that will help you successfully achieve the expectations for Standard 8:

1. Relationships
2. Communication and advocacy
3. School as the center of the community

Relationships

In educational leadership, a common phrase reiterated by professors in principal and superintendent preparation programs is "It's all about the relationships." A valuable skill taught early in the preparation of administrators is to know how to begin to cultivate relationships. Time spent at the beginning of a new job and throughout your leadership journey getting to know your staff and allowing them to get to know you will form the foundation of a trusting, authentic relationship. The investment of time to cultivate relationships with the community pays dividends throughout your career. Leadership is a lifelong process, a journey you go on that requires vision, determination, focus, and discipline. The process allows your commitment of excellence to shine through in your daily actions that others see; it is built on trust, integrity, and passion. According to expectation "b" of this standard an effective leader must "Create and sustain positive, collaborative, and productive relationships with families and the community for the benefit of students" (PSEL, 2015, p. 16).

Consider the following actions as you build strong, lasting relationships in your school community with teachers, staff, students, parents, and community members:

1. **Listen**—be present in the conversation. Dr. Stephen R. Covey (2020, p. 273), in his highly acclaimed series of Seven Habits, says in Habit 5, "Seek first to understand, and then to be understood." He explains, "Most people do not listen with the intent to understand; they listen with the intent to reply." Practice active listening with everyone; stop what you are doing to give them the attention they deserve. Look them in the eye, even if that means kneeling for a child, and have good interpersonal skills and body language. Paraphrase what you thought you heard the person say, in a positive, non-judgmental way. Follow through on a request that was made

2. **Be humble**—servant leadership takes humility. Understand you are serving the members of your community to the best of your ability. It is ok not to have all the answers. It is important to be visible and approachable. You will soon see many conversations happen in the moment, including when you are walking the halls, on lunch duty, before and after school drop-off and pick-up, at the grocery store, or athletic events and concerts. These impromptu conversations serve to enhance relationships. Expectation "a" states that effective leaders "Are approachable, accessible, and welcoming to families and members of the community" (PSEL, 2015, p. 16). People just want to be listened to and heard. They want to make sure you are "in the know" about events in the neighborhood. Daniel Goleman (1995), in his book *Emotional Intelligence*, encourages us to show empathy and understanding about how others are feeling. A simple "Thank you for sharing" or "I truly appreciate you letting me know" goes a long way in building the confidence of others. Not everyone in your school community will feel comfortable calling, emailing, texting, or coming to school; however, as they see you out in the community, they may approach you with information and inquiries. Your receptiveness will be noticed and valued. Theodore Roosevelt has been attributed with sharing, "Nobody cares how much you know, until they know how much you care"

3. **Be a coach**—coaches make observations and give valuable, timely feedback. A good practice is to praise publicly and criticize privately. Carol Dweck (2006), in her book *Mindset: The New Psychology of Success*, says that feedback should be specific and constructive. This is true when coaching adults and children

Standard 8: Families and Community

4. **Be a courageous leader**—be the leader your staff and community are expecting. Provide the vision and actions to go beyond ordinary to extraordinary. Think outside of the box, look for possibilities where others have not, and imagine a school that truly meets the needs of all students. Show vulnerability, make bold decisions. Brene Brown (2010, p. 13) shares in her book *The Gifts of Imperfection* that "Ordinary courage is about putting our *vulnerability* on the line. Vulnerability is the most accurate measure of courage"

5. **Be kind and caring**—follow the Golden Rule of treating others as you would like to be treated. Create an environment of belonging so that all who walk through the school doors feel welcomed and appreciated for who they are and the gifts they possess

Being a part of your community provides valuable insights. Expectation "d" states that an effective leader should "Maintain a presence in the community to understand its strengths and needs, develop productive relationships, and engage its resources for the school" (PSEL, 2015, p. 16). A former superintendent of mine understood this area all too well. He was a true civic leader and expected all principals at every level to also be actively involved in the community. There was a time that all principals were expected to live within the school district boundaries. Active participation in civic affairs was part of our leadership expectations and evaluation. Each year he would ask, how are we involved and what are our plans to cultivate stronger relationships and partnerships with community members? There are many opportunities for you to become involved in your community. Some of the boards and different community events I had the privilege to serve on included being a board member for Boys and Girls Club and helping them build a new youth center in the community, and supporting the Arizona Council on Economic Education and Gilbert Sister Cities board with outreach and travel to China and Northern Ireland. We were able to start pen pal programs with students from different countries. The best part is the opportunity to include your family in most of these events to help establish a sense of community pride and volunteerism. Other administrators chose to belong to the Rotary, Lions, Jaycees, hospital board, etc. In many communities, the school district is the number one employer in the city. Having a strong, contributing presence in the community opens many doors and establishes deep, long-lasting relationships.

Partnerships are also very valuable. Expectation "j" says an effective leader understands how to "Build and sustain productive partnerships with public and private sectors to promote school improvement and student learning" (PSEL, 2015, p. 16). At no other time in our recent history has there been such a need to find students who are not attending any school at all, home school, private, charters, public, parochial, and get them back in school and energized for learning. Before the COVID-19 crisis, the World Education Forum-USA (wefusa.net) estimated 6 million American school-aged children were not attending any type of school. Following school closures nationally, the estimated numbers of students not attending school has skyrocketed to over 15 million (World Education Forum-USA, 2021). On a global scale, a UNESCO (United Nations Educational, Scientific, and Cultural Organization) report summarizes recent global information (2019) on school attendance and reports that, in 2018, at least 258 million children were not attending any type of school. Following the 2020–2021 COVID-19 crisis that number is predictably much higher.

We cannot educate students who are not attending school. Community partnerships are more important than ever in finding these young people. School administrators and local authorities are encouraged to work together to find these children, and make sure it is safe and welcoming for them to return to school. Schools are the front-line support for millions of children. Our educators are key in providing safe spaces for all. Partnerships with the police and fire departments, school districts, inter-faith leaders, chamber of commerce, health care workers, and community resources such as food banks, shelters, and neighborhood service centers allow us to come together in a concerted effort to locate our children. This enables school leaders, educators, and social workers to get them engaged in school. This goes a long way to fostering a community of learners and bridging the achievement and economic gap. A side benefit is that this helps with funding for the school which positively impacts all students as attendance increases.

Other ways to connect with your police department, even if you have a school resource office (SRO) assigned, is to invite local law enforcement to park in front of your school (this slows traffic considerably), have them come in for a break, get a beverage, snack, or a place to complete reports. Every so often, there is a need to call and report a criminal incident. Having police officers who know you and your school community greatly aids in

Standard 8: Families and Community

efficiency and support. A K-9 officer brought his dog for a demonstration at an assembly for the entire school. The students and staff enjoy having police officers on campus. We would ask them to periodically step into a classroom to contribute to a lesson and answer questions. Similarly, connecting with your local fire house is beneficial. Our fire house has offered first aid training in CPR, choking, heat stroke, sun protection, ADE machine usage, and more. During our water day event at the end of the school year, the fire truck comes onto the playground and demonstrates the use of lifesaving equipment and fire hoses, then supports the teachers in dousing the kids who want to participate in getting soaked! It is an event we look forward to each spring. To increase safety protocols, the police and fire departments are invited to the school to observe and offer suggestions on our lockdown and fire drill procedures. On a special day, one fireman who is a double amputee came to school to talk with students whose classmate also recently had surgery to remove both legs below the knee due to sepsis caused by a viral infection. These partnerships, and many others, have proven to be beneficial in promoting school improvement, student learning, safety, and community pride.

Communication and Advocacy

In Chapter 7 Standard 6: Professional Capacity of School Personnel, we addressed the use of a distributed leadership model highlighting leadership team cabinet seats. One such leadership seat was that of Public Relations (PR). The co-chairs of this position included a teacher and parent who were both very involved in the community and school. One of their primary roles is establishing how best to communicate with families and the community, as well as the importance of advocating publicly for the needs of students and families. According to expectation "c" for this standard, effective leaders should "Engage in regular and open two-way communication with families and the community about the school, students, needs, problems, and accomplishments" (PSEL, 2015, p. 16). The use of a survey is a good way to gather information. Does your school use a parent portal to communicate? Have you invited parents in for an open house to demonstrate the portal's use and value in promoting higher student achievement and parent engagement? Students are known to be more successful in school when parents are involved in their learning and communicate regularly with

135

teachers. Back-to-school events such as Meet the Teacher, Science Nights, or Shadow Your Student where parents follow their student's daily schedule are good welcoming events to begin the communication process. Consider creating a video that highlights important information to be shared at the beginning of the year and have available for families who enroll after school starts. It is all about relationships. The more connected parents feel to the school and teachers, the better students do in class.

Some of the events that consistently brought in the largest turn out of families at our school included carnivals, concerts, and athletic events. Another was math and reading nights with focused hands-on experiences and practical information for helping parents work with their children at home. There is a valuable link between parent involvement and student achievement. As an incentive to have parents attend events, students receive "free homework" passes. Personal invitations are mailed home, and phone calls and text messages were also used as a follow-up to the invitation. Parent involvement can make a difference in academic growth of learners when there is an emphasis on shared reading at the elementary level, parent follow-up and support of learning at all levels, and the setting of high expectations for the students. The greater the parent involvement, the greater the family–school bond. Once parents become engaged, they typically remain involved throughout their child's school experience. A systems approach to parent involvement is encouraged which includes parent leadership, teacher training, and creating a welcoming school culture. All children deserve a quality education. Earning at least a high school diploma changes lives dramatically for young people and helps with greater equity in society. All children deserve great teachers, administrators, and schools that have proper resources. Children need adult advocates to speak on their behalf.

As an effective leader, you will need to find your voice. Expectation "h" says you should "Advocate for the school and district, and for the importance of education and student needs and priorities to families and the community" (PSEL, 2015, p. 16). Your students and community are depending on you to understand their needs and to do what it takes to provide the best learning environment possible for all children. Teachers and administrators are in a unique position to understand the needs of each student and understand the knowledge and skills they need to be successful.

Standard 8: Families and Community

The benefits of membership in your state and national associations are bountiful. Especially when you consider the influence they have on state and federal policy due to the size of membership. These organizations have professional staff members researching and sharing timely information and publications to impact your leadership decisions. The National Association of Elementary School Principals (NAESP) and the National Association of Secondary School Principals (NASSP) host an annual National Leaders Conference where principal leaders from around the country meet in Washington, DC to raise their collective voices on topics and policies affecting schools around the country. They schedule time to meet with legislators on Capitol Hill to communicate their stories and inquire as to what message these leaders can bring home and share with local constituents. At the same time, leaders create a network of support and camaraderie to last a lifetime.

In addition, effective leaders (expectation "i") should "Advocate publicly for the needs and priorities of students, families, and the community" (PSEL, 2015, p. 16). It is important to attend your local school board meetings to see what is on their agenda and how decisions will impact your school community. It is sometimes uncomfortable speaking on topics in a public forum, especially legislative action items or public policy. If you do not have a liaison in your district who is active in state legislation, you will need to do some homework to understand and be informed of actions within your state. Consider establishing a legislative liaison within your principal's professional learning community (PLC) to educate and update principals in your group on topics of importance. Set up meetings with your superintendents, who often participate in area consortiums, to share ideas and stand united on topics affecting all children. It is valuable to get to know your state and federal legislators and policy makers. Schedule time to meet with them in person; bring a colleague to enhance the conversation. Before you meet, create a position paper with valuable information and the position you and your colleagues take on an upcoming vote or a bill you would like them to introduce. Go to your state capitol to listen to arguments, maybe a field trip with teachers and students. If you have the opportunity, meet with your federal legislators in Washington, DC. Make an appointment ahead of time for the best chance of meeting with the representative. It is important for both principals and superintendents to be involved and knowledgeable about federal, state, and local politics.

137

School as the Center of the Community

We all feel home should be the safest place for children; however, for many youths, school is the safest place. A place where their physical, emotional, social, psychological, and academic needs are met. Effective leaders, according to expectation "e", should "Create a means for the school community to partner with families to support student learning in and out of school" (PSEL, 2015, p. 16). The school becomes a place to support students before and after the regular school day with clubs and activities, a place to finish homework, receive tutoring, be supervised, participate in organized sporting events, enjoy a hot meal, begin their day ready to learn, or participate in summer school. The school becomes a source of information related to heath care, social-emotional support, parenting, English classes, and community partnerships. Consider creating a pamphlet, as a resource guide, available to parents highlighting community professionals that support family needs. Research shows that where schools are the community center there is an increase in student attendance, academic growth, social-emotional well-being, and parent involvement. These schools recognize and embrace the similarities and differences of individuals that make up their school family. Ask parents what activities, events, or learning would benefit them the most in supporting continuous engagement with home and school. Then work to fulfill those requests.

Schools serve to meet the needs not only of children, but families and community alike. To be a true "center of the community," effective leaders (expectation "g") need to "Develop and provide the school as a resource for families and the community" (PSEL, 2015, p. 16). Be the bridge within the PK-20 education system. Consider the benefit to your community if your school hosts a Parent University where English is taught, and career counseling and job support is offered, or assistance with navigating the bumpy road to higher education with FASFA completion, applications, essay writing, and searching for scholarships. The school can serve as a post for health screenings and social-emotional services. For elementary school principals, you can visit the preschools in your area and share information about your school. Invite incoming kindergarten families to a "Kindergarten Round-up," where parents and students get to meet the teachers, administration, and staff, have a tour of the school, and interact with other families, while providing teachers a chance to complete a

Standard 8: Families and Community

readiness assessment aiding in-class placement for the fall. Offer parents a summer packet of engaging activities to aid in bridging learning gaps.

School activities and events get and hold the attention of students and adults, including sporting events, arts and drama, and cultural events. One activity that our fifth graders look forward to bi-annually is our Fine Dining cultural event. Our school picture day happens twice a year and we leverage this event as a great time to practice etiquette in a fine dining environment. The fifth-grade team of teachers and students present fine dining for the entire school. Based on a particular theme, the café-a-gymatorium is transformed into a fine dining experience for the students. The teachers review dining etiquette prior to lunch and eat with their class to model and reinforce proper table manners and conversation. During the special event, the staff, parents, and administration serve the meal (dressed in theme-appropriate clothing), while the fifth graders practice the roles and responsibilities of working the "front and back of the house," as it is referred to in the restaurant field. This activity also adds to college and career readiness training, giving them insight into opportunities in the culinary arts. Students plan the menu and create the decorations with the art teacher. The cafeteria and front office teams serve as receptionists, set up and bus tables, and create and send invitations for guests. Community and business partners, district leadership, legislators, school board members, parents, and family are all invited. The music and physical education teachers work with students to perform traditional songs and dance based on the theme. This is one of our school's signature events that receives great accolades from the entire community. This tradition has carried on for nearly 20 years, giving us time to explore much of the world's culture through food, music, dance, and art, while enhancing dining etiquette and social awareness, impacting generations. This activity could be performed in the secondary level as well.

For high schools, embrace the tradition of Homecoming, which helps keep the community engaged. Few events can unite a community quite as well as Homecoming. You can use traditional spirit week activities to welcome alumni and community to campus, including a parade, tailgate party, dance, pep rally in the stadium, bonfire, and of course the big game! Welcome back and celebrate past graduating classes; many may still live within the community or within driving distance. Homecoming festivities are part of a classic high school experience that is still popular today. Remember to include the community and past graduating classes in the communication and planning; some may combine this event with their class reunions.

Embrace the uniqueness of your school community. Look at all the things that make it a special place for students and adults. Understand the culture, traditions, foods, music, celebrations, family make-up, language, politics, mean income, educational background, religious practices, and employment status. Find community businesses to partner with that will benefit you both. Expectation "f" of this standard indicates that effective leaders need to "Understand, value, and employ the community's cultural, social, intellectual, and political resources to promote student learning and school improvement" (PSEL, 2015, p. 16). As you may remember, my school is a diverse community with 17 different languages spoken as the main language in the home. Parents/grandparents are invited to school to share their families' traditions, culture, religion, music, food, travel, and their journey to the United States. A popular event for the middle grades is the World's Fair, where students research a nationality and culture; typically they choose their own. They create a poster board of findings and present information to the rest of the school and families. All grade levels can benefit from researching their history by interviewing the eldest family members to learn more about their life journey and the dreams they have for the student and next generations. As part of the student presentations, they are encouraged to wear traditional dress and share music, food, and other cultural and religious influences. It is a highlight of the year for many students and parents.

Well-trained volunteers serve as an invaluable resource benefiting both the school and the volunteer. One year, we calculated the in-kind support of our volunteer brigade to the tune of $65,800. A parent and staff member created a volunteer training program and recruited parents, grandparents, and community members to serve on a consistent basis. It might be once a week or once a month; the point was to have a commitment so we could count on their service. They could volunteer to serve in classrooms, on the playground, in sporting events, in the cafeteria, the front office, or assist with classroom projects. Volunteers should be trained in a variety of responsibilities. The students really benefit both academically and emotionally from the one-on-one time a volunteer provides. Our school paid for the required fingerprint clearance card. Some volunteers served for many years. The teachers became well-versed at tapping into the cultural, social, intellectual, and political talents of community members. Scientists

Standard 8: Families and Community

and engineers are recruited as judges for the Science Fair and guest speakers in class and at STEM/STEAM clubs. Business owners share their entrepreneurial and marketing experiences, energy experts assist students in solar capstone projects, artists and authors demonstrate their talents, chefs share recipes and techniques with the culinary arts club, and musicians enhance the music curriculum. There are numerous opportunities for community partnerships.

Volunteers should be an integral part of your school family. At the end of the year, celebrate them and calculate the hours and salary (if they were paid) and thank them for their selfless contributions to the school's success. The more community and business partners get to know you and your education team, and participate in school events, the greater their level of support. Confidence grows as they see the work you are doing and as they get to know the students and staff. These valuable contributors will be in the community praising your students and the work you and your team are doing to elevate success and professional practices.

Effective educational leaders engage families and the community in meaningful, reciprocal, and mutually beneficial ways to promote *each* student's academic success and well-being. Sometimes, I feel the choice to be a principal is like a pastoral calling, that of a servant leader. The role of building-level principal is the most rewarding career you will ever have. Parents entrust you with the academic, emotional, and social well-being of their children. You will make a difference in the lives of children daily. You will continue to be a teacher as you support your staff member's goal setting, and professional growth and development. The relationships you cultivate will last for years. It is a point of pride when former students move to your area to be able to bring their children to your school or when you hire former students to join your education family. You will be invited to many graduations, weddings, family celebrations, and retirements. Sadly, there will be funerals to attend of students, former students, parents, staff, and community. Even though it may be difficult, make every effort to express condolences during these difficult times and attend funerals when possible. It is all about the people and relationships who have come into your life along your leadership journey. Appreciate each one for they will impact your life in a way you may not realize for many years to come. Thank you for choosing to be a principal.

Robyn Conrad Hansen

 ## Voices from the Field

As a valuable contribution to this *Principal's Desk Reference*, we have collected vignettes shared by award-winning, proven leaders who are effective principals to help you better understand the "how" of implementing each standard. So often we only get the theory, but in this book we want to focus on the "how" of putting it into practice. This exemplar principal has learned many lessons over the years and is eager to share her thoughts and stories with you.

 ## Vignette by Dr. Catarina Song Chen

During my tenure as the head of the American School of Belo Horizonte and as a participant in the international school community, I have found that the acronym CCO represents many different job titles and has a range of meanings across different organizations. CCO can stand for Chief Communication Officer, Chief Compliance Officer, Chief Creative Officer or even Chief Commercial Officer.

The term CCO can easily apply to my duties as "head of school" due to the day-to-day tasks involving communication with various stakeholders, compliance with accreditation standards and local laws, and the development of curriculum, as well as other school services. I have learned that the role of an educational leader can be complex and comprehensive, encompassing all the aforementioned responsibilities and beyond. I have come to believe that a head of school is very much the official ambassador of the school organization, promoting its brand through a myriad of actions. Having served as a head of school for over a decade, I have learned that the first *true* responsibility of the educational leader is indeed to serve as the organization's CCO—Chief Culture Officer.

As the school's Chief Culture Officer, my job is to bridge organizational silos by bringing together our distinct stakeholders—students, parents, faculty, staff, and external organizations—to work together towards a common purpose. The purpose of this role is ultimately to cultivate a school environment where everybody feels a strong sense of safety, support, and belonging, but also feels essential to do their part in sustaining the organization and collaborating to achieve new goals. I was able to do this by bringing the school's mission and core values to life and by making them

Standard 8: Families and Community

a part of the school's ethos. During my initial years of leadership, I asked myself: Do the community members know and embrace the school's mission? Can they identify and define the values of the school? The answer was no. I knew my first action needed to be to reverse this status quo and ensure the mission was known, understood, and embraced. I started with the school's foundational document.

Our mission statement tells our story; it justifies the decisions we make and creates a common language when communicating expectations for learning, collaborating, and responding to change. It transcends time and space, allowing me to cultivate a lasting culture, flexible as the world changes but rigid enough to demand excellence from all constituents. So how have I made the school's mission known and embraced by the school community? And how have I as the CCO communicated the school's expectations and nurtured its ethos? A succinct, easy to remember catchphrase makes a mission easy to remember and recite. But it's through action that the mission can be embraced by the community and consequently come to life.

We involved the entire community when reviewing and revising the mission statement. Starting small with our board and leadership team, as the governing group, we reviewed the foundational document and affirmed the values, mission, and belief statements. Then, faculty, staff, and students were invited to share their input and suggestions for modification. Afterwards, we expanded the process to further solicit the opinion from parents and cross check their understanding to ensure that the intended message of the mission was achieved. Finally, we circled back to the board and leadership for a final adoption based on all stakeholder feedback. In the end, we were able to have engaged all stakeholders through this inclusive process by the time the foundational document was ready for final adoption.

A good CCO should be a standard-bearer, continuously lifting the mission and values in front of every community member to remain at the top of her game. I begin every school year's in-service by revisiting the foundational document with faculty. We review the mission and values and how they live through the school's strategic plan. Most importantly, we hold annual meetings with parents to communicate how our school's mission leads to school success and demonstrate how it's interconnected to student well-being and academic growth to recruit parents as fellow school ambassadors. Students are part of this process and should be

143

empowered to exercise their leadership. Student leaders are encouraged to host town halls, pep rallies, and other gatherings with the student body to share news, solicit feedback, and build school spirit. Staff should never be forgotten! They are often the hidden heroes, the missing link to complete the community's sphere. I also meet with our school secretaries, kitchen staff, and custodians, including all outsourced security guards. I share with them how they personify the school's values and how they uphold the school's mission with their work.

These are just a few initiatives that I led, as Chief Culture Officer, to cultivate a culture in our school community. By including faculty and families in meaningful dialogues and collegial engagements, it has led to student well-being and academic success. Stakeholders become the voice to articulate our school's story, promote mission-aligned actions, and embody our school brand of excellence.

References

Brown, B. (2010). *The gifts of imperfection: Let go of who you think you're supposed to be and embrace who you are.* Hazelden Publishing. www.hazelden.org/store/item/15924

Covey, S. R. (2020). *The 7 habits of highly effective people (30th Anniversary Edition).* Simon & Schuster. www.franklincovey.com/the-7-habits/

Dweck, C. (2006). *Mindset: The new psychology of success.* Ballantine Books. www.audible.com/pd/Mindset-Audiobook/0593150422

Goleman, D. (1995). *Emotional intelligence: Why it can matter more than IQ.* Random House Publishing. www.danielgoleman.info/

National Policy Board for Educational Administration. (2015). *Professional standards for educational leaders.* www.npbea.org/psel/

United Nations Educational, Scientific, and Cultural Organization. (2019, September). *New methodology shows 258 million children, adolescents and youth are out of school.* Fact Sheet no. 56. http://uis.unesco.org/en/topic/out-school-children-and-youth

World Education Forum-USA. (2021). *Help! Strategies needed to find millions of missing kids.* http://wefusa.net/

Standard 9
Operations and Management
Frank D. Davidson

> Effective educational leaders manage school operations and resources to promote *each* student's academic success and well-being.
>
> (PSEL, 2015, p. 17)

Standard 9 involves skills such as managing and monitoring operations and administrative systems, managing staff resources, assigning and scheduling staff, and overseeing budgets and accounting processes (PSEL, 2015, p. 17). These may seem like mundane tasks, but ultimately ensuing the reliability and efficiency of school operations and resources has a huge impact on the day-to-day functioning of the school and ultimately student learning. In a recent examination of ideas by John Kotter, whose academic career has been devoted to exploring the importance of management, he notes we need to be able to make our complex organizations reliable and efficient. We need them to jump into the future—the right future—at an accelerated pace, no matter the size of the changes required to make that happen (Kotter, 2013, para. 10). Part of these management activities for an effective leader are to "Develop and manage productive relationships with the central office and school board" and to "Manage governance processes and internal and external politics toward achieving the school's mission and vision" as stated in expectations "j" and "l" respectively of this standard (PSEL, 2015, p. 17).

Frank D. Davidson

 ## The Varied Dimensions of School Leadership

Successful leadership often involves a more nuanced approach than a forced choice between leading or managing. As has been articulated extensively in this book, school leaders need to prioritize leadership efforts such as engaging their staff in a shared vision and developing coherent systems of curriculum, instruction, and assessment. Leaders also need to effectively manage school operations and resources to promote each student's academic success and well-being, the focus of Standard 9. Expectations "a," "b," and "c" (PSEL, 2015, p. 17) address the management of your school operation where an effective leader should "a) Institute, manage, and monitor operations and administrative systems that promote the mission and vision of the school," "b) Strategically manage staff resources, assigning and scheduling teachers and staff to roles and responsibilities that optimize their professional capacity to address each student's learning needs," and "c) Seek, acquire, and manage fiscal, physical, and other resources to support curriculum, instruction, and assessment; student learning community; professional capacity and community; and family and community engagement."

Leaders must be able to adequately attend to functions in areas as diverse as personnel, budgeting, scheduling, facilities maintenance, communications, food services, and instructional support. Leaders need to have a compelling vision, more than simply head-in-the-clouds visionaries. They also need to effectively attend to the day-to-day operations of a school. This requires not only attention to the core functions of teaching and learning, but also the creation of systems and procedures for routine tasks as varied as attendance reporting, vehicle ingress and egress, and coverage when staff members are absent. As this author was once told by a veteran superintendent of a well-regarded urban school district, "Your leadership isn't worth much of anything if you can't make the trains run on time" (J. Buchanan, personal communication, March 26, 2004). This leadership applies to money as well. Expectation "d" states that effective leaders "Are responsible, ethical, and accountable stewards of the school's monetary and nonmonetary resources, engaging in effective budgeting and accounting practices" (PSEL, 2015, p. 17). In the area of communication and vertical articulation, expectation "i" states that an effective leader

Standard 9: Operations and Management

should "Develop and manage relationships with feeder and connecting schools for enrollment management and curricular and instructional articulation" (PSEL, 2015, p. 17).

There is a substantial body of evidence demonstrating a relationship between school leadership and student achievement. An example of such evidence that is familiar to many practicing administrators is the meta-analysis completed by Waters et al. (2003) that found that the average correlation between leadership and student achievement is .25. A more recent meta-analysis found moderate to large positive effects of leadership on student achievement, teacher well-being, instructional practices, and school organizational health (Liebowitz & Porter, 2019). An important task is to allow teachers the dedicated time needed to accomplish the task of teaching—as expectation "e" states, an effective leader should "Protect teachers' and other staff members' work and learning from disruption" (PSEL, 2015, p. 17). As a principal, you have the difficult task of providing top cover for your staff. One of the many hats worn by principals is dealing with technology resources. Expectation "f" states that an effective leader must "Employ technology to improve the quality and efficiency of operations and management" and expectation "g" says that an effective leader must also "Develop and maintain data and communication systems to deliver actionable information for classroom and school improvement" (PSEL, 2015, p. 17). These expectations often require you to seek the expertise and guidance of resources within and outside your team.

Recent Research on Organizational Leadership

A 2011 study by Grissom and Loeb drew attention to the importance of organizational leadership. Grissom and Loeb note that the study grew from a realization "that much of the principal's day-to-day activity in fact *is not* [italics in original] consumed with the core business of teaching and learning" (2011, p. 1094). While instructional leadership is important, the authors reasoned, much of what principals do daily involves directing and overseeing school operations. The study sought to assess the relationship between five task categories and various indicators of success. From a sample of 314 elementary, middle, and high school principals, the researchers found that, out of five skill categories in a 42-item task inventory, only

147

organization management skills predicted student achievement growth and other measures of success. This finding suggests that the tasks involved in managing an organization are important to a school's success. These researchers concluded that the most effective approach to instructional leadership would combine "an understanding of the instructional needs of the school with an ability to target resources where they are needed, hire the best available teachers, and keep the school running smoothly" (2011: p. 1119).

The findings from the above study by Grissom and Loeb are quite similar to those from a 2010 study by Horng and colleagues (Horng et al., 2010; Horng & Loeb, 2010). That study found that the time that principals spend on organizational management is related to positive outcomes including student achievement, staff perceptions of the school learning environment, teacher satisfaction, and parent assessment of the school. Clearly, this line of inquiry demonstrates that effective leadership requires not only the principal's attention to instructional practices, but also the broad array of responsibilities involved in operating a school.

The study by Liebowitz & Porter (2019) mentioned above used the construct of five task categories similar to that employed in the above Grissom and Loeb study. In examining 51 studies completed after 2000 that explored principal behaviors and student, teacher, and school outcomes, they conclude that, while research indicates that principal leadership produces moderate to large positive effects on student achievement, teacher well-being, instructional practices, and school organizational health, there are leadership behaviors other than those characterized as instructional leadership that make as much of a difference. In other words, "principal behaviors other than instructional management may be equally important mechanisms to improve student outcomes" (Liebowitz & Porter, 2019, p. 789). These authors point out that this should not lead to a conclusion that instructional leadership is unimportant. Indeed, instructional leadership behaviors such as evaluating teachers, planning professional development, engaging in instructional planning, or analyzing data are important and valuable in improving student outcomes. Their findings suggest that "a more equal balance of time across the task categories may be of value" (2019, p. 814). In other words, overemphasizing instructional leadership and diverting energies away from other noninstructional tasks may be counterproductive. It is important to understand how to balance the two. This is consistent with the conclusions of Grissom and Loeb that "Principals

Standard 9: Operations and Management

devoting significant energy to becoming instructional leaders—in the narrow sense—are unlikely to see school improvement unless they increase their capacity for Organization Management as well" (2011, p. 1119). Additional tasks requiring attention include the legal aspects of teaching. Expectation "h" states that an effective leader must "Know, comply with, and help the school community understand local, state, and federal laws, rights, policies, and regulations so as to promote student success" (PSEL, 2015, p. 17). Conflict management is another area this standard addresses by stating in expectation "k" that an effective leader should "Develop and administer systems for fair and equitable management of conflict among students, faculty and staff, leaders, families, and community" (PSEL, 2015, p. 17).

The Challenges of Managing One's Time

Both novice and veteran principals can struggle to effectively manage the limited amount of time available in the day. They can face countless competing demands and are sometimes called upon to make informed decisions on matters large and small, and much of their work happens in full view of students, staff, and parents where it comes under near-constant scrutiny. Research on principals' allocation of time to various tasks by Grissom et al. (2013) found that, overall, principals spend an average of 12.7% of their time on instruction-related activities. Somewhat surprisingly, this study found a negative association between time on classroom walkthroughs and school outcomes, which could lead to a conclusion that untrained or ineffective walkthroughs may not be the most effective use of one's time. A more granular examination of this finding reveals, however, that walkthroughs that are effectively geared toward supporting coaching and professional development may be more beneficial. In the Follow-Through section of Chapter 5, time management concepts are presented, including *BreakThrough Coaching*.

Balancing Competing Demands

It is important to avoid sweeping conclusions about "a false dichotomy between management and instructional leadership" (Grissom & Loeb,

149

2011, p. 1119). Instead, school leaders should recognize the value in both, and strive to create a supportive culture that values contributions from every member of the organization. By focusing on people, through strong recruitment and retention practices, and through capitalizing on the unique strengths in everyone, a leader can exert significant influence on both the instructional and organizational domains. Knowing one's own limitations is important, as a leader who is overly and unjustifiably confident in his or her ability to singlehandedly operate a school will likely fail to develop talent within the school and ultimately hinder the school's progress. Appreciating the limits of what we can individually do, while seeking to tap the strengths, skills, and knowledge of others, will help to bring a greater sense of balance to the challenge of providing both organizational management and instructional leadership.

Voices from the Field

As a valuable contribution to this *Principal's Desk Reference*, we have collected vignettes shared by award-winning, proven leaders who are effective principals to help you better understand the "how" of implementing each standard. So often we get the theory, but in this book we want to focus on the "how" of putting it into practice. They have learned many lessons over the years and are willing share their thoughts and stories with you.

Vignette by Dr. James Driscoll

Stephen Covey (2014) states, "We only get one chance to prepare our students for a future that none of us can possibly predict. What are we going to do with that one chance?"

As an educational leader (Principal), the most important decision you make is the hiring of teachers. Research clearly shows the impact that teachers have on student achievement. Teachers set the foundation and bring to life the dreams of their students. However, leaders create the environment and provide direction that allows teachers to flourish and create authentic relevant learning experiences that captivate our students and change the trajectory of their lives. To do this important work, leaders need to have a foundation and a complete understanding of the standards

Standard 9: Operations and Management

to strategically manage staff resources that optimize staff members' professional capacity to address diverse student learning needs.

Leaders must be present and in the arena, but also have the humility to understand that their teachers in the classrooms are often the most qualified person to inform them of what students need, but more importantly what they need to be successful. It is the leader's responsibility to ensure that staff members have the resources and training to provide an optimal learning environment for students that cultivates positive relationships focused on students' needs.

As a leader, I met with each of my teachers individually to learn from them about their hopes and dreams. I listened for ideas that my staff members had to improve the school and learning experience for our students. I provided a space for them to generate ideas and cultivated an environment that was centered around continuous improvement. I believe the work we did truly changed the lives of our students, as the culmination of this was more than 80% of our third-grade students passing the state reading examination.

Vignette by Mr. Jeff Lavender

The Keeper of the Mission and Vision. One of the challenges principals face is creating and maintaining a balance between the management and leadership aspects required for their position. The job of a principal as crisis manager falls under the domain of management. The day starts by monitoring staff absences and determining what changes to coverage are necessary to ensure the campus is safe. Frequently, as staff start arriving for the day, several stop by to say "Hi" or share a classroom incident they need to process or to receive guidance. Throw in a few unscheduled parent visits and phone calls to resolve issues, and I have just described a typical morning for a principal. The rest of the day is spent putting out fires usually started by poor classroom management and a lack of emotional coping skills by students and staff.

A substantial percentage of educators that work for the principal spend the bulk of their time in a reactive state of mind as they deal with the challenges of managing students, delivering instruction, and being the emotional support system for students they serve each day. On any given day, a school's staff frustration level can be overwhelming. It falls squarely

151

upon the shoulders of the principal to keep the organization healthy, grounded, and moving in a positive direction. This is a responsibility I refer to as "The Keeper of the Mission and Vision."

When you are in a reactive state of mind it is challenging to put aside current circumstances and transition into a proactive mindset. As a leader, I have found a solid, well-understood, and published set of core values, mission statement, and clear vision can provide the elements needed to anchor your organization. Developing these should be a collaborative process involving all stakeholders. These elements form a consistent foundational resource to guide decision making and actions taken in the best interest of students and the learning community.

The sustainability of the core values, vision, and mission is also the responsibility of the principal. Once a consistent team has been established, it can become easy to fall into auto-pilot mode. Each year, it is imperative to spend time revisiting and reinforcing these cultural tenets with existing staff as well as with any potential new staff. As new staff are brought on board, witnessing the enthusiasm expressed toward our core values, vision, and mission can become the cornerstone for camaraderie and positive culture.

Finally, the core values, vision, and mission should be evolving as necessary to make adjustments that address current conditions. Recently we have had a significant change in personnel, and we also lost a school year of normal operations because of the pandemic during the 2020–2021 school year. We will be doing a reforming exercise to get all staff on the same page and also allow for changes to be made if they are needed. I am calling the process our Recommitment Convention.

References

Covey, S. R. (2014). *The leader in me: How schools and parents around the world are inspiring greatness, one child at a time.* Simon and Schuster.

Grissom, J. A., & Loeb, S. (2011). Triangulating principal effectiveness: How perspectives of parents, teachers, and assistant principals identify the central importance of managerial skills. *American Educational Research Journal, 48*(5), 1091–1123. https://doi.org/10.3102/0002831211402663

Grissom, J. A., Loeb, S., & Master, B. (2013). Effective instructional time use for school leaders: Longitudinal evidence from observations of principals. *Educational Researcher, 42*(8), 433–444. https://doi.org/10.3102/0013189X13510020

Horng, E., Klasik, D., & Loeb, S. (2010). Principal's time use and school effectiveness. *American Journal of Education, 116*(4), 491–523. https://doi.org/10.1086/653625

Horng, E., & Loeb, S. (2010). New thinking about instructional leadership. *Phi Delta Kappan, 92*(3), 66–69. https://doi.org/10.1177/003172171009200319

Kotter, J. P. (2013, January 9). Management is (still) not leadership. *Harvard Business Review.* https://hbr.org/2013/01/management-is-still-not-leadership

Liebowitz, D. D., & Porter, L. (2019). The effect of principal behaviors on student, teacher, and school outcomes: A systematic review and meta-analysis of the empirical literature. *Review of Educational Research, 89*(5), 785–827. https://doi.org/10.3102/0034654319866133

National Policy Board for Educational Administration. (2015). *Professional standards for educational leaders.* www.npbea.org/psel/

Waters, T., Marzano, R. J., & McNulty, B. (2003). *What 30 years of research tells us about the effect of leadership on student achievement* (p. 23). Mid-Continent Regional Educational Lab.

Standard 10
School Improvement
Frank D. Davidson

> Effective educational leaders act as agents of continuous improvement to promote *each* student's academic success and well-being.
>
> (PSEL, 2015, p. 18)

Mark Elgart describes continuous improvement as

> a journey that takes more time and greater effort from a wider range of stakeholders than most school initiatives. When implemented patiently, however, it enables schools to identify and meet all students' needs—which is the ultimate destination for all of us who have a stake in the future of our schools and our society.
>
> (2017, p. 59)

Meeting all students' needs is the unquestioned goal of all who care about schooling and the future of our world. We have yet to meet a school leader who does not profess commitment to this ideal. Despite the dedication of school leaders in individual schools across the US, and despite decades of accountability policies and sanctions, this goal often remains an unachieved ideal. The fact that it has remained unachieved should not deter us from passionately pursuing its fulfillment.

There are sound reasons for looking to leadership as a pathway to achieving the above ideal. Evidence has demonstrated a strong positive relationship between leadership and student achievement (Leithwood et al., 2010; Liebowitz & Porter, 2019; Waters et al., 2003). In fact, some findings suggest that leadership may be the second most important school-based factor affecting student achievement after teacher quality (Leithwood

Standard 10: School Improvement

et al., 2010). Standard 10 of the PSEL (2015, p. 18), with its focus on continuous improvement, capacity-building, evidence-based analysis and planning, and systemic change, articulates the elements of leadership that are believed to promote student academic success and well-being. Expectation "a" for this standard states that an effective leader should "Seek to make school more effective for each student, teachers and staff, families, and the community" and expectation "j" states that an effective leader should "Develop and promote leadership among teachers and staff for inquiry, experimentation and innovation, and initiating and implementing improvement" (PSEL, 2015, p. 18).

Even with sufficient resources and access to an ample pool of highly qualified teachers, improving schools is challenging work. Most school leaders do not find themselves in such circumstances. Years after the financial crisis of 2007–2008, schools in two-thirds of the states in the US had still not seen their funding levels restored to pre-crisis levels (Baker et al., 2013). In the face of enrollment in teacher preparation programs that decreased by as much as 53% (Castro et al., 2018), many states chose to respond by creating lower standards for becoming a teacher. Despite facing such challenges, expectations from state and federal accountability policies remain high. Schools can dedicate every ounce of will and effort to the task of meeting such expectations and earning a higher grade in a state ranking system, only to be disappointed by the news that the school's grade has not changed, or worse yet, has dropped from the preceding year.

State and federal policies in the last decade have tended to focus on short-term gains in student achievement to demonstrate to elected officials, parents, and other stakeholders that meaningful improvement is underway. Sometimes this has incentivized prioritizing "bubble" students who are in striking distance of proficiency goals, without producing genuine systemic changes within the school (Munter & Haines, 2019). Typically, picking low-hanging fruit does have its benefits, for instance in identifying and remedying obvious misalignments between curricular content and student assessments. Quick wins in student achievement can build confidence, bolster morale, demonstrate the capacity for further improvement, and lead to changes in cultural norms. Hitt and Meyers states that turnaround "requires initial significant and rapid student achievement gains" (2017). Quick wins may be a critical factor in launching more comprehensive long-term systemic change (Meyers & Hitt, 2018). However, there is

Frank D. Davidson

compelling evidence that soon after quick wins (typically, gains in reading or math achievement) have been achieved, many schools tend to either cease improving or lose some of the ground they have gained (Duke, 2012; Meyers & Hitt, 2016). While quick wins may help to set the stage for further improvement, it is important for leaders to look beyond the achievement of quick wins toward the systemic changes needed for continuous and ongoing improvement. Scholars have agreed that schools need a minimum of three years to seek and shift resources, enact organizational changes, and begin to build the organizational capacity for improvement (Hewitt & Reitzug, 2017). The competencies of leaders that have been successful in leading schools to produce measurable improvement can provide important insights for practitioners.

Support for School Improvement

As noted in Chapter 6 of this book, Bryk and colleagues identified five supports that were effective in advancing school improvement (Bryk, 2010; Bryk et al., 2018; Bryk & Schneider, 2002; Sebring et al., 2006). These researchers found that these five essential supports (coherent planning, capacity-building, parent–community–school ties, a student-centered learning climate, and school leadership) individually and collectively had a substantial effect. They found that "schools strong in most of the essential supports were at least ten times more likely than schools weak in most of the supports to show substantial gains in both reading and mathematics" (Sebring et al., 2006, p. 2). These supports strike a needed balance between academic demands, the school's sense of community, and students' social and emotional needs. One study of leaders in high-performing school districts shed light on the importance not only of celebrating achievements when a goal is achieved, but also of not being satisfied that the present level of performance is the best that can be achieved (Papa et al., 2013, p. 59). At a very practical level, this is the core of how continuous improvement is experienced in schools and districts that are successful in sustaining gains that have been made. Expectation "b" of this standard says that an effective leader should "Use methods of continuous improvement to achieve the vision, fulfill the mission, and promote the core values of the school" and expectation "c" states an effective leader should "Prepare the school and the community for improvement, promoting readiness, an imperative

Standard 10: School Improvement

for improvement, instilling mutual commitment and accountability, and developing the knowledge, skills, and motivation to succeed in improvement" (PSEL, 2015, p, 18).

Essential Role of School Leaders

An essential role for the school's leadership is to maintain the focus on shared goals to which stakeholders have committed. Dr. Jon Sheldahl, one of the practitioners who contributed to this chapter, refers to this as "sticking to the knitting." Many schools lose this focus over time, when the challenges of achieving or sustaining hard-fought gains come to be seen as fixed and permanent barriers. Because of this, expectation "d" states that an effective leader should "Engage others in an ongoing process of evidence-based inquiry, learning, strategic goal setting, planning, implementation, and evaluation for continuous school and classroom improvement" (PSEL, 2015, p. 18). With changes in staff, evolving expectations emanating from local, state, and federal authorities, and the appearance of promising new programs and strategies, it can be tempting to abandon earlier commitments to create the organizational bandwidth to embrace such promising opportunities. However, our experience has taught us that organizational capacity is expanded in large part through organizational coherence, which requires a willingness to stay the course with respect to the collective commitments made by the school. Expectation "e" says an effective leader should "Employ situationally-appropriate strategies for improvement, including transformational and incremental, adaptive approaches and attention to different phases of implementation" (PSEL, 2015, p. 18).

Maintained Focus on School Goals

Maintaining focus also requires narrowing the focus to that which can realistically be achieved. In describing schools and districts that undertake ambitious but voluminous and flawed improvement plans, Elgart correctly asserts that "a 50-page improvement plan simply cannot be implemented—no school or system has the capacity to take on every issue at once" (2017, p. 56). Elsewhere, we have discussed that

Frank D. Davidson

> Effective leaders have a clear sense of purpose. They center their actions and the actions of others on the organization's mission and goals. They also pay attention to systemic barriers that, if properly addressed, can amount to mere speed bumps. Most importantly, they shield themselves and the staff from the distractions of a minor crisis or a passing fad.
>
> (Davidson, 2015, p. 409)

Expectation "f" deals with developing capacity and states that an effective leader should "Assess and develop the capacity of staff to assess the value and applicability of emerging educational trends and the findings of research for the school and its improvement" and expectation "g" says an effective leader should *"Develop technically appropriate systems of data collection, management, analysis, and use, connecting as needed to the district office and external partners for support in planning, implementation, monitoring, feedback, and evaluation"* (PSEL, 2015, p. 18).

Balanced Approach to Leadership

In addition to maintaining a focus on shared goals, there is value in achieving a balanced approach to leadership. Expectation "h" deals with a systems perspective in that an effective leader should "Adopt a systems perspective and promote coherence among improvement efforts and all aspects of school organization, programs, and services" (PSEL, 2015, p. 18). It also addresses prioritization and communication, where an effective leader, in expectation "i," should "Manage uncertainty, risk, competing initiatives, and politics of change with courage and perseverance, providing support and encouragement, and openly communicating the need for, process for, and outcomes of improvement efforts" (PSEL, 2015, p. 18). In a meta-analysis of 51 studies of principal behaviors and student, teacher, and school outcomes, Liebowitz & Porter (2019) found evidence of positive effects for those principals who pursued a balanced approach to leadership. Such an approach is described more fully in Chapter 7 and is also alluded to by both practitioners who contributed to this chapter. As was noted by a study of experienced leaders, "Finding the proper balance between competing demands, while still attending to the trust-building work of being visible and available, is a constant struggle" (Davidson & Hughes, 2019, p. 59).

Voices from the Field

As a valuable contribution to this *Principal's Desk Reference*, we have collected vignettes shared by award-winning, proven leaders who are effective principals to help you better understand the "how" of implementing each standard. So often we only get the theory, but in this book we want to focus on the "how" of putting it into practice. They have learned many lessons over the years and are willing share their thoughts and stories with you.

Vignette by Ms. Darlene A. McCauley

Continuous improvement is both simple and complex. In my experience as a school leader, I can characterize school improvement as a systems process where change models are implemented to gain the highest outcomes possible. I am a firm believer in laying a strong foundation to build solid practices that will lead the school or school district toward goal attainment. This begins with building positive relationships. School improvement relies heavily on transformation of the organizational culture. Positive changes can only flourish in a strong culture that supports positive change. I have had the opportunity to lead in a few situations where the schools were labeled as underperforming. In the first situation, I had been a teacher for many years in the district prior to taking the lead position as principal of the middle school and I currently have a dual role as superintendent and secondary principal.

Through both experiences I learned it was crucial to build collaboration and to embed those collaborative practices into the standard operational plan. The saying "You can never be an expert in your own backyard" has some truth. Implementing change in my home district began with a few painful years of convincing colleagues that I understood educational improvement. As changes took longer than I had hoped, I hired consultants to convey some very important conversations and introduce some of the proposed changes. Over three years, the positive changes took root and systems set in place continue to this day.

In my current assignment, the challenge is not just in transformational change in a single school but in an entire district. I began where the fires were occurring most frequently. I concentrated most of my time on that school, eventually removing barriers to establish working, professional relationships. There was an almost complete turnover in teaching staff and administrators after that initial year. The school took a little while to settle in and is now focusing on building their systems with a new site administrator. I completed initial foundational work with my own school, but the reflective work began the second year. We enjoyed setting up collaborative practices and seeing results not only in our benchmark scores but in the general atmosphere and culture. We were headed into last year's state testing optimistic that we could move ourselves from underperforming status; then there was news of pandemics and distance learning. This has left us a little deflated and we try to reconnect with our plan as we edit and revise many times this year. We haven't lost hope, and we embrace a growth mindset.

Collaborative practice: The idea of collaboration seems easy when thought of as teams of educators working toward a common goal: the education and success of students. However, the complexities that lie within building collaborative practices include group dynamics, interpersonal relationships, communication structures, motivation, shared vision, negotiation/consensus, role assignment, and other factors involving human behavior and social psychology. When I entered school administration with a master's degree in educational leadership, I also had a master's degree in counseling, emphasizing human relations. I had years of previous experience in social services prior to my teaching experience. I didn't realize how much I would rely on my training in the field of counseling. I felt very fortunate to have had the extra strategies gained by working with people and in difficult situations in my toolbox.

School improvement process: As a school administrator and change agent, I lead schools and my district through a systemic change process for improvement. This includes building and strengthening collaborative practices, improving student performance scores, and improving effective instructional practices. I have relied heavily on change models such as Kotter's 8-Step change model (2012), beginning with:

1. Creating a sense of urgency
2. Relying on the development of building positive relationships with key leaders, both formal and informal, to positively influence the change

Standard 10: School Improvement

3. Creating a vision for change requires finding out what is valued

4. Continuous communication of the vision. A leader must "walk the walk and talk the talk" of what is to be expected of all employees. Be a leader by example. Demonstrate consistency and you will have fewer people resist the positive changes needed for the improvement

5. Celebrate and recognize people for being on board and do not be fearful of removing barriers that are contrary to the vision for change. I strive to have conversations with individuals that are respectful, even when addressing behaviors that are in opposition to the plan for change. When I first began, it took some courage and practice with some talking points and an excellent and supportive mentor. Do not avoid these difficult conversations because they are sometimes needed

6. Set short-term goals and celebrate the small wins but know that there is work ahead. I always referred to these as "cautious celebrations"

7. As a team, evaluate things that go well and what did not. Once the positive changes are set, they become the foundation to build upon and reflect upon. As you develop these practices and reflective discussions it becomes easier to be intentional to guide the positive movement toward your desired outcomes

8. These are the practices that will build continuous improvement and become your new framework. Kotter refers to this final step as "anchoring the changes." These effective changes will become part of your day-to-day operations and appear each year in your list of non-negotiables. This is a continuous cycle that school administrators must understand and be willing to devote their time, energy, and attention to

Through my experiences with school improvement, I have had some frustrating times, and some extremely joyous times. I would describe school improvement as an eloquent dance between having a creative vision and completing a reality check. Focus on incremental change, celebrating small wins, devotion to the action steps, and nurturing positive relationships among all stakeholders. I wish all my educational colleagues much success in their respective journeys.

Frank D. Davidson

 Vignette by Dr. Jon Sheldahl

When I was asked to think about Standard 10 and continuous improvement in schools, I thought of two old but important leadership axioms. I honestly can't remember where I picked these up. I know I didn't come up with them myself. The first axiom that came to mind was "it is the function of leadership to define reality and give hope." The other axiom I thought was that successful and continuously improving systems know how to "stick to the knitting."

Leaders who excel in Standard 10 define reality by keeping all stakeholders systematically engaged in data analysis over time. They keep truth and transparency at the forefront of their school improvement efforts. They build cultures where data is routinely analyzed and owned by the adults in the system. They don't tolerate excuses, but neither do they place blame. They make sure that all stakeholders know how all kids are always performing. They put faces to the data and consistently emphasize the moral imperative that all kids will learn.

Those who lead effective continuous school improvement efforts do more than just confront current reality through ongoing data analysis. They also give kids and teachers hope. They understand the importance of teachers having self-efficacy and a growth mindset. They make sure that teachers have the necessary tools to plan, execute, and evaluate instructional strategies with confidence. Effective leaders make sure teachers learn how to effectively use some type of cyclical continuous improvement system. They give teachers not only the skills, but the time and autonomy they need to continuously improve instruction and student learning. They professionalize their learning communities by balancing autonomy with responsibility. They create cultures where risk is rewarded and where teachers and kids alike are not afraid to fail because they know they will learn something in the process. They make sure all successes are celebrated and are always on the lookout for incremental improvements to point out as evidence that teacher efforts are paying dividends. All these things create a culture of hope.

Sticking to the knitting is a metaphor I like to use to emphasize the importance of keeping systems simple and aligned. Leaders who lead consistent school improvement efforts over time stick with systems that have been shown to work. They understand the antecedents that lead to consistent improvement and have the courage to say no to new ideas that are not consistent with current priorities. They understand the importance of avoiding distractions and being able to focus on doing fewer things, but doing those things very well. This not only leads to higher levels of teacher self-efficacy; it protects teachers from the burnout associated with trying to integrate too many competing initiatives. This type of leadership takes courage because it involves having to say no to a lot of good ideas. Political pressure to move on the next new instructional panacea can come from any direction at any time, but good leaders understand that trying to do everything often leads to doing nothing well. So, they stick to their knitting.

References

Baker, B. D., Sciarra, D. G., & Farrie, D. (2013). *Is school funding fair? A national report card* (p. 49). Education Law Center of the Rutgers Graduate School of Education. https://files.eric.ed.gov/fulltext/ED570455.pdf

Bryk, A. S. (2010). Organizing schools for improvement. *Phi Delta Kappan, 91*(7), 23–30.

Bryk, A. S., & Schneider, B. L. (2002). *Trust in schools: A core resource for improvement.* Russell Sage Foundation.

Bryk, A. S., Sebring, P. B., Kerbow, D., Rollow, S., & Easton, J. Q. (2018). *Charting Chicago school reform: Democratic localism as a lever for change.* Routledge.

Castro, A., Quinn, D. J., Fuller, E., & Barnes, M. (2018). *Addressing the importance and scale of the U.S. teacher shortage* [Policy Brief]. University Council for Educational Administration. https://files.eric.ed.gov/fulltext/ED579971.pdf

Davidson, F. D. (2015). Secrets of creating positive work cultures: The work lives of teachers. In F. W. English (Ed.), *The SAGE guide to educational leadership and management* (pp. 401–417). Sage Publications, Inc. http://dx.doi.org/10.4135/9781483346649.n39

Davidson, F. D., & Hughes, T. R. (2019). Exemplary superintendents' experiences with trust. *Education Leadership Review, 20*(1), 51–68.

Duke, D. L. (2012). Tinkering and turnarounds: Understanding the contemporary campaign to improve low-performing schools. *Journal of Education for Students Placed at Risk (JESPAR), 17*(1–2), 9–24. https://doi.org/10.1080/10824669.2012.636696

Elgart, M. A. (2017). Can schools meet the promise of continuous improvement? *Phi Delta Kappan, 99*(4), 54–59. https://doi.org/10.1177/0031721717745546

Hewitt, K. K., & Reitzug, U. (2017). Turnaround as Faustian bargain. In C. V. Meyers (Ed.), *Enduring myths that inhibit school turnaround* (pp. 277–296). Information Age Publishing.

Hitt, D. H., & Meyers, C. V. (2017). School turnarounds and the test of time. In C. V. Meyers (Ed.), *Enduring myths that inhibit school turnaround* (pp. 319–338). Information Age Publishing.

Kotter, J. P. (2012). *Leading change*. Harvard Business Press.

Leithwood, K., Patten, S., & Jantzi, D. (2010). Testing a conception of how school leadership influences student learning. *Educational Administration Quarterly, 46*(5), 671–706. https://doi.org/10.1177/0013161X10377347

Liebowitz, D. D., & Porter, L. (2019). The effect of principal behaviors on student, teacher, and school outcomes: A systematic review and meta-analysis of the empirical literature. *Review of Educational Research, 89*(5), 785–827. https://doi.org/10.3102/0034654319866133

Meyers, C. V., & Hitt, D. H. (2016). School turnaround principals: What does initial research literature suggest they are doing to be successful? *Journal of Education for Students Placed at Risk*, 1–19. https://doi.org/10.1080/10824669.2016.1242070

Meyers, C. V., & Hitt, D. H. (2018). Planning for school turnaround in the United States: An analysis of the quality of principal-developed quick wins. *School Effectiveness and School Improvement, 29*(3), 362–382. https://doi.org/10.1080/09243453.2018.1428202

Munter, C., & Haines, C. (2019). "Students get what flows downward": District leaders' rationalizations of the standardized testing of children. *The Educational Forum, 83*(2), 160–180. https://doi.org/10.1080/00131725.2019.1567891

National Policy Board for Educational Administration. (2015). *Professional standards for educational leaders*. www.npbea.org/psel/

Papa, R., English, F. W., Davidson, F., Culver, M., & Brown, R. (2013). *Contours of great leadership: The science, art, and wisdom of outstanding practice*. Rowman & Littlefield Education.

Sebring, P. B., Allensworth, E., Bryk, A. S., Easton, J. Q., & Luppescu, S. (2006). *The essential supports for school improvement.* Consortium on Chicago School Research at the University of Chicago, 1–72.

Waters, T., Marzano, R. J., & McNulty, B. (2003). *What 30 years of research tells us about the effect of leadership on student achievement* (p. 23). Mid-Continent Regional Educational Lab.

Mentoring as an Integral Part of a Comprehensive Evaluation System

Robyn Conrad Hansen

A comprehensive evaluation system positively impacts the quality of work and provides accurate, timely feedback that is performance-based, strengthening leadership capacity and improving schools and student performance. After creating a comprehensive evaluation system, the next step is establishing a robust mentoring program that allows beginning principals, assistant principals, and deans to gain the skills and knowledge necessary to become proficient. In this chapter, we introduce concepts behind an effective evaluation system and explain why they need to be aligned closely with the standards and expectations detailed within PSEL. We also provide actionable steps in developing your own principal mentor program that is based on research and provides a consistent path toward mastering the expectations.

 Principal Pipeline

One of the key values in developing both a principal performance evaluation system and a mentoring program is that districts are able to attract and retain high-quality principals to better meet the needs of students and the communities they serve. Developing a principal pipeline is affordable and sustainable. All graduate students in my principal and superintendent preparation courses are required to read an article published by the School Leaders Network called "Churn: The High Cost of Principal

Mentoring

Turnover" (2014). The high cost is representative of both the monetary cost of onboarding new principals, approximately $75,000 in 2014, but more importantly, the high cost of declining student academic achievement and the students' decreased lifelong earning potential, especially in the lowest socio-economic schools.

The general concept of the principal pipeline includes high-quality principal preparation programs at the university level aligned with the leadership standards, i.e., NELP (National Educational Leadership Preparation) Standards for Building Level and District Level (2018) and PSEL (2015). Superintendent preparation courses align with the NELP District Level Standards (2018) and PSEL (2015), with ample opportunities for field experience under the supervision of a campus site mentor and professors with greater depth of knowledge and experience in educational administration and application of the standards. Districts are charged with the responsibility for attracting and retaining well-prepared administrators with purposeful placement based on experience, talent, and aligned dispositions to the needs of the school community. Supervisors of principals, who have their own set of standards, *Model Principal Supervisor Professional Standards* (Council of Chief State School Officers [CCSSO], 2015), are tasked with helping principals grow as instructional leaders, understand district policies and procedures, and develop principal mentoring programs for at least the first year of service. The downloadable *Model Principal Supervisor Professional Standards* document is available at https://ccsso.org/resource-library/model-principal-supervisor-professional-standards. Understanding how complex and isolating the role of a principal and superintendent can be, the need for at least a one-year, preferably a two-year mentoring program, is paramount for the health, success, and longevity of new principals and superintendents.

According to the School Leaders Network article, "Churn: The High Cost of Principal Turnover" (2014), a high percentage of principals exit the job within the first three years, often leaving the school in gridlock due to decreased consistency in leadership, lack of progress toward the strategic plan, and school improvement goals. Likewise, superintendent turnover is also extremely high. Mentorship is the key to enabling the influx of less-experienced superintendents, principals, assistant principals, and deans to navigate the PK-12 educational landscape that is changing at an ever-increasing rate. School leadership is more complex than ever before and we must provide these incoming and less-experienced professionals with the tools to be successful, ensuring a high-quality education for all students while providing a positive, welcoming school environment that is inclusive with culturally responsive classrooms and activities. For this reason, we recommend all first- and second-year administrators be assigned or seek out a proven leader to help them negotiate the ever-changing responsibilities of leading our nation's schools.

Developing a Comprehensive Principal Evaluation System

If you ask principals and superintendents what components should be included in a comprehensive performance evaluation system to positively impact the quality of work they should accomplish, these leaders want a system that provides accurate, timely feedback based on performance that strengthens their leadership capacity to improve schools and student performance. In fact, the National Association of Elementary School Principals (NAESP) and the National Association of Secondary School Principals (NASSP) convened a Principal Evaluation Committee to examine such practices, supported by senior research scientist Matthew Clifford from the American Institutes for Research (AIR) and Steven Ross, professor of education at the Center for Research and Reform in Education at Johns Hopkins University.

This Principal Evaluation Committee comprises proven leaders from across the United States representing elementary, middle, and high schools, including leaders from diverse backgrounds and from small and large schools to rural and urban schools. This chapter captures the essence of multiple conversations that occurred both in person and electronically over the course of several months. As a lifetime member of NAESP and member of NASSP, it was an honor to represent the voices of elementary and middle-level principals from around the country and abroad on the Principal Evaluation Committee. As a result of several robust conversations based on review of research, policy, and looking at current best practices, the committee designed a "comprehensive, research-based framework that links performance evaluation to professional development" in the publication *Rethinking Principal Evaluation: A New Paradigm Informed by Research and Practice* (NAESP & NASSP, 2012). Through these conversations and research, the committee outlined a framework for principal evaluations

Mentoring

that can be transferred for use with superintendent evaluations, based on the following beliefs highlighted in the *Rethinking Principal Evaluation: A New Paradigm Informed by Research and Practice* (2012, p. 8) document. Principal evaluations should be:

- Created by and for principals
- Part of a comprehensive system of support and professional development
- Flexible enough to accommodate differences in principals' experiences
- Relevant to the improvement of principals' dynamic work
- Based on accurate, valid, and reliable information, gathered through multiple measures
- Fair in placing a priority on outcomes that principals can control
- Useful for informing principals' learning and progress

A well-designed performance evaluation system, aligned with the Professional Standards for Educational Leaders (PSEL, 2015), strengthens leadership capacity and aids in improving schools and districts for children and families across our country, as well as globally. The same process used for developing your teacher evaluation program can be adapted to generate your principal evaluation system. As stated in the *Rethinking Principal Evaluation: A New Paradigm Informed by Research and Practice* (NAESP & NASSP, 2012, p. 1) publication:

> Realizing the potential of principal evaluation as a strategy for strengthening leadership and improving schools requires systemic change to ensure that evaluation systems support valid performance results and that principals have a clear path to improve their performance and access to resources that strengthen their leadership.

Since this publication, the majority of states have adopted the PSEL and set forth to create principal performance evaluation systems that are supportive of continuous leadership development. Those who have yet to put the development of effective evaluation systems as a priority are seeing higher turnover and lower than expected student growth and achievement. Typically, their practices are not informed by the research

169

and are too heavily focused on high-stakes test scores without considering multiple measures of success and what it takes to educate the whole child, academically, psychologically, physically, socially, and emotionally. We recommend districts and states implement a systematic change model that includes information gathered from the same research that informed the development of *Principal Pipelines* published in cooperation with NAESP and the Wallace Foundation (Gates et al., 2019). In October of 2019, Wallace updated *Principal Pipelines*, which can be viewed at this link: www.wallacefoundation.org/knowledge-center/principal-pipeline-infographic/index.html

Effective Leadership Matters! Research has consistently demonstrated school leadership is second only to effective instruction in impacting student achievement (Leithwood & Louis, 2012). Especially for low-performing schools, it is critical that building leaders focus on effective instruction and higher student achievement for all students. In a recent Wallace Foundation report, *How Principals Affect Students and Schools: A Systematic Synthesis of Two Decades of Research* (Grissom et al., 2021, p. xiii), they cite new empirical evidence that says:

> We find that a 1 standard deviation increase in principal effectiveness increases the typical student's achievement by 0.13 standard deviations in math and 0.09 standard deviations in reading. To translate this result, we estimate that the impact of replacing a below-average elementary school principal (i.e., one at the 25th percentile of effectiveness) with an above-average principal (i.e., at the 75th percentile) would result in an additional 2.9 months of math learning and 2.7 months of reading learning each year for students in that school.
>
> (Kraft, 2020, cited in Grissom et al., 2021)

As the Wallace Report points out, a teacher's sphere of influence is contained within the classroom based on the number of students they instruct each year. A principal's influence is far reaching when considering the effect on all students enrolled in the school for multiple years. With this being said, principals need to be well-prepared, strong, confident instructional leaders capable of making bold, courageous decisions that positively impact the overall school community—leadership does matter in the success of our students.

A high-quality, comprehensive principal performance evaluation system supports administrative growth and development throughout the administrator's career. Research by Clifford et al. (2014) found that quality principal evaluation systems support teaching and learning, giving leaders a sense of accountability for strong instructional practices. Furthermore, the evaluation system should be linked to personalized, job-embedded ongoing professional development. A key component associated with an inclusive evaluation system is the use of administrative self-reflection. In Appendix B we provide a leadership self-assessment based on the National Policy Board for Educational Administration's PSEL (2015). By taking this self-assessment and being reflective of your current reality, you (and your mentor or supervisor) will be able to begin to design a professional development plan that will positively impact your leadership development focused on your professional growth and learning over the next three to five years.

Clifford et al. (2014) state that effective evaluation systems that are impactful need to be based on research and clearly outline performance indicators of what the administrator is expected to know and be able to do. Researcher David C. Berliner from Arizona State University published a book back in 1988 that is still very relevant today, titled *The Development of Expertise in Pedagogy*. Even though the research discusses the continuum of growth and development for teachers, this concept is easily transferrable to administrative development as well. For example, Dr. Berliner outlines five stages in his theory of development:

- **Stage 1**: Novice—uneasy, cautious
- **Stage 2**: Advanced Beginner—developing rational decision making
- **Stage 3**: Competent—rational
- **Stage 4**: Proficient—intuitive
- **Stage 5**: Expert—ease of performance, confident

It is understandable that educators move through these stages at different rates of development throughout their career. Job changes, new policies, and new standards sometimes cause a backward slide in development as the teacher needs to learn new curriculum, assessments, and instructional styles based on expectations and the needs of the learner. Likewise, an administrator may also see a slide or regression of skills based on several external forces such as new job assignment, changes in federal and/or state law and policies, shift in demographics, or personal concerns.

When designing a principal or superintendent performance evaluation system, you may want to consider using the following performance-level indicators aligned to the PSEL. Your state may already have performance-level indicators in place that you can use.

- **Novice**: Application of knowledge and skills is inconsistent, awkward, unsure
- **Developing**: Expansion of knowledge and skills is progressing
- **Proficient**: Confident and capable of the application of knowledge and skills
- **Exceeds**: Intuitive, consistently goes above and beyond expectations

An additional set of performance-level indicators you might consider using are:

- **Ineffective**: The principal/superintendent does not demonstrate acceptable levels of proficiency related to the standard
- **Developing**: The principal/superintendent demonstrates the knowledge and skills needed to be an effective leader; however, is inconsistent or ineffectively executes the standard
- **Effective**: The principal/superintendent consistently meets expectations for good performance related to the standard
- **Exemplary**: The principal/superintendent distinguishes themselves as an expert by continuously demonstrating sustained growth and development of the standard

Use an evaluation committee to decide on the performance levels and definition. This is an excellent group activity usually with a robust discussion. Choose the terms and definitions that resonate with the majority of administrators. An argument against rating individual performance comes often as a result of inconsistency of supervision and truly understanding and valuing the context of the school challenges.

The supervisor must be able to consider the contextual variables from school to school and not compare one principal to another. The supervisor meets with the principal early in the year, before school begins, to review data and expectations with each principal individually, set attainable goals with action steps, consider beneficial professional development, visit the

Mentoring

school, and meet with the principal several times during the year. Schedule a summative review with the principal, usually around the end of the third quarter of school, to review progress toward the goals. It is advisable for the principal to collect artifacts of success and evidence of progress to share with the supervisor, understanding they will be on campus on a limited basis. Any concerns of inadequate performance must be brought to the attention of the principal immediately, with discussion and support as to how to improve. Providing quality feedback takes time. The role of the supervisor of principals has become very important, thus the reason for the timely development of the *Model Principal Supervisor Professional Standards* (CCSSO, 2015).

Looking at a continuum of growth, what should be the expected time for a new principal to move from one level to the next, understanding personalized, job-embedded professional development is a key to an administrator's growth and development? Our district found, on average, a novice administrator would take from one to three years to move from novice to developing. The following levels of expected growth and development were agreed upon with groups we are familiar with:

- **Novice to Developing** = up to the 3rd year in the profession
- **Developing to Proficient** = 3rd–6th year in the profession
- **Proficient to Exceeds** = 7th–10th year in the profession

Included in the formula for continuous improvement and success of administrators, in addition to a quality performance evaluation system and professional development, is a well-designed principal and superintendent mentor program for at least the first year in the profession, timely feedback, self-reflection, professional development, and membership in professional organizations.

Developing a performance evaluation system is a process that needs input from many perspectives. Begin by bringing members of the principalship, superintendency, and teacher representation together to first discuss the purpose of the evaluation. A teacher's perspective provides an important insight that needs to be considered. It is critical that the evaluation system not be punitive; rather it should be designed to inform practice and support continuous improvement of the administrator in a collaborative environment. In a group setting, we recommend that you

173

discuss the six key domains of principal leadership found in *Rethinking Principal Evaluation: A New Paradigm Informed by Research and Practice* (NAESP & NASSP, 2012, p. 12):

1. **Professional Growth and Development**—measure how the administrator followed through on plans to improve
2. **Student Growth and Achievement**—measure the primary goal of schools, that of teaching and learning
3. **School Planning and Progress**—measure how well the administrator can manage the school planning process
4. **School Culture**—measure how well the administrator can develop and maintain a positive school/district culture
5. **Professional Qualities and Instructional Leadership**—measure the administrator's leadership knowledge, skills, and behavior competencies
6. **Stakeholder Support and Engagement**—measure the administrator's ability to build strong community relationships with stakeholders inside and outside the school/district

Discuss what these domains would look like in practice and how can they be measured. What evidence or artifacts could be collected to show proficiency and growth for each domain?

Next, unpack the ten Professional Standards for Educational Leaders (2015) by analyzing the content of the standard to extract the essential knowledge and skills an administrator is expected to know and be able to do to not only show proficiency, but exceed the expectation in the eyes of the administrator, supervisor, board, community, and/or tribal council.

Most people are visual learners, so it is helpful to create a framework showing the relationship with the six domains and the ten PSEL, which allows you to see how the standards align to the six domains. Table 12.1 provides a fictitious example of how the table might be used. The number in the cell refers to the standard and the letter in the cell refers to the applicable PSEL expectation for that specific standard. There is not one correct or best answer. You as a committee may decide to not include all the expectations for a standard within your performance evaluation system based on the contextual complexity of your district. The value you gain in populating the table is the rich, robust discussions that will happen because

Table 12.1 Example of Mapping PSEL Expectations into Leadership Domains

Domains Standard Competencies	1 Professional Growth and Learning	2 Student Growth and Achievement	3 School Planning and Progress	4 School Culture	5 Professional Qualities and Instructional Leadership	6 Stakeholder Support and Engagement
1 - Mission, Vision, and Core Values		1. a				1. c
2 - Ethics and Professional Norms			2. e		2. a	
3 - Equity and Social Responsiveness		3. c		3. f		
4 - Curriculum, Instruction, and Assessment					4. g	
5 - Community of Care and Support for Students						5. d
6 - Professional Capacity of School Personnel			6. a			
7 - Professional Community for Teachers and Staff				7. e		
8 - Meaningful Engagement of Families and Community						8. a
9 - Operations and Management			9. b			
10 - School Improvement	10. c					

Source: Created by Dr. Robyn Hansen

of your coming together and reviewing the alignment of the standards to the six domains.

In developing your district's and/or state's administrative performance evaluation system, agree upon the methodology that will best support valuable and timely feedback directly related to the competencies expected of administrators with focus on the anticipated trajectory of professional growth and development. Doug Reeves (2006), in his book *The Learning Leader: How to Focus School Improvement for Better Results*, emphasizes the need to use current, "real-time data" to provide timely and accurate feedback to principals based on their performance. Concentrate on developing a principal evaluation system that truly aligns to the PSEL (2015) and focuses on building leadership capacity throughout a respectable continuum of time supported by personalized, job-embedded professional development. Ensure the administrators and other stakeholders are at the table aiding in the design of the new principal evaluation system. Districts will have greater capability for hiring high-quality leaders, and the benefit of retaining exceptional leadership with a systems approach to building leadership capacity anchored by supporting the principal pipeline with purposeful evaluations, mentoring, and professional development. As part of the conclusion in *Rethinking Principal Evaluation: A New Paradigm Informed by Research and Practice* (NAESP & NASSP, 2012, p. 24), the authors project:

> Rethinking principal evaluation systems according to the framework presented in this document has the potential to create a new paradigm of practice for equipping leaders in the 21st century to improve our nation's schools and propel every student to reach his or her highest potential.

Developing a Robust Mentoring Program

We provide an example of a comprehensive principal mentoring program as a starting place that you are welcome to copy and modify as needed to help support the creation of a principal mentor program within your district. It was created as a final project for the NAESP National Principal Mentor Training Program (2015, www.naesp.org/programs/professional-learning/mentor-program) by myself and a colleague of mine, Karen Coleman, Ed.D.

Mentoring

The purpose of this principal mentoring program is to provide a framework for beginning principals to accelerate their development as educational leaders with a focus on impacting student growth and achievement. We believe a formal principal mentoring program is one way to attract and retain the best administrators while providing students and families with well-prepared school leadership. On a quantitative level, the success of a mentoring program should ideally be demonstrated by establishing measurable indicators in five areas of improvement:

1. Student outcomes
2. Culture of the school
3. Increased teacher effectiveness
4. Increased principal effectiveness as outlined by a principal performance evaluation system based on the PSEL
5. Leader's self-efficacy

Sample Principal Mentoring Program

Purpose for Principal Mentoring Program

The purpose of this Principal Mentoring Program is to provide a framework for beginning principals to accelerate their development as educational leaders with a focus on impacting student growth and achievement, school culture, increased teacher effectiveness, health and wellness of the administrator, and principal self-efficacy. This program is intended for beginning principals, assistant principals, and deans.

Goals of This Mentoring Program

1. Develop a comprehensive induction plan for all beginning principals.
2. Provide beginning principals with a non-threatening/non-evaluative, meaningful, and relevant mentoring support to help them navigate the multifaceted role.

3. Provide beginning principals with mentoring support and professional development opportunities to help them grow as instructional leaders focused on high standards and success for all students.

4. To help beginning principals understand performance expectations and develop a deep understanding of the Professional Standards for Educational Leaders (2015).

Characteristics of a Principal Mentor

The characteristics of a principal mentor program are based on curriculum from the NAESP National Principal Mentor Training Certification Program (2015):

1. The mentor should be a proven leader within the school district
2. The mentor should have the ability to assist the beginning principal reflect and develop solution options
3. The mentor should be empathetic, with the ability to relate to challenges of beginning principals, and serve as a coach
4. The mentor should have extensive knowledge of current leadership best practices, including educational law
5. The mentor should have knowledge of the school district's principal performance evaluation system
6. The mentor should respect the confidential nature of the mentoring relationship
7. The mentor should be a data-driven decision maker with the ability to interpret data
8. The mentor should be current on research and participate in ongoing, shared professional development
9. The mentor should be a neutral party and should not play a role in the evaluation of the mentee
10. The mentor should have good interpersonal relationship skills when working with adults
11. The mentor should have room in their schedule to commit the necessary time to be available for the mentee, to meet with the mentee, and model skills for the mentee

Mentoring

Assessment of the Principal Mentor Program

Ideally, the success of the mentoring program should be demonstrated by evaluating the measurable indicators for quantitative success in the following five areas:

1. Improved student learning
2. Culture of the school
3. Increased principal effectiveness
4. Increased teacher effectiveness
5. Improved principal self-efficacy

In support of this quantitative assessment, student learning can be demonstrated in data on student achievement, student progress, and the academic performance of student subgroups. The culture of the school can be measured with the use of surveys. Improved principal and teacher effectiveness can be demonstrated by those measures and by the overall professional growth as demonstrated by the administrative and teacher performance evaluation systems. Improved self-efficacy can be determined with the use of a self-efficacy scale.

Starting the program required an initial half-day "Welcome to the District" in-service where the new principals received an overview of policies and procedures needed to start the year. They were also introduced to their administrative peer coach who would mentor them for the year, and most likely many years beyond. As a whole group, we met monthly, focusing on topics that were timely and relevant for their continued success, in addition to many individual mentor sessions and phone or virtual calls with peer coaches.

The mentoring program continues throughout the school year meeting on at least a monthly basis, where as a group each of the ten standards in PSEL are unpacked and the new principals gain a deeper understanding of the associated expectations during the next seven months to align them with the principal evaluation system.

The following is a sample one-year calendar containing multiple events beginning before the start of the school year. You are free to adjust the schedule as needed based on the hire dates of the new administrators, understanding that late hires may happen each year.

179

Sample Year One Calendar for Beginning Principals (Elementary, Middle, and High School)

Five Weeks Before School Starts

Whole Group with All Beginning Principals

- Welcome to the district by the superintendency
- Introduce mentee to their mentor
- Review vision and mission of the school district—discuss the core values
- Review administrative handbook
- Principal evaluation system with expectations
- Complete the PSEL self-assessment (found in Appendix B in this book)
- Data notebook—presentation by district's data specialist:

  - Time for mentee and mentor to look over their school's data

  - Create SMART goals based on data and vision and mission

- Check to see if the schools are fully staffed, review hiring procedures
- District safety committee with evacuation/lockdown drills
- Discuss meeting your administrative team, coaches, support staff
- Letter of introduction to parent and community (add to school's website)

Five Weeks Before School Starts

Individual Meeting on Mentee's Campus with Mentor

- Have mentee give a tour of the school to their mentor
- Allow mentee to share reflections—mentor asks reflective questions
- Review school's vision and mission statements, community core values

Mentoring

- Review data notebook, PSEL self-assessment and SMART goals
- Review staff lists/class counts
- Review school's safety plan, opening of school, traffic routes
- Plan time to meet staff, i.e., a meeting, social, etc
- Look at master calendar and class schedules, make needed adjustments
- Schedule time to meet with parent group/stakeholders

Four Weeks Before School Starts

Individual Meeting on Mentee's Campus with Mentor

- Time for reflection and sharing
- Plan agenda for first faculty/staff meetings/leadership
- Data—share principal's SMART goals
- Schedule meeting with parent group (PTSO/PTA/site council)
- Schedule open house or back-to-school events
- Schedule time to meet with student council and other student groups

Four Weeks Before School Starts

Whole Group with All Beginning Principals

- Human resources—teacher performance evaluation system
  - Progressive documentation
- Curriculum and assessment
  - Title I, ELL, Gifted, Special Education, AP, IB, Honors, SEL plans for all
- Transportation
- Community education
- Special education and related services/psychology
- Business services—to manage resources efficiently and equitably
- Technology services

Robyn Conrad Hansen

- Food services
- Mentor will touch base to see how they are getting along

Three Weeks Before School Starts

Individual Meeting Between Mentor and Mentee

- Make sure all staff are hired, backup plan as needed
- Discuss school social with PTSO/PTA/student government/parent boosters
- Discuss open house or back-to-school events
- Review class rosters and master schedule

Two Weeks Before School Starts

Individual Meeting with Mentee

- Review staff meetings
- Review open house and first few days of school
- Discuss student behavior protocols
- Discuss first leadership/faculty/staff meeting
- Make sure site council meeting is scheduled with invitations to members
- Review administrative team calendar of meetings, events, sports, activities

One Week Before School Starts

Meet with All New Administrators (Elementary, Middle, and High School)

- Meet with all district-level curriculum directors/coordinators

182

Mentoring

Continue to Meet Monthly with Mentoring Teams to Discuss

Topics Specific to the New Administrator and Their Campus

- Review district meetings
- Review benchmark data
- Check teacher evaluation timeline
- How are professional learning communities and master schedule going?
- Facility and plant management
- Planning for and executing the budget
- Climate and culture of the school
- Parent and community involvement
- Student and staff well-being
- Student or staff concerns?
- Health and wellness of administration

Principals Make a Difference

We believe a high-quality principal mentoring program provides a bridge between preparation programs and practice. These programs help develop highly effective principals who have the skills necessary to successfully lead our schools. We also believe that great principals stay in the principalship longer, are more successful, and sustain an enjoyable, healthy career. We conducted a survey at the end of the first year of the mentor program and our results support what the research says—that principals desire a personal mentoring relationship and guidance from an experienced principal. Both new principals to a district and novice principals desire mentoring through their first year. As a mentor principal, with years of experience, skills, and expertise in the profession, we have a moral imperative to work with our newest administrators. We are seeing too many administrators with health issues and making decisions to leave the field after a couple years in the principalship because of isolation and lack of leadership support in their first years in the profession. If we are going to make continuous improvement and real change in our schools, we need consistency in leadership. We need to take the time to design a quality principal mentor program to meet the needs of novice or struggling principals in our districts.

Even today, 30 years after choosing to become an administrator, it is enjoyable to be part of preparing the next generation of school leaders by serving as a professor, as well as a principal and superintendent intern supervisor with Northern Arizona University. We believe that quality leadership truly matters. Achieving success as a school leader does not come in isolation. Find a mentor early in your career and offer to be a mentor to those who come after you. In other words, "Find a Mentor, Be a Mentor." You have chosen the greatest profession, one where you make a difference in the lives of children and families every day! Don't underestimate your value and contributions to society.

References

Berliner, D. C. (1988). *The development of expertise in pedagogy*. American Association of Colleges for Teacher Education. https://eric.ed.gov/?id= ED298122

Clifford, M., Hansen, U. J., & Wraight, S. (2014). *A practical guide to designing comprehensive principal evaluation systems* (revised ed.). National Comprehensive Center for Teacher Quality. https://gtlcenter. org/sites/default/files/PracticalGuidePrincipalEval.pdf

Council of Chief State School Officers. (2015, January 1). *Model principal supervisor professional standards*. https://ccsso.org/resource-library/ model-principal-supervisor-professional-standards

Gates, S. M., Baird, M. D., Master, B. K., & Chavez-Herrerias, E. R. (2019, April). *Principal Pipelines: A Feasible, Affordable, and Effective Way for Districts to Improve Schools*. Rand Corporation. www. wallacefoundation.org/knowledge-center/Documents/Principal-Pipelines-A-Feasible-Affordable-and-Effective-Way-for-Districts-to-Improve-Schools.pdf

Grissom, J. A., Egalite, A. J., & Lindsay, C. A. (2021). *How principals affect students and schools: A systematic synthesis of two decades of research*. The Wallace Foundation. www.wallacefoundation.org/ principalsynthesis

Kraft, M. A. (2020). Interpreting effect sizes of education interventions. *Educational Researcher, 49*(4), 241–253. https://scholar.harvard.edu/ mkraft/publications/interpreting-effect-sizes-education-interventions

Leithwood, K., & Louis, K. S. (Eds.). (2012). *Linking leadership to student learning*. Jossey-Bass. www.academia.edu/19639999/Linking_Leadership_to_Student_Learning

National Association of Elementary School Principals & National Association of Secondary School Principals. (2012). *Rethinking principal evaluation: A new paradigm informed by research and practice*. www.naesp.org/sites/default/files/PrincipalEvaluationReport.pdf

National Association of Elementary School Principals. (2015). *National mentor training and certification*[TM] *program*. www.naesp.org/programs/professional-learning/mentor-program/

National Policy Board for Educational Administration. (2018a). *National educational leadership preparation (NELP) program standards: Building level*. www.npbea.org/nelp/

National Policy Board for Educational Administration. (2018b). *National Educational Leadership Preparation (NELP) Program Standards: District Level*. www.npbea.org/nelp/

National Policy Board for Educational Administration. (2015). *Professional standards for educational leaders (PSEL)*. www.npbea.org/psel/

Reeves, D. B. (2006). *The learning leader: How to focus school improvement for better results*. Association for Supervision and Curriculum Development. www.ascd.org/publications/books/118003.aspx

School Leaders Network. (2014, November 26). *CHURN: The high cost of principal turnover*. Carnegie Corporation of New York. www.carnegie.org/news/articles/the-high-cost-of-principal-turnover/

13

Grow Your Own
A Program for Aspiring Leaders
Frank D. Davidson

Many school districts across the US have undertaken initiatives to develop succession plans and manage the development of aspiring leaders, though recent survey data indicates that the vast majority of school districts have not undertaken any form of succession planning. This chapter provides information about features of such programs that can be implemented in districts of all sizes.

Fusarelli and colleagues point to the importance of succession planning as follows:

> In the athletic world, succession planning is thought of as bench strength. How strong are the players sitting on the bench during the game? Whether the sport is football, basketball, baseball, soccer, or any other team sport, the bench must contain players prepared to play in case of injury, illness, poor performance, or other unforeseen issue. This same concept of bench strength can be applied to education. Whether the need is a result of retirements or growth, school districts need to have a strong bench of candidates to fill administrator positions.
>
> (Fusarelli et al., 2018, p. 291)

Generally speaking, the development of succession plans or "grow your own" programs is a less common practice in the US educational system than it is in business or, for that matter, in other nations' educational systems. Evidence from high-performing school districts in Ontario, Singapore, Hong Kong, and Shanghai reveals comprehensive, cohesive, and systemic approaches to leadership development, qualities which are

Grow Your Own

less common in the US (Sparks, 2017). Practices in the above systems include the following elements:

- Linking leadership development to the district's vision
- Identifying and preparing teachers for leadership roles
- Building in training that prepares leaders with the problem-solving and critical thinking skills needed in a constantly shifting educational and cultural landscape
- Continuing professional development throughout a principal's career

An American Association of School Administrators (AASA) study from 2016 found that approximately 10% of large school districts in the US have any form of succession planning (Domenech, 2016). Some large districts that have undertaken substantial efforts to develop future leaders are described in an analysis by Fusarelli and colleagues (Fusarelli et al., 2018). Rosenberg (2016) described the efforts of "grow your own" initiatives supported by the Wallace Foundation. Another such analysis is provided by Corcoran et al. (2012), who conducted research on New York City's Leadership Academy. Yet another analysis of a district–university partnership in Newark, New Jersey is provided by Gutmore and colleagues (Gutmore et al., 2001).

Whether referred to as "succession planning" or "leadership development," districts of all sizes would benefit from taking steps to prepare for future openings caused by anticipated events such as enrollment growth or the retirement of baby boomers, as well as the unanticipated illness or death of administrators. Given the demand for new leaders, this is an essential step for large districts and for districts of any size that are experiencing rapid growth. As practicing school leaders, the authors of this book both worked in districts during periods of rapid enrollment growth and witnessed firsthand the critical demand for leaders. Unless they have prepared for growth by engaging in succession planning that includes leadership development, during periods of rapid growth districts run the risk of assigning inexperienced and underprepared leaders to schools. In a time of significant accountability and competition, this could lead to lasting consequences from which it may be difficult for a school to recover.

Features of Effective Leadership Development Efforts

In an extensive review of literature on leadership and leadership development, Daniëls and colleagues (Daniëls et al., 2019) identify five characteristics of effective professional development for leaders that are relevant to "grow your own" programs.

- First, to the extent feasible, programming should be tailored to the individual needs and experiences of aspiring leaders
- Second, learning experiences must be based on a meaningful context and must be experiential in nature, focusing on the real-world problems and challenges that leaders face. Significant benefits can be gained from engaging aspiring leaders in addressing actual problems in the school districts where they work
- Third, programs should use a variety of ways of learning, to include lecture, collaborative group projects, and peer- and self-evaluation
- Fourth, time should be provided for networking and relationship-building with aspiring and practicing principals
- Fifth, professional development should be ongoing, and as indicated above, should be aligned to the knowledge, needs, and experiences of participants

Leadership development can take the shape of formal or informal mentoring, partnering with neighboring districts or a university to provide training, shadowing experiences, action research, project-based learning, or monthly district-sponsored sessions with aspiring leaders. One study of principals' perceptions of the effectiveness of a leadership development program pointed to the importance of providing exposure to real-life situations and building relationships with a cohort of future leaders (Tingle et al., 2019). Aside from the obvious benefit of developing leadership capacity within the organization, "grow your own" efforts afford districts the opportunity to essentially conduct a year-long interview with prospective leaders and assess the alignment of candidates' values, skills, and goals with the needs of the district. A district's leadership development approach can also be designed to develop leaders not only for administrative positions, but also for other leadership roles, such as instructional specialists, department chairs, grade-level leads, school leadership teams, or advisory councils. In research on one medium-sized district's leadership development initiative, Searby and Shaddix (2016) noted that participants in the program moved on to other critically important leadership roles including teacher mentors, student teacher supervisors, and professional development specialists. Stakeholder perspectives on existing leadership development efforts are described later in this chapter.

Prevalence of District Leadership Development Programs

Survey data collected in conjunction with a recent multi-state study (Davidson et al., 2021) revealed that the most common practice that was undertaken by districts to prepare potential leaders was verbal encouragement, which was reported by 82% of districts. Just over half of the respondents to this survey reported that the district engaged in a practice of identifying potential candidates for future openings. One-fourth indicated that plans for developing leaders were in place, and one-fourth reported assigning mentors to individuals with leadership potential. One-third responded that the district offered leadership development training to aspiring leaders. Understandably, a district's size is an important factor in determining whether or not a leadership development program is offered. While just 18% of districts with enrollment under 1,000 reported offering a leadership development program, this percentage rose to 60% for districts enrolling 10,000–20,000 students. For districts enrolling over 20,000 students, 91% reported offering leadership development training to aspiring leaders.

Risks to Consider

There are costs associated with failing to engage in succession planning or leadership development. With respect to succession planning in business, Charan wrote that "the result of poor succession planning is often poor performance, which translates into higher turnover and corporate instability" (2005, p. 74). A change in leadership can result in a high organizational cost, in the form of lost momentum and organizational confusion, as a school attempts to adjust to both the abandonment of practices and initiatives embraced by a predecessor, as well as the introduction of changes promoted by a successor. In order to successfully lead a school following a change in leadership, leaders must be effectively vetted and prepared for the problem solving and emotional resiliency required to help a school navigate a change in leadership. A mismatch between the needs of a school and the skills and dispositions of a new principal can create frustration, conflict, and chaos. No school can effectively meet the needs of students if such conditions exist.

There are also certain risks associated with offering leadership development to prospective leaders. A district that offers leadership development training to aspirants is, in effect, communicating that district leaders: 1) anticipate future openings, 2) see potential leaders emerging within the organization, and 3) are committed to serious consideration of internal candidates. If completers of "grow your own" programs see little likelihood of positions becoming available, or if they see a trend of external candidates being selected, then they may choose to move on to other opportunities. Conger and Fulmer observe that organizations "must make sure that high potential employees have enough options that they don't grow restless—royal heirs can be expected to show impatience when waiting for the throne, but corporate heirs have many other options" (2003, p. 82). Consequently, a district's leadership development efforts need to be matched to the district's needs. A leadership development program that is designed, as described above, to prepare individuals to serve not only in administrative capacities but in a variety of other roles may help to avoid creating the expectation that the destination for all program completers is a position in administration.

Addressing Existing Inequities

By widely advertising a leadership development program, seeking recommendations for promising candidates from teachers and administrators, and providing direct encouragement to individuals, districts can begin to ensure more equitable representation of the community. Corcoran and colleagues provide evidence of such an outcome (Corcoran et al., 2012). Historically, the percentages of female principals and principals of color do not reflect their percentages in the student population or the community at large, and a leadership development program with provisions for outreach and recruitment could be a constructive means for bringing about much-needed change. Models are emerging of "grow your own" programs that are designed to address both teaching shortages and lack of diversity in the teaching workforce (Gist, 2019; Rogers-Ard et al., 2019). "Grow your own" programs for leaders would benefit from similar approaches that focus on both the need for leaders and the need for leaders that represent the diversity of the community.

Unique Challenges of Small and Rural Schools

As indicated from the research cited above, "grow your own" programs are relatively common in larger districts. They are much less common in small and rural settings. The rural setting provides unique challenges. In comparison with their counterparts in larger districts, administrators in smaller districts tend to wear many hats, pitching in to fulfill functions in human resources, state and federal projects, professional development, and curriculum planning; as a result, there may be less time available to devote to leadership development or mentoring. Moreover, given the smaller number of leadership positions in small and rural districts, the demand for new leaders may be insufficient to warrant ongoing, annual leadership development efforts.

For many small and rural districts, the erosion of rural tax bases often implies less competitive salaries for small and rural districts, thereby compounding the difficulties of competing with more metropolitan districts for the most desirable candidates for both teaching and leadership positions (Ayers, 2011). In some cases, the difficulty of attracting candidates from elsewhere increases the likelihood that rural districts will look to internal candidates for upcoming leadership positions. It stands to reason that creating opportunities to grow such leaders through mentoring, coaching, or a more formal approach would benefit both the aspiring leader and the district.

An option pursued by many small and rural districts is to identify promising leaders, appoint them to a leadership position, and provide

Frank D. Davidson

mentoring intended to help them to grow into the job. However, there are risks to employing a noncompetitive process. In a study carried out by Versland, such a noncompetitive selection process "caused jealousy and compromised the leaders' ability to build relationships" (2013, p. 6). The transition from the classroom to a leadership role can strain existing relationships in the best of conditions, and if there is a perception that a candidate has been plucked from the ranks without an open and competitive process, this can create resentment that would certainly not be helpful to a new administrator. The use of a competitive process for selecting candidates for leadership development opportunities would help to alleviate such resentments and would likely increase the likelihood of a successful transition to a new leader. Versland advises expanding the pool of potential leaders by partnering with other small and rural schools in close proximity and using an open application process to foster an impartial approach. Fusarelli and colleagues (Fusarelli et al., 2018) describe the experiences of a school–university partnership to provide leadership development support to small and rural districts. Another such partnership involving rural school districts and a university is described by Lindsay (2008).

The Need for Ongoing Mentoring and Coaching

Leadership development cannot stop with the hiring of a new administrator. The authors of this book had the opportunity to be mentored by others, and in turn, became mentors to many leaders. We observed that leaders at all stages of their careers can benefit from the support and guidance of a mentor. Additional details on developing a robust mentoring program can be found in Chapter 12.

Districts that continue to support new administrators through the early years in a new role, through efforts such as regular meetings or mentoring, are likely to see a greater degree of success in such leaders. Although there appears to be increasing attention given to mentoring or coaching, ten-year-old data from the Schools and Staffing Survey revealed that only around half of the nation's principals had access to such support (Manna, 2015). Leadership development efforts need to be ongoing once new principals are in their new roles. Such efforts typically continue through the initial 2–3 years in the principalship (Korach & Cosner, 2016). Although there is

Grow Your Own

still a great deal to learn about what specific approaches to coaching and mentoring of early-career principals are most effective, there is reason to believe that such support is important in the development of leadership skills for leaders at all stages of their careers.

Implementing a School District Leadership Development Program

Based on the experiences of the authors, existing research on leadership development, and interviews with both administrators of and participants in leadership development programs, we offer these strategies and features to consider in creating such a program.

Application Process

Districts often open the application process during the spring, so that participants can be notified regarding their acceptance before the end of the school year. This time frame can also facilitate coordination with participants' university internships so that both can be completed simultaneously.

Program Coordination

It goes without saying that a program of this nature should be coordinated by leaders who are widely respected in the district. One district that has a long history of a successful leadership development program is the Paradise Valley Unified School District in Arizona. For three decades, this 30,000-student PK-12 district has offered the AIM Program ("Administrative Internship and Management") to develop aspiring leaders. Oversight of the program is the responsibility of two of the district's assistant superintendents. One of the assistant superintendents who administers the AIM Program is Dr. Steven Jeras, Assistant Superintendent of Leadership (Elementary). Prior to becoming a school principal, Dr. Jeras himself completed the AIM program. Moreover, the principal of the school where he was a teacher had completed the program. In fact, during a conversation with Dr. Jeras as

193

Frank D. Davidson

this manuscript was being prepared, he noted that "there is probably not a single administrator in PV who was hired internally who did not come through the AIM program."

For districts that have such a position, it makes sense for oversight of the program to be carried out by a principal coach. This is the approach taken by the Creighton Elementary School District in north-central Phoenix, as reported by the district superintendent, Dr. Donna Lewis. For districts without such a position, some have opted to select an accomplished principal to fill that role, which is an approach that was employed in the Casa Grande Elementary School District in south-central Arizona. Jeff Lavender, one of the practitioners who contributed to this book, served in such a role, sharing his experiences as a principal for 24 years.

Topics

Districts typically include a variety of topics of district-wide interest and invite district administrators or heads of departments such as transportation, finance, or food service as guest speakers. Over the course of a school year, participants take part in monthly meetings, many of which focus on shared leadership, which is central to the district's approach. Similar to the program in Paradise Valley, Creighton's program offers regular sessions that include guest speakers and that focus on topics such as systems thinking, finance, and instructional leadership. In Creighton, participants must carry out a project that has a district-wide impact. In Paradise Valley, participants must complete a written assignment and undergo an exit interview with the two assistant superintendents who facilitate the program.

The relationships among participants can prove to be an important source of ongoing support. Kimberly Koda, an administrator in Paradise Valley who took part in the program, noted that "The connection to the people whom I met through the program was very valuable. That familiarity was very important as I moved into an administrative position."

Recruitment

As explained above, it is important to use a competitive application process in selecting participants for a "grow your own" program. However, it is also important to identify and encourage promising leaders to apply. For many successful leaders, that initial nudge from a mentor or colleague was just the spark they needed. This can also be a strategy for addressing the underrepresentation of people of color in the leadership ranks. Creighton's superintendent, Dr. Donna Lewis, cites this as a high priority of the district's governing board and administration. Marta Maynard, a National Board for Professional Teaching Standards certified teacher and principal who participated in the AIM program in Paradise Valley, cited the encouragement of two administrators in recalling what had inspired her to take part.

Shadowing

In the Paradise Valley Unified School District, participants in the AIM program are provided five days of release time to shadow a leader, and they are encouraged to gain new experience by shadowing someone in a setting and/or grade level that is different from what they are accustomed to. Similarly, Creighton encourages aspiring leaders to learn from leaders who are similar to them and from those whose styles are quite different; in doing so, they learn a great deal about the range of effective approaches to being a leader.

Teachers-on-Assignment

An approach we used in the Casa Grande Elementary School District was to build on our "grow your own" program by creating "Teachers-on-Assignment" positions. This is an approach commonly used by many districts. These serve as entry-level leadership positions where individuals can gain experience in roles like that of a dean of students or assistant principal under the mentorship of a principal. In our experience, these positions proved to be a vital pathway to the principalship, as, for a period of several years, most principals in the district both participated in the year-long leadership development program and entered formal leadership as a teacher-on-assignment.

Initiating a Grow Your Own Program

Planning for a district's leadership development program should be carried out by a diverse yet manageably sized leadership team to include district administrators, principals, teachers, and support staff. The group's work should be guided by the district's mission and vision and informed by the collective experience and knowledge of the leadership team. Together, members of this team need to address questions such as:

- What is the program's purpose? Is the focus only on the principalship, or is the program intended to develop leadership skills for a variety of roles, including, for instance, administration of support programs (such as food services, transportation, human resources, etc.), instructional support, and department or grade-level leadership?
- What topics are important?
- Who will lead the program?
- What type of application process will be used? Must applicants be recommended by their principal or another administrator? If applicants are rejected, what level of due process is available? Can they reapply the following year?
- Will participants be expected to complete a project or culminating activity?
- Will the program include a shadowing component?
- What costs are involved?
- How will feedback on the program's effectiveness be collected? How will we measure success?

A commitment to transparency in leadership development will go a long way toward gaining trust and credibility. As has been discussed throughout this book, the quality of principal leadership has a significant effect on the quality of schooling that students receive. The level of support that a district provides to the development of leaders, and the authenticity of that support, speaks volumes about the promise and potential of leadership.

References

Ayers, J. (2011). *Make rural schools a priority* (p. 9). Center for American Progress. https://files.eric.ed.gov/fulltext/ED535987.pdf

Charan, R. (2005). Ending the CEO succession crisis. *Harvard Business Review, 83*(2), 72–84. https://hbr.org/2005/02/ending-the-ceo-succession-crisis

Conger, J. A., & Fulmer, R. M. (2003). Developing your leadership pipeline. *Harvard Business Review, 81*(12), 76–84.

Corcoran, S. P., Schwartz, A. E., & Weinstein, M. (2012). Training your own: The impact of New York City's aspiring principals program on student achievement. *Educational Evaluation and Policy Analysis, 34*(2), 232–253. https://doi.org/10.3102/0162373712437206

Daniëls, E., Hondeghem, A., & Dochy, F. (2019). A review on leadership and leadership development in educational settings. *Educational Research Review, 27,* 110–125. https://doi.org/10.1016/j.edurev.2019.02.003

Davidson, F. D., Schwanenberger, M., & Carlson, H. (2021). Superintendents' perceptions of the assistance provided by their predecessors during a change in leadership. *Journal of Scholarship and Practice, 17*(4), 24–41.

Domenech, D. A. (2016). Corporate impact on leadership succession. *The School Administrator, 73*(6), 3.

Fusarelli, B. C., Fusarelli, L. D., & Riddick, F. (2018). Planning for the future: Leadership development and succession planning in education. *Journal of Research on Leadership Education, 13*(3), 286–313. https://doi.org/10.1177/1942775118771671

Gist, C. D. (2019). For what purpose?: Making sense of the various projects driving grow your own program development. *Teacher Education Quarterly, 46*(1), 9–22.

Gutmore, D., Strobert, B., & Guttmore, R. F. (2001). Meeting the needs: A best practice grow your own school leader program. *Journal of Scholarship and Practice, 6*(1), 32–69.

Korach, S., & Cosner, S. (2016). Developing the leadership pipeline: Comprehensive leadership development. In M. D. Young & G. M. Crow (Eds.), *Handbook on the education of school leaders* (pp. 262–282). Routledge.

Lindsay, S. R. (2008). Grow your own leaders. *School Administrator, 65*(7), 20–23.

Manna, P. (2015). *Developing excellent school principals to advance teaching and learning: Considerations for state policy*. The Wallace Foundation. www.wallacefoundation.org/knowledge-center/Documents/Developing-Excellent-School-Principals.pdf

National Policy Board for Educational Administration. (2015). *Professional standards for educational leaders.* www.npbea.org/psel/

Rogers-Ard, R., Knaus, C., Bianco, M., Brandehoff, R., & Gist, C. D. (2019). The grow your own collective: A critical race movement to transform education. *Teacher Education Quarterly, 46*(1), 23–34.

Rosenberg, M. (2016). Building bench strength. *School Administrator, 73*(6). https://my.aasa.org/AASA/Resources/SAMag/Jun16/Rosenberg.aspx

Searby, L., & Shaddix, L. (2016). Growing teacher leaders in a culture of excellence. *Counterpoints, 466,* 214–221.

Sparks, S. D. (2017, October 19). *Principal-training secrets shared by the world's top school systems.* Education Week. www.edweek.org/leadership/principal-training-secrets-shared-by-the-worlds-top-school-systems/2017/10

Tingle, E., Corrales, A., & Peters, M. L. (2019). Leadership development programs: Investing in school principals. *Educational Studies, 45*(1), 1–16. https://doi.org/10.1080/03055698.2017.1382332

Versland, T. M. (2013). Principal efficacy: Implications for rural "grow your own" leadership programs. *The Rural Educator, 35*(1), Article 1. https://doi.org/10.35608/ruraled.v35i1.361

14 | The Future of PK-12 School Administration

Frank D. Davidson

 Anticipating an Uncertain Future

The title of this chapter brought to mind this author's two efforts to prepare for potential crises. The first anticipated crisis involved preparations for Hurricane Nora, which was expected to enter Arizona from the Gulf of California in the fall of 1997 and extensively inundate low-lying areas. Having experienced devastating flooding in both 1983 and 1993, the intrepid superintendent of a 400-square-mile school district was intent on taking proactive steps to alert parents, prepare plans for emergency shelters, and anticipate transportation challenges. Emergency response teams were activated, preparations were coordinated with municipal and county authorities, and a communications center was established. In the end, not a drop of rain fell on the school district. For some years, any time the superintendent spoke of the need to prepare for some anticipated challenge, the response from some colleagues was a shake of the head and a chuckled "Here we go again—Hurricane Nora."

The second anticipated crisis involved an extensive pandemic plan that had been developed in preparation for the possible impact of the H1N1 virus in 2009. The plan was explored and considered in lengthy white papers, parent communications, and advisories from the Centers for Disease Control. Thick binders with plans for addressing every conceivable challenge were distributed throughout the district. Early in the development of the plan, there was a smattering of "Hurricane Nora" comments; however, when case counts began to rise and the H1N1 influenza was officially declared a pandemic in June 2009, it became evident that the

DOI: 10.4324/9781003145332-14

Frank D. Davidson

threat was taken quite seriously by the Centers for Disease Control and needed to be taken seriously by educators.

The preparations for the H1N1 pandemic, involving greater attention to hygiene, handwashing, sanitizing surfaces, PPE, case counts, remote learning from home, and social distancing, only hinted at the overwhelming measures that schools would be forced to undertake during the 2020–2021 global pandemic. While there certainly were those who viewed the pandemic as a hoax or an overhyped crisis akin to "Hurricane Nora," this was a disease that took over 600,000 lives (as of this date) and produced unprecedented disruptions to daily life.

 ## Future Trends

There are three key challenges that we would like to explore in this chapter as we consider the future of school administration. We have introduced the chapter with the above recollections to illustrate both how difficult it is to anticipate what the future will bring, and to highlight the challenges which may lie ahead for school leaders.

In March of 2018, the Organisation for Economic Co-operation and Development (OECD) identified three categories of challenges in a position paper called *The Future of Education and Skills 2030* (OECD, 2018). This work was based on an acknowledgement that societies and educational leaders would be expected to contend with environmental, economic, and social challenges in the coming years. *Environmental* challenges are becoming evident with each passing day, as communities and regions experience the effects of climate change and the exhaustion of natural resources. Evidence of *economic* challenges is seen in the disruptions produced by unprecedented technological innovations and a shared global economy. Increasing migration, social and cultural diversity, inequitable standards of living, and a loss of trust in government are producing unprecedented *social* challenges. Lying in the interstices of these challenges are interdependencies that increase their complexity.

School leaders across the globe will need to engage in thoughtful planning with stakeholders around the question of how schools can develop students with the knowledge, skills, attitudes, and values to confront challenges effectively, creatively, and collaboratively. We believe that our best hope for our schools and our societies lies in effective, creative, and collaborative leaders.

Effective Leadership

Throughout this book, as we have examined the practical and research support for the PSEL standards, I have attempted to provide our view of effective leadership from our perspective as both practitioners and scholars. Central to our view is the belief that, in order to be effective, leaders must be ethical, inclusive, committed to equity, disciplined, purposeful, self-aware, and open to sharing leadership. In addition to being instructionally competent, they must also be competent managers who are capable of administering complex organizations. In an increasingly diverse world with escalating conflicts around historical perspectives and cultural stereotypes, they must be able to provide moral leadership as schools grapple with how the delivery of content affects minority students, and whether the content represents a comprehensive picture and context.

Collaborative Leadership

Despite the polarized and polarizing times in which we live, we believe that school leaders can and must build the collaborative relationships among stakeholders that the above challenges will require. The environmental, economic, and social challenges that our communities face are so great and so complex that the only way they can be effectively addressed is through respectful and cooperative relationships and alliances. This is extremely difficult work, yet those leaders who are able to effectively navigate the contentious and conflict-laden times ahead will be those who have found a way to bridge the divides and remain in relationship with both adversaries and allies. Rather than following the example of those leaders who seek to fuel divisions and fan the flames of hatred, school leaders must look to those moral leaders among us who, in their best moments, refuse to sacrifice either their principles or potential partnerships. As was voiced by so many of the practitioners who contributed to this book, leaders must deeply understand that they lead by example, and that there are many impressionable witnesses who will learn from that example.

Voices From the Field

As a valuable contribution to this *Principal's Desk Reference*, we have collected vignettes shared by award-winning, proven leaders who are effective principals to help you better understand the topics presented. This exemplar leader has learned many lessons over the years and is eager to share her thoughts and story with you.

 ## Vignette by Dr. Kristi Wilson

I gave remarks recently to a large group of educators in China. The theme was based on innovation, technology, and educational reform. How the US and China can continue with its partnerships—its exchange programs—what and how we can learn from each other during this pandemic. Specifically, how we can move forward in a positive direction.

From preschoolers to postgraduates, these students form the foundation of everything that everyone today dreams about for the future. Cooperation, quality international curriculums, and education reform that is supported and empowered by technological innovation is on everyone's minds throughout the world.

For me and the approximately 13,000 US superintendents AASA represents, our work is focused on the term "cooperation" because it is essential to success in the workplace and the classroom, in the boardroom, and to the chambers of government. Without cooperation, we have a myriad of competing interests, locked in a zero-sum game that fails to maximize potential, stifles creativity and innovation, and dissuades the next generation from seeking to participate in an unrewarding experience. I believe that we are better than that because I know that we all strive to instill in students the value of collaboration. There is a need for cooperation, moreover the need for continual collaboration and the need to transform education. Parents will demand it; educators are now responding to needs differently and the entire preK-21 system will not be able to return to life as it knew it before COVID-19.

Not only in China but throughout my term as president of AASA, I used my platform to speak about the fact that it is understood and undeniable that cooperating minds leveraged in healthy competition can yield incredible

The Future of PK-12 School Administration

outcomes. Those outcomes will not be "yours" or "mine," because the potential lies in them being "ours."

I believe it is imperative that we embrace a principle that is widely regarded as fundamental to cooperative learning in education: positive interdependence. Positive interdependence promotes a cooperative, sharing, and caring learning community. In contrast negative interdependence creates an unfriendly, competitive, or even hostile learning environment in which classmates are at odds with each other. In the business community the application of positive interdependence encourages participation and teamwork in the classroom by preparing students for the modern workplace where ability to work well with others is the single most important employability skill.

In short, to spur success, teachers must design cooperative situations in which the team cannot be successful without every member of that team experiencing success, and principals must learn how to assess their effectiveness. My success depends on you, as much as you depend on me. Note that this is different from scenarios where I might receive a personal failing score because you did not do what was expected. In the classroom, we might be "graded" differently in the end, but our team task, itself, cannot succeed unless we all have positive gains in some form. As you know, however, individual "grading" is generally an artificial classroom construct somewhat unique to our system.

In the classroom, we strive to create such artificially structured tasks for a purpose: it helps to maximize learning by eliminating a zero-sum approach to tasks. Not everything has to have winners and losers; conversely, "when one wins, we all win" is an expectation we should establish, whenever possible. This helps to incorporate in the minds of students that there is a benefit to employing cooperative strategies and, logically, this suggests that investing one's time into sharpening the requisite skills has inherent value. Ironically, there is something "in it for me," if I stop just focusing on "me."

The call of our work parallels this concept and is the sensible correlate of such efforts in education. Indeed, the demand for such skills and attitudes in the global economy is well-documented. It's never been more important. In our communities of business and education our win can be your win; we don't always need a loser, as the loser creates a gravity that pulls on even the biggest winner over time.

There is value in creating situations of positive interdependence for our students. When students experience situations of positive interdependence often enough, their social orientation is transformed from an "against others" to a "with others" orientation. When those students encounter a new person, they are less likely to ask, "Who is up and who is down; who is better, who is worse?" They are more likely to ask, "How can we work together; how can we enhance each other's outcomes?" And at that point, we have created a better world.

References

National Policy Board for Educational Administration. (2015). *Professional standards for educational leaders.* www.npbea.org/psel/

Organisation for Economic Co-operation and Development. (2018). *The future of education and skills 2030.* www.oecd.org/education/2030/E2030%20Position%20Paper%20(05.04.2018).pdf

Appendix A
Professional Standards for Educational Leaders (PSEL)

These professional standards are grounded in current research and real-life experiences. They are student-centric and designed to ensure that educational leaders are ready to effectively meet the challenges and opportunities of the principalship (PSEL, 2015, p. 1). The following are the ten standards defined within the Professional Standards for Educational Leaders (PSEL, 2015, p. 27).

Standard 1: Mission, Vision, and Core Values

Effective educational leaders develop, advocate, and enact a shared mission, vision, and core values of high-quality education and academic success and well-being of *each* student.

Standard 2: Ethics and Professional Norms

Effective educational leaders act ethically and according to professional norms to promote *each* student's academic success and well-being.

Professional Standards

Standard 3: Equity and Cultural Responsiveness

Effective educational leaders strive for equity of educational opportunity and culturally responsive practices to promote *each* student's academic success and well-being.

Standard 4: Curriculum, Instruction, and Assessment

Effective educational leaders develop and support intellectually rigorous and coherent systems of curriculum, instruction, and assessment to promote *each* student's academic success and well-being.

Standard 5: Community of Care and Support for Students

Effective educational leaders cultivate an inclusive, caring, and supportive school community that promotes the academic success and well-being of *each* student.

Standard 6: Professional Capacity of School Personnel

Effective educational leaders develop the professional capacity and practice of school personnel to promote *each* student's academic success and well-being.

Professional Standards

 ## Standard 7: Professional Community for Teachers and Staff

Effective educational leaders foster a professional community of teachers and other professional staff to promote each student's academic success and well-being.

 ## Standard 8: Meaningful Engagement of Families and Community

Effective educational leaders engage families and the community in meaningful, reciprocal, and mutually beneficial ways to promote each student's academic success and well-being.

 ## Standard 9: Operations and Management

Effective educational leaders manage school operations and resources to promote each student's academic success and well-being.

 ## Standard 10: School Improvement

Effective educational leaders act as agents of continuous improvement to promote each student's academic success and well-being.

National Policy Board for Educational Administration (2015). Professional Standards for Educational Leaders 2015. Reston, VA: Author. Used with Permission.

Appendix B
PSEL Knowledge and Skill Self-Assessment

We created the following knowledge and skills self-assessment to help you gauge your performance level for each of the expectations under each of the ten standards. Within this book, we expanded on these expectations to aid you in better understanding what effective leaders should know and be able to do to achieve success with each standard, including the use of the PSEL standards in the principal performance evaluation, mentoring, and grow your own leadership development programs.

In each table, carefully read the description of the skill (expectation) that effective leaders should know and be able to do under each standard. Place a check in the box (E, M, D, N) that most closely represents your current level of knowledge and skill in that area. Leadership development is a never-ending journey of continuous improvement. Be honest as you self-reflect upon your current skill set based on the PSEL.

 Definition of Column Headings

E = Exceeds, M = Meets, D = Developing, N = Novice

 Definition of Performance Indicators

Exceeds: Performs at a higher, more sophisticated level than what is indicated.

PSEL Knowledge and Skill Self-Assessment

Meets: Performs at a consistent, predictable level as stated.
Developing: Performs hesitantly or unsure based on the statement.
Novice: Struggles to know what steps to take to proceed with the skill stated.

Standard 1: Mission, Vision, and Core Values	E	M	D	N
a) Developing an educational mission for the school to promote the academic success and well-being of each student.				
b) In collaboration with members of the school and community, using relevant data, develop and promote a vision for the school on the successful learning and development of each child and on instructional and organizational practices that promote such success.				
c) Articulate, advocate, and cultivate core values that define the school's culture and stress the imperative of child-centered education; high expectations and student support; equity, inclusiveness, and social justice; openness, caring, and trust; and continuous improvement.				
d) Strategically develop, implement, and evaluate actions to achieve the vision for the school.				
e) Review the school's mission and vision. Adjust them to changing expectations and opportunities for the school and changing needs and situations of students.				
f) Develop shared understanding of and commitment to mission, vision, and core values within the school and the community.				
g) Model and pursue the school's mission, vision, and core values in all aspects of leadership.				

Standard 2: Ethics and Professional Norms	E	M	D	N
a) Act ethically and professionally in personal conduct, relationships with others, decision-making, stewardship of the school's resources, and all aspects of school leadership.				

209

PSEL Knowledge and Skill Self-Assessment

Standard 2: Ethics and Professional Norms	E	M	D	N
b) Act according to and promote the professional norms of integrity, fairness, transparency, trust, collaboration, perseverance, learning, and continuous improvement.				
c) Place children at the center of education and accept responsibility for each student's academic success and well-being.				
d) Safeguard and promote the values of democracy, individual freedom and responsibility, equity, social justice, community, and diversity.				
e) Lead with interpersonal and communication skill, social-emotional insight, and understanding of all students' and staff members' backgrounds and cultures.				
f) Provide moral direction for the school and promote ethical and professional behavior among faculty and staff.				

Standard 3: Equity and Cultural Responsiveness	E	M	D	N
a) Ensure that each student is treated fairly, respectfully, and with an understanding of each student's culture and context.				
b) Recognize, respect, and employ each student's strengths, diversity, and culture as assets for teaching and learning.				
c) Ensure that each student has equitable access to effective teachers, learning opportunities, academic and social support, and other resources necessary for success.				
d) Develop student policies and address student misconduct in a positive, fair, and unbiased manner.				
e) Confront and alter institutional biases of student marginalization, deficit-based schooling, and low expectations associated with race, class, culture and language, gender and sexual orientation, and disability or special status.				
f) Promote the preparation of students to live productively in and contribute to the diverse cultural contexts of a global society.				

PSEL Knowledge and Skill Self-Assessment

Standard 3: Equity and Cultural Responsiveness	E	M	D	N
g) Act with cultural competence and responsiveness in their interactions, decision-making, and practice.				
h) Address matters of equity and cultural responsiveness in all aspects of leadership.				

Standard 4: Curriculum, Instruction, and Assessment	E	M	D	N
a) Implement coherent systems of curriculum, instruction, and assessment that promote the mission, vision, and core values of the school, embody high expectations for student learning, align with academic standards, and are culturally responsive.				
b) Align and focus systems of curriculum, instruction, and assessment within and across grade levels to promote student academic success, love of learning, the identities and habits of learners, and healthy sense of self.				
c) Promote instructional practice that is consistent with knowledge of child learning and development, effective pedagogy, and the needs of each student.				
d) Ensure instructional practice that is intellectually challenging, authentic to student experiences, recognizes student strengths, and is differentiated and personalized.				
e) Promote the effective use of technology in the service of teaching and learning.				
f) Employ valid assessments that are consistent with knowledge of child learning and development and technical standards of measurement.				
g) Use assessment data appropriately and within technical limitations to monitor student progress and improve instruction.				

PSEL Knowledge and Skill Self-Assessment

Standard 5: Community of Care and Support for Students	E	M	D	N
a) Build and maintain a safe, caring, and healthy school environment that meets the academic, social, emotional, and physical needs of each student.				
b) Create and sustain a school environment in which each student is known, accepted and valued, trusted and respected, cared for, and encouraged to be an active and responsible member of the school community.				
c) Provide coherent systems of academic and social supports, services, extracurricular activities, and accommodations to meet the range of learning needs of each student.				
d) Promote adult–student, student–peer, and school–community relationships that value and support academic learning and positive social and emotional development.				
e) Cultivate and reinforce student engagement in school and positive student conduct.				
f) Infuse the school's learning environment with the cultures and languages of the school's community.				

Standard 6: Professional Capacity of School Personnel	E	M	D	N
a) Recruit, hire, support, develop, and retain effective and caring teachers and other professional staff and form them into an educationally effective faculty.				
b) Plan for and manage staff turnover and succession, providing opportunities for effective induction and mentoring of new personnel.				
c) Develop teachers' and staff members' professional knowledge, skills, and practice through differentiated opportunities for learning and growth, guided by understanding of professional and adult learning and development.				
d) Foster continuous improvement of individual and collective instructional capacity to achieve outcomes envisioned for each student.				

PSEL Knowledge and Skill Self-Assessment

Standard 6: Professional Capacity of School Personnel	E	M	D	N
e) Deliver actionable feedback about instruction and other professional practice through valid, research-anchored systems of supervision and evaluation to support the development of teachers' and staff members' knowledge, skills, and practice.				
f) Empower and motivate teachers and staff to the highest levels of professional practice and to continuous learning and improvement.				
g) Develop the capacity, opportunities, and support for teacher leadership and leadership from other members of the school community.				
h) Promote the personal and professional health, well-being, and work–life balance of faculty and staff.				
i) Tend to their own learning and effectiveness through reflection, study, and improvement, maintaining a healthy work–life balance.				

Standard 7: Professional Community for Teachers and Staff	E	M	D	N
a) Develop workplace conditions for teachers and other professional staff that promote effective professional development, practice, and student learning.				
b) Empower and entrust teachers and staff with collective responsibility for meeting the academic, social, emotional, and physical needs of each student, pursuant to the mission, vision, and core values of the school.				
c) Establish and sustain a professional culture of engagement and commitment to shared vision, goals, and objectives pertaining to the education of the whole child; high expectations for professional work; ethical and equitable practice; trust and open communication; collaboration; collective efficacy; and continuous individual and organizational learning and improvement.				
d) Promote mutual accountability among teachers and other professional staff for each student's success and the effectiveness of the school as a whole.				

PSEL Knowledge and Skill Self-Assessment

Standard 7: Professional Community for Teachers and Staff	E	M	D	N
e) Develop and support open, productive, caring, and trusting working relationships among leaders, faculty, and staff to promote professional capacity and the improvement of practice.				
f) Design and implement job-embedded and other opportunities for professional learning collaboratively with faculty and staff.				
g) Provide opportunities for collaborative examination of practice, collegial feedback, and collective learning.				
h) Encourage faculty-initiated improvement of programs and practices.				

Standard 8: Meaningful Engagement of Families and Community	E	M	D	N
a) Are approachable, accessible, and welcoming to families and members of the community.				
b) Create and sustain positive, collaborative, and productive relationships with families and the community for the benefit of students.				
c) Engage in regular and open two-way communication with families and the community about the school, students, needs, problems, and accomplishments.				
d) Maintain a presence in the community to understand its strengths and needs, develop productive relationships, and engage its resources for the school.				
e) Create means for the school community to partner with families to support student learning in and out of school.				
f) Understand, value, and employ the community's cultural, social, intellectual, and political resources to promote student learning and school improvement.				
g) Develop and provide the school as a resource for families and the community.				
h) Advocate for the school and district, and for the importance of education and student needs and priorities to families and the community.				

PSEL Knowledge and Skill Self-Assessment

Standard 8: Meaningful Engagement of Families and Community	E	M	D	N
i) Advocate publicly for the needs and priorities of students, families, and the community.				
j) Build and sustain productive partnerships with public and private sectors to promote school improvement and student learning.				

Standard 9: Operations and Management	E	M	D	N
a) Institute, manage, and monitor operations and administrative systems that promote the mission and vision of the school.				
b) Strategically manage staff resources, assigning and scheduling teachers and staff to roles and responsibilities that optimize their professional capacity to address each student's learning needs.				
c) Seek, acquire, and manage fiscal, physical, and other resources to support curriculum, instruction, and assessment; student learning community; professional capacity and community; and family and community engagement.				
d) Are responsible, ethical, and accountable stewards of the school's monetary and non-monetary resources, engaging in effective budgeting and accounting practices.				
e) Protect teachers' and other staff members' work and learning from disruption.				
f) Employ technology to improve the quality and efficiency of operations and management.				
g) Develop and maintain data and communication systems to deliver actionable information for classroom and school improvement.				
h) Know, comply with, and help the school community understand local, state, and federal laws, rights, policies, and regulations so as to promote student success.				

PSEL Knowledge and Skill Self-Assessment

Standard 9: Operations and Management	E	M	D	N
i) Develop and manage relationships with feeder and connecting schools for enrollment management and curricular and instructional articulation.				
j) Develop and manage productive relationships with the central office and school board.				
k) Develop and administer systems for fair and equitable management of conflict among students, faculty and staff, leaders, families, and community.				
l) Manage governance processes and internal and external politics toward achieving the school's mission and vision.				

Standard 10: School Improvement	E	M	D	N
a) Seek to make school more effective for each student, teachers and staff, families, and the community.				
b) Use methods of continuous improvement to achieve the vision, fulfill the mission, and promote the core values of the school.				
c) Prepare the school and the community for improvement, promoting readiness, an imperative for improvement, instilling mutual commitment and accountability, and developing the knowledge, skills, and motivation to succeed in improvement.				
d) Engage others in an ongoing process of evidence-based inquiry, learning, strategic goal setting, planning, implementation, and evaluation for continuous school and classroom improvement.				
e) Employ situationally appropriate strategies for improvement, including transformational and incremental, adaptive approaches and attention to different phases of implementation.				
f) Assess and develop the capacity of staff to assess the value and applicability of emerging educational trends and the findings of research for the school and its improvement.				

PSEL Knowledge and Skill Self-Assessment

Standard 10: School Improvement	E	M	D	N
g) Develop technically appropriate systems of data collection, management, analysis, and use, connecting as needed to the district office and external partners for support in planning, implementation, monitoring, feedback, and evaluation.				
h) Adopt a systems perspective and promote coherence among improvement efforts and all aspects of school organization, programs, and services.				
i) Manage uncertainty, risk, competing initiatives, and politics of change with courage and perseverance, providing support and encouragement, and openly communicating the need for, process for, and outcomes of improvement efforts.				
j) Develop and promote leadership among teachers and staff for inquiry, experimentation, and innovation, and initiating and implementing improvement.				

Developed using PSEL 2015, by Dr. Robyn Hansen

After you complete the tables by taking an honest look at your current reality in terms of leadership knowledge and skills based on the ten PSEL standards, we recommend that you create a three- to four-year plan for development in the areas marked as Novice (N) or Developing (D). You may want to work in concert with your supervisor or mentor on this plan, so that you are able to receive timely and focused feedback on your professional growth and development.

If you are a more experienced administrator with mostly Developing (D) or Meets (M) with some Exceeds (E), we recommend that you stretch yourself with a challenging comprehensive professional development plan to strengthen your skills to move to mostly Exceeds. Remember, the role of an administrator is ever-changing. With that said, your knowledge and skills in these areas will continue to be challenged as you move through your long and productive career.

When you have achieved a level with mostly Meets (M) and Exceeds (E), our hope for you is that you would decide to mentor one or two Novice or Developing administrators. The role of school leader can be very lonely

217

PSEL Knowledge and Skill Self-Assessment

and isolating. Extend a hand to someone with less experience to strengthen their abilities as they strive to be an effective school leader. Our students and school communities deserve the best leaders possible. You make a difference in the lives of so many—good leadership matters! Professional development goals should be developed for you to focus on a never-ending, continuous path of school improvement as a role model to those who look to you for advice and leadership. There are many, even if you are not aware of who is watching and learning from you daily.

Continue to strive for excellence in all you do. You make a difference in the lives of children and families. Thank you for your commitment to excellence in education!

Glossary

CAEP — The Council for the Accreditation of Educator Preparation, the body which accredits leadership preparation programs.

ELCC — The Educational Leader Constituent Council standards, initially developed and aligned to the ISLLC standards in 2002, provide guidance in developing and reviewing programs that prepare aspiring building- and district-level leaders. The ELCC standards have been replaced by the NELP standards.

ISLLC — The initial professional standards for school leaders, developed in 1996 and revised in 2008. The ISLLC standards have been replaced by the PSEL standards.

NELP — The National Educational Leadership Preparation standards, which are intended to define what novice leaders and preparation program graduates should know and be able to do after completing a high-quality educational leadership preparation program.

PSEL — The Professional Standards for Educational Leaders, adopted in 2015 by the National Policy Board for Educational Administration.

Contributor Biographies

 **Rosemary Agneessens (Vignette in Chapter 4)**

Rosemary, a seasoned leader in education, has served as a teacher, dual language program director, and principal in both Phoenix and Prescott, Arizona. Following her administrative tenure in Prescott, Rosemary returned to her community-organizing roots to focus on education advocacy. In this role, she works with schools all over Yavapai County to educate parents and community members about the serious funding needs in Arizona's educational system.

Her current work is empowering others to have a voice in the future of education. Rosemary shows community members and parents how to inform themselves, present the facts, push for support, and bring about change. She teaches and models how to build relationships with state legislators and others to sustain an ongoing dialog. She works as a community organizer for Yavapai County Education Service Agency and in collaboration with AZ Interfaith Network, an Industrial Area Foundation affiliate.

Connect with Rosemary at: agneessens5935@gmail.com

Contributor Biographies

Liza Caraballo-Suarez (Vignette in Chapter 7)

Liza Caraballo-Suarez is the principal of PS 120, the Magnet School of Architecture, Engineering & Design located in District 14 in Brooklyn, NY. Caraballo-Suarez has served as an educational leader for over 30 years in the same neighborhood she grew up in and is a former teacher, staff developer, and assistant principal. Under her leadership, PS 120 was awarded two Federal Magnet Grants, Lighthouse School Status Leader in Me, Respect for All Recognition, and various grants including one from the Afro Latin Jazz Alliance. She is committed to ensuring all students have access to a high-quality and equitable education through a culturally responsive curriculum that is inclusive and reflects the rich diversity of our children.

Caraballo-Suarez served as president of the National Association of Elementary School Principals (2022–2023), representing all principals nationwide in grades K-8. Caraballo-Suarez is a trailblazer who is breaking barriers, as the first Latina in New York State elected president of the National Association of Elementary School Principals (NAESP). In addition, she is an active member of various professional organizations, community organizations, and boards, including the New York Association of Elementary School Principals, New York Academy of Public Education, New York State Association of Latino Superintendents and Administrators, School Administrators Association of New York State, American Federation of School Administrators, Alliance for Puerto Rican Education and Empowerment, and Council of School Supervisors and Administrators.

Caraballo-Suarez has earned a doctorate from Sage College, Albany NY, and a bachelor's degree in elementary education in special education from Hunter College. She received her second master's degree in special education from Brooklyn College, and an Advanced Certificate in school administration and supervision from Dowling College. She's a proud alumnus of NYC public schools and a Brooklyn native.

Connect with Liza at: docsuarez99@gmail.com

Contributor Biographies

 # Howard C. Carlson (Vignette in Chapter 6)

Howard Carlson retired from the superintendency in June 2020 and now works with the Greater Phoenix Educational Management Council (GPEMC) and its affiliate group, the Arizona Educational Management Council (AZEMC). In addition, Carlson coordinates the Northern Arizona University (NAU) Rural and Small School District Resource Center and serves as an adjunct professor for NAU and Grand Canyon University.

Carlson also works as a superintendent mentor through the American Association of School Administrators (AASA) Superintendent Certification Program and consults on a variety of issues related to leadership, the superintendency, and K-12 education.

In 2015 he was named the Arizona School Administrators' Distinguished Administrator of the Year for the Superintendents' Division and in 2019 served as Arizona's nomination for National Superintendent of the Year to the AASA.

The author of two books, *So Now You're the Superintendent* and *Accelerated Wisdom: 50 Practical Ideas for Today's Superintendent*, and a leadership blog, which can be found at www.acceleratedleadershipwisdom. com, Carlson is a frequent writer and presenter on leadership and the superintendency.

Over the course of his career, Carlson served as superintendent in the states of Washington, Minnesota, and Arizona.

Connect with Howard at: Hcarlsonthesupt@gmail.com

 # Catarina Song Chen (Vignette in Chapter 9)

Prior to moving to Brazil, Catarina was an elementary school teacher in the US for eight years.

She started her international teaching career at the American School of Belo Horizonte (EABH) as the Primary Years Program (PYP) coordinator in 2008 and shortly thereafter promoted to principal/director. Under her leadership, EABH tripled its enrollment and implemented a series of changes that significantly improved the school's overall performance. She involved the entire school community in revising the school's core value, beliefs, vision, and mission statements, as well as establishing a culture of integration and collaboration across all cultural backgrounds, ages, and stakeholders.

Catarina served as the President of the Association of American Schools in Brazil (AASB) from 2012 to 2014 and as a member of the Board of Trustees at the Association of American Schools of South America (AASSA). She earned a bachelor's degree in philosophy from the University of California, Los Angeles (UCLA), and a master's degree in administration from Pepperdine University, Malibu, California. She believes that having fun is an attitude and aptitude necessary to make all hard work relevant and meaningful. She is married to a Chinese-Brazilian-American and has two children.

Connect with Catarina at: Catarina.chen@eabh.com.br

Sarah Gentis Collins (Vignette in Chapter 4)

Sarah Gentis Collins is an elementary school principal in Tempe, Arizona. She has been in public education for 22 years. She has served as a school leader for five years and was previously a dean of students and classroom teacher. Sarah has one master's degree in elementary education and a second master's degree in educational leadership. She has recently earned her doctoral degree in K-12 educational leadership, with her dissertation topic being culturally responsive teaching pedagogy. For the past six years, she has been able to use her experience and education to support teacher candidates as an adjunct faculty member for Rio Salado Community College in the teacher preparation post-baccalaureate program.

Connect with Sarah at: sarahcollinsaz@gmail.com

James Driscoll (Vignette in Chapter 10)

James Driscoll is the superintendent of Tempe Elementary School District in Tempe, AZ. The 23 schools offer exceptional K-8 experiences in exemplary National Blue Ribbon and Arizona Education Foundation A+ Schools with a variety of engaging learning environments suited to meet individual academic and social needs for each child.

He began his career as a classroom teacher having taught both elementary and middle school students in suburban and urban settings.

Contributor Biographies

His administrative experience includes being a dean of students, assistant principal, principal, district hearing officer, director of special education, and assistant superintendent of East Area K-8 schools, as well as assistant superintendent of human resources. His successes include recruitment and retention of personnel, developing equitable and challenging learning experiences for all students, and identifying strengths and weaknesses in collaborative learning communities.

Driscoll holds a Bachelor of Arts in Elementary Education, master's degrees in educational leadership, human relations, special education, and business and administration, and a doctoral degree in educational leadership.

Connect with James at: james.driscoll@tempeschools.org

Steven Jeras (Vignette in Chapter 3)

Steven Jeras is an assistant superintendent of a unified school district serving 30,000 students in Phoenix and Scottsdale, Arizona. He received his doctorate degree in educational leadership from Northern Arizona University, a master's degree in educational leadership from Northern Arizona University, and a bachelor's degree in journalism from Arizona State University. Prior to his current position, he was a director of student services, an elementary principal, middle school assistant principal, and high school teacher. He is a member of the district's equity leadership team of advisors, which has helped identify opportunities for improving equity.

Connect with Steven at: stevenjeras@gmail.com

Rachael George (Vignette in Chapter 2)

From fighting wildland fires with the US Forest Service to putting out fires in the classroom, education was the last place that Rachael thought she'd end up. It was not until a hard conversation with a base manager in Grangeville, Idaho did Rachael realize she needed to put her chainsaw down and make a bigger impact on the world. Rachael is a member of the ASCD Emerging Leaders Class of 2015 and currently serves as the principal of Sandy Grade School in the Oregon Trail School District. Over the past seven years, Sandy Grade School has moved from being one of the lowest-ranked elementary

Contributor Biographies

schools in the state of Oregon to performing in the top 20%. Sandy Grade School has been recognized by the International Center for Leadership in Education (ICLE) as a Model School for closing the achievement gap. Prior to serving as an elementary principal, she was a middle school principal of an "outstanding" and two-time "Level 5: Model School" as recognized by the State of Oregon. Rachael specializes in curriculum development and instructional improvement as well as working with at-risk students and closing the achievement gap. She is also co-author of the book *Principaled: Navigating the Leadership Learning Curve* (2020). Connect with Rachael on Twitter @DrRachaelGeorge or at rachael.george00@gmail.com

Joanne Kramer (Vignette in Chapter 3)

The daughter of a Foreign Service Officer, Joanne Kramer grew up outside of the United States. Her family values were very strong, and they lived in diverse communities and countries. She learned that their family gained the trust and respect of those around them by acting professionally, promoting social justice, and being transparent and resilient when things didn't always go as expected. Every time the family moved to a new country required that they start all over again.
Connect with Joanne at: joanne.kramer@cgesd.org.

Jeff Lavender (Vignette in Chapter 10)

Jeff Lavender has been a building principal for 24 years. He has also served as a principal mentor and supervisor. His schools have been awarded the Arizona Education Foundation A+ School of Excellence three times. He is also a member of the City Council in Casa Grande, Arizona.
Connect with Jeff at: lavenderjeff@ymail.com

Marianne Lescher (Vignette in Chapter 5)

Marianne Lucas Lescher is currently in her 21st year as a school principal (both K-5 and K-8) in the Kyrene School District located in Chandler,

225

Contributor Biographies

Arizona and in her 38th year as a proud public school educator and administrator. Lescher received her Ph.D. from Boston College in Educational Research, Measurement and Evaluation and her M.Ed. from the University of Massachusetts-Boston in Educational Administration. She started her educational journey as a special education teacher and then as an assistant principal and director of curriculum prior to taking on the best job in public schools...as a building principal!

Lescher is an Arizona Exemplary Principal (Maricopa County) and a Circle of Honor Principal (Arizona Department of Education). Lescher's schools have achieved the Arizona A+ School of Excellence Recognition five times and her proudest professional achievement is when her school, Kyrene Traditional Academy, was named a National Blue Ribbon School of Excellence because it reflected the hard work and dedication of her entire school community, teachers, and students.

Connect with Marianne at: mlesc@kyrene.org

Darlene A. McCauley (Vignette in Chapter 11)

Darlene McCauley was born and raised in Winslow, Arizona. She has been an educator in rural Arizona for 30 years and has worked as a teacher, counselor, and administrator. She has served as an administrator in both social services and educational fields, including junior high school principal and currently as a junior high school/high school principal and superintendent on the Arizona Strip. Her current, rural district is geographically remote, requiring travel through Nevada or Utah to reach it. Although her high school was labeled an underperforming school, the school's Academic Olympic team won the regional title and took third place for the State of Nevada in its division last year. (The school competes in Nevada due to its location.) She holds degrees including an M.Ed. in Educational Leadership and an M.Ed. in Counseling from Northern Arizona University (NAU). She has completed coursework in the Ed.D. in Educational Leadership program at NAU and is currently working on her dissertation. She has memberships in Phi Kappa Phi, Golden Key International, Arizona School Administrators, Arizona Rural Schools, and local committees and boards to improve career and college-going efforts in rural Arizona, Nevada, and Utah.

Connect with Darlene at: dam33@nau.edu

Contributor Biographies

Shannon Bruce Ramaka (Vignette in Chapter 2)

Shannon Bruce Ramaka is a passionate educator of 30+ years, who believes that supporting teacher leaders and facilitating deep professional collaboration in schools are the keys to sustained continual improvement. She began her career in Oregon and since 2007 has been an international teacher and leader in Zambia, Hungary, Morocco, Turkey, Kosovo, and the Netherlands. She has taught all ages of students, prekindergarten to the university level, and enjoys integrating the arts, "big ideas," and hands-on learning into all curriculum, whenever possible. She holds a B.S. in Business Administration, M.S. in Curriculum, Instruction and Supervision, and an Ed.D. in Educational Leadership. As an innovative leader, she founded the Renaissance Charter School in Eagle Point, Oregon, and the international virtual professional learning community, VisionaryEd (https://visionaryed.org/). As the head of the International Teacher Education of Secondary Schools (ITESS) in the Netherlands, she introduced a remote teaching practice connecting student teachers with mentor teachers in the Janesville School District in Wisconsin so that students could complete their studies despite the limitations caused by the covid-19 pandemic.

Connect with Shannon at: Shannon.visionaryed@gmail.com

Ines Schreiner (Vignette in Chapter 8)

Ines Schreiner has been an educator for over 20 years in both the United States and Austria. She has experience working in SEN, language and literature, language acquisition, inclusive classrooms, and school counseling and has been appointed as the Head of Secondary at the International School in Velden, Austria. Ines has completed professional development in both elementary and middle school teacher training at the Pädagogische Hochschule Hasnerplatz in Graz, Austria. She is currently enrolled in a master's program for school leadership at the Viktor Frankl Hochschule in Klagenfurt, Austria. She is a mother of four boys and a passionate advocate for teenage brain health and teenage brain informed teaching and learning practices.

Connect with Ines at: i.schreiner@isc.ac.at

Contributor Biographies

Jon Sheldahl (Vignette in Chapter 11)

Jon Sheldahl is currently the Chief Administrator of Heartland Area Education Agency in Johnston, Iowa. Heartland AEA employs 700 staff who provide educational services to 50 school districts and 140,000 students in Central Iowa. He previously served as the superintendent of schools in Ottumwa, Iowa. In his over 30 years in educational leadership, he has served as superintendent, human resource director, building principal, and service agency executive in Arizona and Iowa. He holds a B.A. in English from the University of Iowa and an Ed.D. in Educational Leadership from Northern Arizona University.

Connect with Jon at: jsheldahl@heartlandaea.org

Kristi Wilson (Vignette in Chapter 14)

At the time this manuscript was being prepared, Kristi Wilson was beginning her eighth year as superintendent of the Buckeye Elementary School District in Buckeye, Arizona, one of the fastest-growing cities in America. Prior to her superintendency, Kristi served in a variety of leadership roles, including as an assistant superintendent, executive director of student services, special education director, school administrator, teacher, and adjunct professor in both Arizona and Oregon.

Kristi served as President of the American Association of School Administrators (AASA) and President of the National Minority Student Achievement Network (MSAN) and serves on the American Heart Association and the Executive Board of the Arizona Business and Education Coalition (ABEC) and the Arizona School Alliance Board. She was recognized as the 2020 Arizona Superintendent of the Year. In the past she has been the recipient of the Arizona PTA Honorary Lifetime Achievement Award, and VH1 Save the Music National Superintendent of the Year.

In her spare time, Kristi loves to read, travel, and play golf with her husband. She is also currently writing a book on the importance of empowering women in leadership, and ways in which it can be accomplished.

Connect with Kristi at: kwilson@besd33.org

Michael L. Wright (Vignette in Chapter 6)

Michael L. Wright has led in postsecondary and K-12 education for 20 years. Mike held various executive and senior executive leadership positions, including Chief Operating Officer and President of York Technical Institute in York, Pennsylvania, before becoming Superintendent of Blue Ridge Unified Schools. Mike is also an adjunct professor at Northern Arizona University and serves on the Arizona Board of Education, Professional Practices Advisory Committee, and Arizona's Commission for Post-Secondary Education. He is on the board of directors for Kairos, a non-profit health care administrator for over 20,000 people.

Professional publications include Wright and Papa (2020) "Sustaining and Sustainable Superintendent Leadership," *Oxford Research Encyclopedia of Education*, Oxford University Press; Wright (2020) "The Importance of Decisive Leadership and Clear Direction During Crisis," *International Journal of Entrepreneurship and Economic Issues*, 4(1), 35–38, https://doi.org/10.32674/ijeei.v4i1.24; and Wright (2020) *A Guide to Effective Leadership in Crisis: The Edge*. Arizona School Administrators.

Connect with Mike at: mwright@brusd.org

Printed in the United States
by Baker & Taylor Publisher Services